Religious Perspectives in Faulkner's Fiction

Religious Perspectives in Faulkner's Fiction

YOKNAPATAWPHA AND BEYOND

J. ROBERT BARTH, S.J., Editor

UNIVERSITY OF NOTRE DAME PRESS
NOTRE DAME   LONDON

Library of Congress Catalog Card Number: 75-185896
Manufactured in the United States of America by
NAPCO Graphic Arts, Inc., Milwaukee, Wisconsin

To
My Brothers and Sisters
PHIL, KARL, ERIC, ROGER, SUZIE AND SHARI

Contents

Preface ====

ONCE AN AUTHOR IS GENERALLY ACKNOWLEDGED TO BE A great writer, it is not long before he finds his work at the center of an enormous body of criticism. William Faulkner is no exception.

What then is the justification for yet another study of Faulkner? First, this study is one of the few books on Faulkner to focus entirely on religious aspects of his work. And it differs from books like Hyatt Waggoner's excellent *William Faulkner: From Jefferson to the World,* which does give careful attention to religious attitudes in Faulkner's work, in that it is the work of various critics, considering Faulkner from differing points of view. Second, it differs from general collections of essays, like the splendid anthology of Frederick J. Hoffman and Olga W. Vickery, in that this volume is restricted to the single area of religious problems in Faulkner's work.

Perhaps most importantly, however—and this might be taken as a summary of aim and general structure—this collection hopes to justify itself by its attempt to set up, by means of commentary on each essay, a kind of dialogue among the contributors. It might be objected that there is no single point of view throughout. But a dialogue does not, after all, generally flow from a single point of view. It moves, idea suggesting idea, assertion evoking objection and commentary, by a kind of dialectic process. The editor of this book holds the place of a participating chairman, who has a viewpoint of his own which emerges as time goes on but whose primary function is to elicit responses, to sharpen positions, to keep the meeting in order, and to summarize and draw at least tentative conclusions. If in the process the reader finds himself drawn into the dialogue, then the aim of the discussion will have been achieved.

From this it will perhaps be clear that the ideal reader of this book is one who has read the novels of Faulkner that come under particular discussion. If one is to enter fully into a dialogue, it is helpful for him to be familiar ahead of time with the data and the agenda. The book should also be useful, how-

ever, especially the general essays of chapters 1–5, as an introduction to reading the novels. It is hoped, too, that this volume
might be a starting point for further discussion by college
classes (whether in religious studies or in literature), by discussion groups, and the like. Clearly, its conclusions are tentative enough and its outer limits open enough for the dialogue
to go on.

Finally, since this collection is aimed at students of literature
and of religion, some justification seems called for of this joint
effort—some may call it confusion—of two distinct interests.
That will be the purpose of the first chapter.

My debts in the making of this book are many. I am indebted to the authors and publishers who graciously gave permission for the use of previously published material, and to
whom full acknowledgment is made elsewhere. In addition to
these, I am grateful to the editors of *America* and *The Jesuit
Educational Quarterly* for permission to use (in chapters 1 and
9) several passages from articles of mine which appeared in
those journals. But there are many unacknowledged debts as
well. Anyone who works with Faulkner is in constant debt to
the critics who have gone before him. I am deeply grateful
to all the Faulkner scholars who have opened doors for me
over the years.

I am grateful for the skillful assistance of Donna M. Smith
in the work of proofreading and indexing, and for the services
of a very able typist, Mrs. Martha Robinson.

I owe a special debt of gratitude to two friends—Philip C.
Rule, S.J., of the University of Detroit, and Patricia R. Cannon,
R.S.C.J., of Barat College—who took time to read the manu-
script of this book when other demands on them were pressing,
and who gave criticism and encouragement when both were
needed. In addition to these scholarly obligations, my personal
debts to both these friends are immeasurable.

Cambridge, Massachusetts   J. R. B.
December 1971

Contributors ═══════

J. ROBERT BARTH, S.J., Assistant Professor of English at Harvard University, is the author of *Coleridge and Christian Doctrine,* as well as of articles in such literary journals as *Thought, Renascence,* and *Studies in Romanticism.*

CLEANTH BROOKS, Gray Professor of Rhetoric at Yale University, has published *The Well Wrought Urn, William Faulkner: The Yoknapatawpha Country,* and a wide range of other books and articles.

ROBERT W. DANIEL, Professor of English at Kenyon College, has published *A Contemporary Rhetoric* and is editor of several other volumes.

HAROLD J. DOUGLAS teaches English at Transylvania College in Lexington, Kentucky.

JOHN W. HUNT, Professor of English at Earlham College, is the author of *William Faulkner: Art in Theological Tension* and of articles in such journals as *Critique, Criterion,* and *The Journal of Religion.*

ROMA A. KING, JR., Professor of English at Ohio University, has published widely on nineteenth century and modern literature, and is General Editor of *The Complete Works of Robert Browning.*

HERBERT A. PERLUCK is Assistant Professor of English at Brooklyn College.

PHILIP C. RULE, S.J., Associate Professor of English at the University of Detroit, is former literary editor of the weekly journal *America.*

HYATT H. WAGGONER, Professor of English at Brown University, is the author of *William Faulkner: From Jefferson to the World, Hawthorne: A Critical Study,* and other books and articles on American literature.

AMOS N. WILDER, Hollis Professor of Divinity, Emeritus, Harvard Divinity School, is the author of many books, including *Modern Poetry and the Christian Tradition* and *The New Voice: Religion, Literature, Hermeneutics.*

J. Robert Barth, S. J.

1 ═══

RELIGION AND LITERATURE: THE CRITICAL CONTEXT

THE DEAN OF A GREAT EUROPEAN THEOLOGICAL FACULTY was asked not long ago by a young priest who had just completed his graduate work in theology what should be the next step in his program. The dean replied: "Study modern literature."

To some extent, a new and fresh encounter between theology and imaginative literature has already begun. It is, in fact, one of the most hopeful developments in modern culture. As Nathan Scott points out in *Modern Literature and the Religious Frontier,* the modern writer, "in his reflection upon the issues of existence that in a time of crisis have engaged the modern imagination, has often found himself peering into those vacuums of tragedy and mystery whose terrors it has traditionally been the office of religion to assist us in confronting."[1] For their part, the interpreters of Christianity, in their efforts to speak to the disintegrated consciousness of modern man, are often turning today to the vast body of modern religiously oriented literature in order to discover what Scott calls "a point of entry into the mind inhabited by the men of our time."[2]

While both the theologian and the critic might dread the encounter, our generation must come to terms with this problem of the relationship between literature and theology. All too frequently in the past, when such a relationship has been so much as hinted at, the critic has cried "didacticism." The theologian, too, has often scorned the relationship: the literary man, according to him, has no right to theological ideas.

But the problem can no longer be ignored. To post the "No trespassing" sign is not enough. Literature today is perhaps more serious in intent than it has been since Greek tragedy and

1

epic incarnated the theology and the religious ideals of a whole race. The novel and drama are more than media of entertainment; they are, usually quite intentionally, carriers of serious ideas. Poetry is as much as it ever was a fast, dazzling, serious game, "with barracking and broken bones."

Let there be no mistake. Neither the writer of imaginative literature nor the literary critic is a theologian, nor does either claim to be. Theology is, and must remain, a discipline with a methodology of its own. Our discussion joins theology only at that point—wherever it is—at which the study of theology becomes the study of religion. It is at that point of juncture, where theology becomes religion—where the theologian's traditional *fides quaerens intellectum* becomes *fides practica*—that the theologian and the literary critic become professionally interested in some of the same objects and values. Whether we like it or not, the novelist, the dramatist, and the poet are intensely aware that Western man exists in a concrete historical situation—that of the Judaeo-Christian tradition—and that he must take his position, pro or con, within this historical framework. The literary critic, being a critic of literature, must follow him. The literary man is not a theologian but, like the theologian, he does traffic in religious ideas.

There is hardly a major writer today for whom this seriousness of intent and this fascination with religious ideas are not crucial. Graham Greene's preoccupation with grace and the problem of evil, Mauriac's concern with the sacramental system and the redemptive role of the Church, Faulkner's mystique of predestination, Joyce's anguished attempt to reconcile art and belief, Kafka's eschatological forebodings, Camus' often agonized agnosticism, Hemingway's self-conscious nihilism—all these give the lie to the view that religious belief has nothing to do with literature. The catalogue could go on to include almost any modern writer of consequence: F. Scott Fitzgerald, D. H. Lawrence, Thomas Wolfe, Robert Penn Warren, Bernard Malamud, Saul Bellow, Flannery O'Connor, Léon Bloy, Georges Bernanos, Ignazio Silone, José María Gironella—all of them in deadly earnest about man and his ultimate values. Never before in its three-hundred-year history has the novel been so much a vehicle for serious ideas.

Drama, too, has been marked by a pronounced philosophical and theological bent: Eliot, Claudel, Cocteau, Anouilh, and (closer to home) Eugene O'Neill, Tennessee Williams, Arthur

Miller, Edward Albee. Even beyond this merely theological bent, the drama seems to have been chosen almost as a specifically philosophical or theological tool by writers like Jean-Paul Sartre and Gabriel Marcel.

Modern poets have been equally concerned with the problem of ultimate values and of man's relationship to God. Specifically Christian poets like Edith Sitwell, T. S. Eliot, W. H. Auden, and Allen Tate, and less specifically religious poets, too, like Dylan Thomas, John Crowe Ransom, E. E. Cummings, Marianne Moore, Karl Shapiro, and Wallace Stevens betray their concern with ultimate reality and with man's destiny.

There is little question that the most significant literature of our day deals with moral and metaphysical themes. Amos Wilder has even insisted (in his book *Theology and Modern Literature*) that "the deeper moral and spiritual issues of man today are often more powerfully canvassed by such writers than by theologians themselves." Wilder turns for his examples to Eliot, Auden, Claudel, Joyce, André Gide, Christopher Fry, Robert Lowell, and Robert Penn Warren, as well as to the "long line of modern agnostics or rebels, from Blake and Shelley, Whitman and Melville, to D. H. Lawrence, Kafka, Yeats." Such writers are for him "a kind of lay order in Christendom, engaged in tasks which the official Church has not yet fully encountered or assumed."[3]

If it is true that modern literature has been greatly concerned with religious ideas, either on the philosophical level or more specifically on the level of religious experience, then it is not surprising to find that modern criticism is beginning to reflect this concern.

The volume *Literature and Belief,* a selection from the 1957 Columbia University English Institute, is a case in point. Here we have critics like M. H. Abrams, Douglas Bush, Walter Ong, Cleanth Brooks, and Nathan Scott basically in agreement on the much-vexed problem of the relationship between literature and belief. The common denominator that becomes apparent in this volume is the view that since literature is a specifically human activity, the poet's beliefs are a constitutive element of his poetry and are thus an important object of the critic's attention. This is clearly an important and much-needed corrective for the excesses of some practitioners of the New Criticism, who emphasized too much the "poem-as-organism." If modern literature is more than "pure poetry," and is indeed intensely preoccupied with religious and theological values, then criticism must be prepared to deal with such a religious value structure.

This new realization of the pertinence of an author's religious commitment (or lack of it) to the critical endeavor is reflected in the spate of critical works which, during the past few years, have studied this problem.[4] In all these books, despite the vast differences in the backgrounds against which they are written, there is agreement that the religious commitment of an author is pertinent, indeed essential, to the critical endeavor. Basically, these critics would agree with Amos Wilder that "the theological aspect of literature and art bear on the very substance of the work, on the literary form and style."[5]

To substitute such a "theological" or "philosophical" criticism for all the other legitimate areas of criticism—historical, structural, semantic—is obviously not the point; it is simply a matter of insisting that such criticism has its proper place within the rubric of a complete criticism. Far from forgetting that discussion of structure and style is central to the critical endeavor, it must be insisted that the complexities of language are themselves charged with "value-significance." Literature, of its very nature, must begin with the word, then build with "rhetoric as skeleton and style as body of meaning"; it is language (especially metaphorical language) which enunciates, delimits, and evaluates theme, and thus reveals the particular poise and attitude of any imagination. A dichotomy between content and form is inadmissible; one is necessarily a function of the other. Both express, or at least imply, judgments of value; both are important objects of the critic's attention.

William Lynch, writing in *The Image Industries* of the relationship between theology and the arts, insisted cogently that "the immediately human materials of art have far greater theological connotations than we suppose and should engage the positive and creative attention of the theologian."[6] It is nonsense, he says, to think that a real theology could be "uninterested in the state of human sensibility in any civilization," but at the same time he acknowledges that "the theologians have not sufficiently illuminated the vital relationship of Christology to the arts and to all the concrete modes of human life."[7]

This relationship of theology to literature and the arts is not simply that of the moral theologian, necessary though his intervention may sometimes be. It is rather the positive analysis of creative theologians who, "if they will say the right thing about what Christianity and men really are," will help thereby "to unleash wonderful energies in all those artists who wish in their own way and according to their own powers to say the same thing."[8] But they will be helped toward mutual understanding only if each respects the methodology of the other, "if they both recognize that they run along different paths toward the same goal. That goal is nothing less than the reality of man."[9]

Just as it is risky for the literary artist to divorce the world of art from the world of reality, to retire into the realm of "pure poetry," so it seems equally dangerous for the theologian to accept too clear-cut a dichotomy between the world of dogma and the world of human art and sensibility. In any work of art, literary or otherwise, there is at least implicit a view of reality; and precisely here is the point of tangency with the theologian, who is concerned with the religious revelation as God's revealed view of reality. Surely the one has a profound relevance for the other.

There is an urgent practical aspect, too, of the rapport between literature and theology. In the secular colleges which are educating the great mass of collegiate America, the greater number of students take no formal courses in philosophy or theology. As one college professor remarked ruefully, "The only opportunity we have to handle problems of belief and human values is through literature." Perhaps this phenomenon is a long-term result of existentialist thinking with its emphasis on the concrete existent; perhaps it is the inevitable by-product of an age of science. Whatever the reason, the fact remains that intellectual America today is being exposed to philosophical and theological ideas not in the abstract, but through the very concrete medium of imaginative literature. It is useless to insist that the frontiers be maintained between these two ways of knowing, the theological and the literary; we must face up to the fact that the lines are being crossed, and there is (and should be) communication across the border.

Basically, the problem is that the relationship between these two ways of knowing, the theological and the literary, remains undefined. What is most important about the theologian vis-à-vis the artist is, I suppose, that he can help the artist to understand more clearly the workings of God in human history, elucidating as well as he can—by means of his own theological tools and methodology—the data of revelation.

The artist, for his part, can help the theologian by giving him a sense of the immediacy of the modern world. Theologians, from the nature of their science, must be formal and abstractive. It may be that the presentation of the concrete, dramatic, and phenomenological in literature might help them to relate the religious revelation more immediately to the modern mind. If their reading is restricted to *Death Comes for the Archbishop*, they are safe in the past; but if they read *A Farewell to Arms* or *Brighton Rock*, they may be forced to ask themselves what it means to modern man to say that the world is now redeemed.

Revelation, even while it speaks always the same truth, speaks to each age in its own terms. Revelation comes to us in an interpersonal mode of utterance, in sacred Scripture; this gives way to a metaphysical, or dogmatic, mode of discourse, in which theology is properly developed. Perhaps literature, as a statement of the mind and sensibility of contemporary man, can help theologians to return the developed theology to the interpersonal mode of discourse in which man's life must be lived.

The relationship between the critic and the theologian is more difficult to determine. If it is true that the artist is more and more frequently dealing with ideas that are properly theological—original sin, predestination, redemption, grace—does the literary critic, whose concern is the total literary work of art, have the right to judge these ideas? Perhaps the need is for the theologian-critic, one who will be able to appraise the literary work of art in all its literary dimensions, including that of the theological. This seeming anomaly is no longer a rarity, as men like the University of Chicago's Nathan Scott and Harvard's Amos Wilder testify by their work. To determine whether such an anomaly really should exist is part of the problem that remains.

This would indeed be a late date to revive the confusion of Matthew Arnold, by making literature a surrogate for theology. Neither poetry nor theology would be served by the confusion; the result could only be the emasculation of religion and the destruction of true poetry. But surely the time has come for dialogue between two branches of knowledge that are both so vitally concerned with the human situation. Let literature and its critics, for the fullness of their view of man, listen to the theologian's interpretation of the religious message; let the theologian turn to the artist to discover that important "point of entry into the country of the mind inhabited by the men of our time."

It is perhaps easy enough to enunciate general principles about the growing rapport between literature and theology, but finally one must come down to cases.

Faulkner, or indeed any writer of worth, must be approached cautiously in this regard. The critic must be always aware of just what he is about. It is not, as we have already insisted, a question of translating literature into dogma or dogma into literature, as if a novel or poem were somehow a translation of Thomas Aquinas's *Summa* or Calvin's *Institutes* into its imaginative equivalent. Faulkner, like any artist, must be met on his own terms. And Faulkner's terms are often demanding ones indeed.

Beyond the evident problem of Faulkner's involuted style there is the problem of his use of time—sometimes static, sometimes fluid, rarely limited by ordinary chronology, always psychologically significant, frequently bearing religious implications as well.

Another complicating factor is the matter of Faulkner's dramatic "voice," the problem of distinguishing Faulkner's attitude from those of his characters. This has been a recurring and often troublesome element in thirty years of Faulkner criticism. Herbert Perluck's essay on "The Bear," for example, sheds new light on the theological implications of this story, and particularly on Faulkner's own religious stance, precisely because he has realized—as too many others have not—that Ike McCaslin is not a spokesman for Faulkner.

Finally, there is the problem of the mixture of religious traditions that becomes evident on a careful reading of Faulkner. Faulkner knew, and was influenced by, not only the Judaeo-Christian tradition, but also the several religious traditions of Greece and Rome; and within the Christian tradition itself there are in Faulkner traces of more than one of the American Protestant theologies.

The essays which follow are not special pleading for any theological tradition, or any sect, or any literary theory. Nor are they biographical essays, attempting to determine the nature of Faulkner's own religious beliefs; the authors are con-

cerned rather with religious attitudes as they are found incarnated in Faulkner's fiction, and as they are operative in deter-
mining the inner structure of his art. Nor, finally, are they
exercises in theology. Theology and literature have many values, attitudes and concepts in common, as we have seen, and
so have relevance one for the other. Their disciplines and
methodologies must not be confused, however. Interrelated
though they are, the one is not the other.

The first four essays are general ones, not limited to a consideration of one or another of Faulkner's novels. They attempt
to define various aspects of religious experience and attitudes
in Faulkner's works: the particular cast of the Protestant Christianity found there; regional aspects of religion in the American South; the nature of good and evil, sin and redemption,
free will and predestination; the influences on Faulkner of the
ancient religions of Greece and Rome.

The six essays that follow are studies of individual works of
Faulkner. They represent no single point of view, and employ
no single methodology. They include close analysis of imagery,
study of interrelated patterns of symbolism, definition of dramatic situation and persona, analysis of theme, of character
development, of the nature of allegory. What is common to
them is their interest in the religious dimensions of Faulkner's
art, in whatever aspect of his work they may be seen.

There will be—of necessity, it seems to me—no further
attempt to define and follow through a theme common to all
the essays. To do so would be, in a sense, to close off the necessary openness of the critical endeavor. As he moves through the
essays, the reader will no doubt find certain themes, images, and
attitudes recurring, as Faulkner's work is turned around and
around, to be looked at from different points of view. Common
notes and conclusions may at length appear, and from them
perhaps a brief epilogue can be written. For the most part,
however, whatever conclusions can be drawn about the nature
of religious experience in Faulkner's fiction—and some will
be tentative at best—must emerge from the reader's careful
appraisal of the essays and commentaries themselves in the
light of his own reading of Faulkner.

2 ≡≡≡≡

This essay has been chosen to open the discussion simply because, of all the essays, it is the most general in scope and intent, and as such may serve—at least at the outset—as a kind of matrix for more detailed discussion. It attempts to discern a pattern of religious values and attitudes not in one or another novel but throughout the whole corpus of Faulkner's work. The editor finds its suggestions and assertions sometimes confirmed, sometimes supplemented, often qualified, by the other essays which follow it.

This essay was first published in *Thought*, 39 (1964), pp. 100–120, and is used with permission.

J. Robert Barth, S. J.

FAULKNER AND THE CALVINIST TRADITION

A PROFESSOR OF ENGLISH ONCE SUGGESTED THAT THE long-awaited American epic has already been written—a Calvinist epic, jointly authored by Nathaniel Hawthorne, Herman Melville, and William Faulkner. One may have serious reservations theologically as to the meaning and ultimate value of this epic, but its importance can hardly be denied. Whether epic or not, it is there and it is part of our tradition; it has contributed toward making us what we are.

The few critics of Faulkner who touch on his theological background have been content to situate him in a general way as a part of the American Protestant ethos. William Van O'Connor, for example, in his excellent essay on Faulkner's attitude toward religion in *Light in August,* speaks of "the spirit of Protestantism in the southern mores" and of "Protestant orthodoxy."[1] Taken *tout court,* this is true enough, but in the light of the complex nature of the Protestant tradition it leaves much to be said. It will be suggested here that Faulkner belongs, in the particular bent of his imagination, to one of several lines of tradition in American Protestantism—that he stands strongly and unmistakably within the Calvinist camp, in a direct line of kinship with Cotton Mather and Jonathan Edwards, with Hawthorne and Melville.

In a general way, it may be said that the main stream of American literary thought and sensibility flows in a more or less direct line from the crucial age of American Puritanism. All too often, the term "Puritanism" has been equated with Calvinism pure and simple. Although this identification might be made with somewhat more truth in the case of English

11

Puritanism, American Puritanism, even in its nascent stages, was already theologically ambivalent.

Today we must demur from the somewhat oversimplified version of Parrington, dividing American Puritanism into its constituent Calvinist and Lutheran elements.[2] At the same time, his basic insight remains valid, that American Puritanism was in conflict with itself. There was indeed a stern foundation of Calvinist thought in much of American Puritanism. The strict Puritan "was sure that the universe centered not on man, but on God, and that all man's energies must be devoted to God's service. God absolutely controlled all creation. Man was his creature, inherently sinful, and could be freed from evil only by the arbitrary gift of divine grace. Neither his own deeds nor the intercession of a church could help him. . . ."[3] Calvin's two fundamental postulates of predestination (the elect to salvation, the non-elect to damnation) and the total depravity of human nature after the fall, are surely characteristic of much of the theological literature of American Puritanism. This is the stern and unflinching Calvinism of John Winthrop, of Increase and Cotton Mather, of Jonathan Edwards.

At the same time, it must be recognized that there were other currents of thought moving strongly through the age. Perry Miller has shown, in his studies of men like John Cotton, Thomas Hooker, Thomas Shepard, and Peter Bulkley, that "they worked out a special and peculiar version of theology which has a marked individuality and which differentiates them considerably from the followers of unadulterated Calvinism."[4] Particularly by renewed study of the nature of the covenant between God and man, these founders of the "federal theology" strove "to bring Calvinism into harmony with the temper of the seventeenth century."[5] The effect of their speculation was "to introduce an element of historical relativism into the absolute dogmatism of original Calvinism. God is seen deliberately refraining from putting His decisions fully into effect until man can cope with them and profit by them."[6] Miller's summary of the federal theologians' view of grace and free will is a far cry from Cotton Mather's stern view of predestination and depravity:

> The covenant of grace defines the conditions by which Heaven is obtained, and he who fulfills the conditions has an incontestable title to glorification, exactly as he who

pays the advertised price owns his freehold. God may continue to choose the elect in the impenetrable fastness of
His will, but according to the covenant He has agreed to
give the individual discernible grounds for His decision.[7]

In addition, there were other liberal elements: Separatists,
Antinomians, Seekers, and others. Roger Williams fought for
the separation of Church and State, with its concomitant principle of toleration in religion, and was banished from the
Massachusetts Bay Colony for this opposition to the Calvinist
theocracy. John Wise justified the principle of Congregational-
ism by applying to ecclesiastical government the principle of
democracy in civil affairs, precipitating counterblasts from the
Presbyterian party. This struggle between the theocratic and
the democratic principles was simply a reflection, on the level
of external organization, of the deep conflict within Puritan
thought itself.

In short, then, the heritage left to us by American Puritanism
was a double one. It already contained within itself the seeds
of two contradictory ideologies, determinism and extreme indi-
vidualism. The one is found in the strict Calvinistic theological determinism of the right-wing Puritan divines, such as Cotton Mather and Jonathan Edwards; the other is manifested
in the liberal Puritanism of men like Thomas Hooker, Roger
Williams, and John Wise.

But our concern here is with the place of Faulkner in the
Puritan heritage. In relating Faulkner to this tradition, a
clear line must be drawn between the two elements of the Puritan theology; he stands quite unmistakably within the orthodox
Calvinist strain.

Roughly speaking, the general lines of development began
with the rigidly Calvinist determinism of right-wing Puritans
of the stamp of Mather, Winthrop, and Edwards. All the
actions of men, they believed, have been predestined and predetermined from the beginning; man is not a free and responsible agent. The dominant stress was not on man's striving
toward his last end, but on God's absolute sovereignty with
respect to salvation and damnation. Jonathan Edwards' spec-
tacular sermon "Sinners in the Hands of an Angry God" leaves
little room for human striving, any more than does the whole
Calvinist economy of salvation.

Between the death in 1758 of Jonathan Edwards, the great

master of American Calvinism, and the first publications of Nathaniel Hawthorne in the 1820's, America lived through a strange and turbulent period. Hand in hand with the Revolution of the young republic came a revolution, long brewing, in the realm of ideas. The influences of French liberalism and German romantic transcendentalism were felt more and more strongly, and the voices of Rousseau and Schelling were heard in the land, if only through the medium of English writers like Locke, Coleridge, and Carlyle. From French liberalism came William Ellery Channing and Unitarianism; from the mating of Unitarianism with German thought came, not long after, the American brand of romantic transcendentalism.

The clash of the new ideas with the Calvinist orthodoxy was inevitable. The guardians of Calvinist theology were not to allow this incursion upon orthodoxy without a battle; the Calvinist tradition was still alive in the midst of a world turned liberal. The Unitarians won control of Harvard College in 1805, but the Calvinists countered with the founding of Andover Theological Seminary in 1808. While Unitarianism continued to win converts and popular acclaim, the stern orthodoxy of Edwards was kept alive by men like Jedidiah Morse, Timothy Dwight, Nathaniel Walker, and Samuel Hopkins.

With the flowering of New England transcendentalism in the 1820's, however, it might seem that Calvinism was dead. The liberal conviction of man's innate goodness and endless perfectibility held the field, and the young nation was bursting with optimism. But it must be remembered that transcendentalism had not grown in a vacuum. Despite the important influences from abroad, it had grown from native soil; its roots were in the American Puritan past, to which it owed, above all, its intense moralism. The balance had swung toward a new and rarefied kind of left-wing Puritanism, but the old right-wing Puritanism of Mather and Edwards was only awaiting its chance to make an entrance.

Its re-emergence, in altered but still recognizable form, may perhaps have been due to an inevitable disillusionment in certain quarters with some of the Rousseauian sentimentalities and unrealities of Unitarianism and Transcendentalism. At any rate, epitomizing this opposition to the new romantic liberalism were two men who stand clearly in the Calvinist line, Hawthorne and Melville.

Nathaniel Hawthorne was born into the Calvinist tradition,

and lived his whole life in its shadow. Although he ceased early in his life to believe in its dogmas, Hawthorne always remained a Calvinist in the sense that the bent of his mind was Calvinistic. As Parrington expresses it:

> Although he was a child of the liberation and had broken the web that Calvinism had woven about the mind of New England, he did not choose to quit the world from whose bondage he had freed himself. . . . It appealed to his imagination after his reason had rejected its dogmas; it determined his art after it had ceased to command his loyalty.[8]

Not only is sin the central fact in the most characteristic of Hawthorne's work, but this fact is consistently stated with unmistakable overtones of divine determinism and human depravity.

But Hawthorne was not content with his New England birthright. He dared to question the Calvinist tradition. He questioned, but he could not find it in himself either to fashion another image of man, or to look beyond his vision of God the Father as this "great stone face"—calm, benign, and somehow provident, but not to be moved by our laughter or our tears.

Herman Melville at times seems to reject this vision of life's mystery, but the very vehemence of his disavowal reveals how heavily the tradition weighed upon him. Ultimately, there seemed to him but one logical solution to the Calvinist dilemma, to the problem of reconciling the supposed goodness of God with the existence of predetermined evil in the world. His solution was that of the Manichees, a dualism which admitted a dynamic principle of evil within the godhead. Melville's very belief in the existence of Moby Dick (in whom "all evil, to crazy Ahab, was visibly personified") was an implicit avowal of the existence of God.

Melville, like Newman, could readily see that if there is a God, then "the human race is implicated in some terrible calamity." For Newman this calamity is original sin, weakening man but not condemning him. For Melville, it is every man's predetermination to catastrophe.

It is into this literary line that Faulkner was born. The strong thread of predestination that runs through his work, together with his preoccupation with guilt and man's depravity, put the unmistakable Calvinist stamp upon him. He is not simply in the Protestant tradition; he is in the Calvinist Protestant tradition.

The basic Faulknerian theme of predetermination is always present underlying the action, and is frequently the subject of explicit and extended treatment. It has many synonyms in Faulkner's vocabulary. Sometimes it is fate, sometimes it is doom; most frequently he simply refers to it as "the curse."

It should be made clear from the outset that the concept of "the curse" is not a univocal one. It is not simply Calvin's conception of man caught in the clutches of an angry and vengeful God; it is an analogous concept shifting with character and situation. For Thomas Sutpen it is the memory of his "poor-white" ancestry, driving him to a life of greed and exploitation; for the suicide Quentin Compson it is the oppressive weight of a whole family's immorality, as felt in "the contradiction between proclaimed ethic and daily defeat";[9] for the cursed McCaslin family it is the injustice inherent in the whole Southern tradition, the ravaged land and the exploitation of the slaves. Whatever it is that takes away man's freedom—whether it is the consequence of sin or circumstances, of ancestry or race or character, of uncharity or injustice—that is what constitutes the curse. The curse, Faulkner seems to say, is the human condition.

As early as *Soldier's Pay* (1926) the theme of predetermination, of "the inevitable," is enunciated. Donald Mahon, returning from World War I scarred and war-weary and near death, is completely helpless in the hands of the fate toward which he moves. In the midst of all the human forces that play about him, he remains passive and inert, carried along by "the wheel of the world, the terrible calm, inevitability of life."[10] After Donald's death, the book closes on the same note: "Then the singing died, fading away along the mooned land inevitable with to-morrow and sweat, with sex and death and damnation" (p. 319).

In *Sartoris* (1929) this theme is brought into sharp focus with Faulkner's first treatment of the ill-starred Sartoris family, which figures prominently in much of the saga of Faulkner's mythical Yoknapatawpha County. The Sartoris curse is a type of the curse of the South, the curse of slavery and exploitation, lasting through four generations. All the Sartorises are doomed to moral decay and eventual extinction: Colonel John, who fought in the Civil War; old Bayard, the politician; the wild young Bayard, who toys with death; and young Benbow, who, even with a different name, cannot escape the family doom.

> It showed on John Sartoris' brow, the dark shadow of fatality and doom. . . . The railroad was finished, and that day he had been elected to the state legislature after a hard and bitter fight, and doom lay on his brow, and weariness.[11]

And of old Bayard, Faulkner says: "Yes, it was a good gesture, and old Bayard sat and mused quietly on the tense he had unwittingly used. Was. Fatality; the augury of a man's destiny peeping out at him from the roadside hedge . . ." (p. 93).

Young Bayard's wife Narcissa, as well as Bayard himself, is aware of the doom that sits upon him:

> She took his face between her palms and drew it down, but his lips were cold and upon them she tasted fatality and doom. . . . And they would lie so, holding to one another in the darkness and the temporary abeyance of his despair and the isolation of that doom he could not escape (p. 289).

Indeed, Narcissa herself is the instrument by which the curse is passed on to the child she is to bear:

> . . . she was cherishing the child under her own heart with all the aroused constancy of her nature: it was as though already she could discern the dark shape of that doom which she had incurred, standing beside her chair, waiting and biding its time (p. 356).

As the book closes, the master of the story, the punisher of the guilty (and the not-guilty), is briefly glimpsed:

> The music went on in the dusk softly; the dusk was peopled with ghosts of glamorous and old disastrous things. And if they were just glamorous enough, there was sure to be a Sartoris in them, and then they were sure to be disastrous. Pawns. But the Player, and the game He plays . . . He must have a name for His pawns, though. But perhaps Sartoris is the game itself,—a game outmoded and played with pawns shaped too late and to an old dead pattern, and

of which the Player Himself is a little wearied. For there is death in the sound of it, and a glamorous fatality, like silver pennons downrushing at sunset, or a dying fall of horns along the road to Roncevaux (p. 380).

In his important work *The Sound and the Fury* (1929), Faulkner handles the fatality theme just as explicitly, this time in his poetic narration of the decay of the Compson family. As Quentin Compson comes to realize just before his suicide: "there's a curse on us its not our fault."[12] Doom runs throughout the book as if it were a *leitmotiv* for the Compsons themselves. "No battle is ever won," Mr. Compson tells his son. "They are not even fought. The field only reveals to man his own folly and despair" (p. 95). And again: "One day you'd think misfortune would get tired, but then time is your misfortune Father said. A gull on an invisible wire attached through space dragged. You carry the symbol of your frustration into eternity" (p. 123). Man is, he tells Quentin, "a problem in impure properties carried tediously to an unvarying nil: stalemate of dust and desire" (pp. 142–143).

It is in such a context of fatality that Caddy's daughter Quentin is forced to say: "If I'm bad, it's because I had to be" (p. 277). Jason, too, realizes that his destiny is not under the control of his will: "He could see the opposed forces of his destiny and his will drawing swiftly together now, toward a junction that would be irrevocable" (p. 323).

The story of the Compsons is a brooding tale of a family caught in the web of its own past, living out the contradiction between what it pretends to be and what it is; as Faulkner makes clear in an Appendix written for the book, the family is paying the price for its ancestors' rapacity and greed. The father drinks himself to an early death; the mother lives out an ineffectual life, helplessly watching the ruin of her children; Quentin III falls in love with his sister Candace, and commits suicide shortly after her marriage; Candace becomes the town slut, in which calling she is later followed by her daughter Quentin; Jason, Quentin's uncle, is drained of all human affection and sympathy, and is brought to ruin by his niece Quentin's theft of his savings; Benjy the last-born, an idiot, is gelded after an attack on a little girl and is ultimately committed to the state asylum. This tale of horror is spun out in the context of a view of man as a creature "whose every breath is a fresh cast with dice already loaded against him," and who comes to realize "that even the despair or remorse or bereavement is not particularly important to the dark diceman" (p. 196).

Light in August (1932) gives us, in the figures of Joe Christmas, the Reverend Hightower, and Miss Joanna Burden, what Richard Rovere has called Faulkner's "feeling for the past as the arbiter of present destinies."[13]

Joe Christmas' fatal past is the parentage that left him "tainted," even though uncolored, by Negro blood; it brought him to suffering and solitude and violent death. As he thinks of the road down which he has fled all his life, Christmas reflects:

> . . . he is entering it again, the street which ran on for thirty years. . . . It had made a circle and he is still inside of it. . . . I have never got outside that circle. I have never broken out of the ring of what I have already done and cannot ever undo (p. 296).

And again:

> . . . he believed with calm paradox that he was the volitionless servant of the fatality in which he believed that he did not believe. He was saying to himself *I had to do it* already in the past tense; *I had to do it* (p. 245).

Christmas knows he is going to commit a murder even before he has made any decision. Suddenly the razor is in his hand.

> "Something is going to happen. Something is going to happen to me"; and a moment later, already speaking in the past, he adds, even though he has not yet committed the act: "*I had to do it. . . . I had to do it*" (p. 245).

It is possible to foresee, but not to determine, the course of human events.

For the Reverend Hightower, the curse is the lost glory of the Civil War, which is perpetuating its defeat in his life; he is caught between dream and reality.

> "If I am the instrument of her [his wife's] despair and death, then I am in turn instrument of someone outside

myself. And I know that for fifty years I have not even been clay: I have been a single instant of darkness in which a horse galloped and a gun crashed" (p. 430).

In the case of the spinster Joanna Burden, who is murdered by Joe Christmas, the curse is "the white man's curse" left by the cruelty and injustice of slavery.

"Your grandfather and brother are lying there, murdered not by one white man but by the curse which God put on a whole race before your grandfather or your brother or me or you were even thought of. A race doomed and cursed to be forever and ever a part of the white race's doom and curse for its sins. I had seen and known Negroes since I could remember. I just looked at them as I did at rain, or furniture, or food or sleep. But after that I seemed to see them for the first time not as people, but as a thing, a shadow in which I lived, we lived, all white people, all other people. I thought of all the children coming forever and ever into the world, white, with the black shadow already falling upon them before they drew breath. And I seemed to see the black shadow in the shape of a cross. And it seemed like the white babies were struggling, even before they drew breath, to escape from the shadow that was not only upon them but beneath them too, flung out like their arms were flung out, as if they were nailed to the cross. I saw all the little babies that would ever be in the world, the ones not yet even born—a long line of them with their arms spread, on the black crosses" (pp. 221–222).

The simple Lena Grove, one of Faulkner's most appealing characters, might seem to tip the scale in favor of freedom. She and the admirable Byron Bunch do, indeed, serve as a counterpoint for the tragic figures of Christmas, Hightower, and Miss Burden, but it must be pointed out that Lena is predetermined to good just as ineluctably as Joe Christmas is to evil. Christmas and Hightower are destroyed because, even though doomed to defeat, they accept the challenge of their humanity; Lena, the "good unruffled vegetable Lena," survives in her stupidity. The only truly free agent among them is Byron Bunch, who alone seems free to assert a destiny of his own choosing.

It is in the sustained dark brilliance of *Absalom, Absalom!* (1936) that Faulkner's fatality theme receives its fullest expression. The curse on Thomas Sutpen is that of his "poor-white" background of poverty and neglect, driving him on to wrest a plantation from the wilderness by fair means or foul, while the curse on his family is the result of his cruelty and injustice. But there seems to be another and deeper dimension. The curse on Sutpen's family is also the curse on the South for its inhumanity and greed, for cheating the Indians of their land and the Negroes of their human dignity. On an even deeper level, is it the curse that broods over fallen mankind?

Sutpen himself is the first object of his own curse. All the while he was cheating and clawing his way to wealth and position,

> he was unaware that his flowering was a forced blooming too and that while he was still playing the scene to the audience, behind him Fate, destiny, retribution, irony— the stage manager, call him what you will—was already striking the set and dragging on the synthetic and spurious shadows and shapes of the next one.[14]

But it was Sutpen's family, for generations afterward, that was to pay the price. Quentin Compson, narrator of the tragedy of Sutpen's son Henry, says of him:

> "Maybe he knew there was a fate, a doom on him. . . . Maybe he knew then that whatever the old man had done, whether he meant well or ill by it, it wasn't going to be the old man who would have to pay the check; and now that the old man was bankrupt with the incompetence of age, who should do the paying if not his sons, his get, because wasn't it done that way in the old days" (p. 325).

This is the "current of retribution and fatality which Miss Rosa said Sutpen had started and had doomed all his blood to, black and white both" (p. 269). And by Faulkner's imaginative use of time, telescoping past and present to show the inescapable impact of one on the other, Sutpen's curse is brought vividly into present reality. Quentin Compson (the doomed suicide of *The Sound and the Fury*) relates Sutpen's curse to his own curse that comes to him from his father:

> "Maybe we are both Father. Maybe nothing ever happens once and is finished. Maybe happen is never once but like ripples maybe on water after the pebble sinks, the ripples moving on, spreading. . . . Yes, we are both Father. Or maybe Father and I are both Shreve, maybe it took Father and me both to make Shreve or Shreve and me both to make Father or maybe Thomas Sutpen to make all of us" (pp. 261–262).

In the larger view, Sutpen's curse stands for the doom that hangs over the South. Rosa Coldfield, whose family is linked to Sutpen's through the marriage of her sister, says it is

> "as though there were a fatality and curse on our family and God Himself were seeing to it that it was performed and discharged to the last drop and dreg. Yes, fatality and curse on the South and on our family as though because some ancestor of ours had elected to establish his descent in a land primed for fatality and already cursed with it, even if it had not rather been our family, our father's progenitors, who had incurred the curse long years before and had been coerced by Heaven into establishing itself in the land and the time already cursed" (p. 21).

In the context of Faulkner's entire saga, there frequently seems to be the suggestion of something even beyond the fatality of the South, something that "grieves on universal bones"—a doom that hangs over all men. Sutpen's daughter Judith seems to be touching on such a vision in the dark defeat of this passage:

> "You get born and you try this and you dont know why only you keep on trying it and you are born at the same time with a lot of other people, all mixed up with them, like trying to, having to, move your arms and legs with strings only the same strings are hitched to all the other arms and legs and the others all trying and they dont know

why either except that the strings are all in one another's way like five or six people all trying to make a rug on the same loom only each wants to weave his own pattern into the rug; and it cant matter, you know that, or the Ones that set up the loom would have arranged things a little better, and yet it must matter because you keep on trying or having to keep on trying and then all of a sudden it's all over and all you have left is a block of stone with scratches on it provided there was someone to remember to have the marble scratched and set up or had time to, and it rains on it and the sun shines on it and after a while they dont even remember the name and what the scratches were trying to tell, and it doesn't matter" (p. 127).

In *Old Man* (1939) Faulkner shows us another face of the same coin. Here he does not speak in terms of "curse" or "fatality," but directly of man's freedom. The tall convict who is the protagonist is caught quite unwillingly in a situation, a responsibility: the care of a pregnant woman who is his fellow refugee from the Mississippi flood of 1927. He has but one aim throughout the whole of the story—to get away from freedom and its concomitant responsibility, back to the unthinking and volitionless life of prison. "All I want in the world is just to surrender."[15] It is, we are told, "as if his own failed and spent flesh were attempting to carry out his furious unflagging will for severance at any price, even that of drowning, from the burden with which, unwittingly and without choice, he had been doomed" (p. 177). He speaks of "the old primal faithless Manipulator of all the lust and folly and injustice" (p. 247), of the "cosmic joker" who toyed with him (p. 264), of "the gambit which he had not elected" (p. 266).

When the convict has returned voluntarily to prison, "safe, secure, riveted warranted and doubly guaranteed by the ten years they had added to his sentence for attempted escape" (p. 164), he is finally at peace. After all, Faulkner seems to say, freedom is not natural to man.

Besides the Sartoris, Compson, and Sutpen families, there is another Yoknapatawpha family on whom a doom sits: the McCaslin family, presented principally in *Go Down, Moses* (1942), a series of independent but interrelated narratives. Four of the stories deal with the ancestry and character of Isaac McCaslin,

while two of them are concerned with the Negro offshoots of
the family. Over all the events narrated there broods the over-
whelming fact of the curse brought down on the family by its
founder, Carothers McCaslin, when he seduced the daughter
born to him by a Negro slave. Implicit here (and sometimes
explicit) is an equivalence with the South's rape of the land
which the black race had helped it to conquer and tame, and
its betrayal of the black race itself. The central moral action of
Go Down, Moses, especially as recounted in the moving story
"The Bear" and its postscript "Delta Autumn," is Isaac Mc-
Caslin's recognition of the shame and injustice that corrupt his
inheritance.

In "The Bear," the narrowing strip of wilderness to which
the hunters go is a kind of pilgrimage shrine, to which they set
out in the hope of shedding the guilt of society. But even in
their coming they realize that the woods are doomed, just as
the great bear Ben is doomed. "Dont you see?", McCaslin says
to the Negro Lucas Beauchamp.

> "This whole land, the whole South, is cursed, and all of us
> who derive from it, whom it ever suckled, white and black
> both, lie under the curse? Granted that my people brought
> the curse onto the land: maybe for that reason their
> descendants alone can—not resist it, not combat it—maybe
> just endure and outlast it until the curse is lifted."[16]

Indeed, Lucas himself had already found long since "that no
man is ever free and probably could not bear it if he were"
(p. 281).

Besides these full and explicit expositions of the fatality
theme, there are many other less extended treatments of it in
Faulkner's work. In *Pylon* (1935) the reporter-protagonist lives
in the conviction that the ordinary passage of human events
suffocates hope, that you "walk the earth with your arm
crooked over your head to dodge until you finally get the old
blackjack at last and can lay back down again."[17] As late as *The
Town* (1957), Faulkner presents in the man-destroying Eula
Varner a breathing symbol of passivity in the face of an inevitable destiny. In the short story "That Evening Sun," the Negro
Nancy sits waiting for a fate she cannot escape: "'Twont do no
good. . . . Putting if off wont do no good."[18] In "Red Leaves,"
the Indian Issetibbeha's Negro body servant is doomed by

Indian custom to be buried with his master, and the story portrays the struggle between his will to live and his ineluctable fate.

It is in the story "A Justice" that doom becomes synonymous with man himself. In it, the old Indian chief is known as "the Man," in French "Du Homme."

> "My name is Doom now," Doom said. "It was given me by a French chief in New Orleans. In French talking, Doo-um; in our talking, Doom."
>
> "What does it mean?" Herman Basket said.
>
> He said how Doom looked at him for a while. "It means the Man," Doom said (*Collected Stories*, p. 348).

When Cotton Mather and Jonathan Edwards spoke of man's predestination, they were asserting not only the frailty of man but also the greatness of God. The elect were chosen only because of the gratuitous mercy of an all-powerful God; the damned were predestined to hell precisely because they were "in the hands of an angry God." Faulkner, on the other hand, as will be evident by this time, is not so much concerned with the relationship between man and God that is implied in the "curse" as he is with the human situation itself and with man's causality in bringing it about. He does refer, it is true, to the "Player," the "Manipulator" of men's lives and of the human doom, but his focus of attention is the curse itself in all its analogous manifestations—Negro blood, a family's slow decay, an idiot son, hatred and lust and incest, and behind it all, the curse on all of fallen mankind. And beyond all these are the distant causes of the curse—the ravaged land, the exploitation of the slaves, the greed and injustice of the South, and, perhaps, some great primeval fault in the years beyond telling. Because the South has sinned, Faulkner seems to say, because our fathers have sinned, man is no longer free to work out his destiny.

The other Calvinist attitude found in Faulkner—his preoccupation with depravity and evil, corruption and guilt—may be treated more expeditiously, for it is even clearer in Faulkner's work than the theme of predestination; besides, its pervasive influence has already been glimpsed in the fate motif. Quite clearly, the predetermination we have seen in Faulkner's characters is generally toward evil, that of "the curse."

In a more consciously Christian writer, one might be inclined to call Faulkner's portrayal of evil simply a "sense of original

sin." But in his work the emphasis on depravity is so strong,
while the freedom to overcome it is so generally withheld, that
it must be more sharply defined; it must be reckoned closer to
the Calvinist notion of depravity than to any other interpretation of the concept of original sin. In *The Sound and the Fury*
it is "the sequence of natural events and their causes which
shadows every mans brow" (p. 195); in *Light in August* it is
"the devil's walking seed unbeknownst among them, polluting
the earth" (p. 335); in *Absalom, Absalom!* it is "that sickness
somewhere at the prime foundation of this factual scheme"
(p. 143).

One of the most obvious manifestations of Faulkner's preoccupation with man's depravity is his frequent description of
sexual perversions, which are often crucial elements in his
story. Numerous examples come to mind: Benjy's attack on the
little girl in *The Sound and the Fury;* Popeye's perverted attack
on Temple Drake in *Sanctuary;* the wife shared by the pilot
and the mechanic in *Pylon;* the incest either planned or per-
petrated by Quentin in *The Sound and the Fury,* by Charles
Bon in *Absalom, Absalom!,* by Carothers McCaslin in *Go
Down, Moses;* the extended description of the idiot Ike Snopes's
act of bestiality in *The Hamlet;* Miss Emily's necrophilia in
"A Rose for Emily."

Faulkner's harsh treatment of women offers an interesting
insight into the frequent occurrence in Faulkner's work of what
is very close to "total depravity." No one better sums up Faulkner's recurring attitude toward women than does old Doc
Hines in *Light in August,* when he furiously denounces "the
bitchery and abomination of womanflesh." There are few
writers who have so fiercely attacked what Irving Howe calls
"the young American bitch": Cecily Saunders, the nympho-
maniac of *Soldier's Pay;* Patricia, the flapper of *Mosquitos;*
Temple Drake of *Sanctuary,* who thoroughly enjoys her stay in
a Memphis brothel. Faulkner lashes out, too, at women like
Laverne in *Pylon* and Charlotte in *The Wild Palms,* who sin
not through malice but through the impersonal mechanics of
their sex; at Joanna Burden in *Light in August,* who was "completely corrupt"; at the man-destroying Eula Varner, who
moves through *The Hamlet* and *The Town* like an inverted
fertility symbol, destroying life instead of bringing it into the
world.

There are few women in Yoknapatawpha County who escape

the charge of "bitchery and abomination." Some of Faulkner's colored women, like Dilsey and Nancy Mannigoe, or of his old women, like Granny Millard Sartoris, manage to evoke Faulkner's admiration, but these remain rare exceptions to his general judgment of the depravity of "womanflesh." Even an exceptional character like gentle Lena Grove is good rather through stupidity than through deliberate choice.

By far the most convincing evidence of Faulkner's emphasis on man's corruption is found in a series of pivotal characters whom Faulkner presents as evil incarnate in the world: Jason Compson in *The Sound and the Fury,* Popeye in *Sanctuary,* Thomas Sutpen in *Absalom, Absalom!,* and Flem Snopes, who appears in *The Hamlet* (1940), *The Town* and *The Mansion* (1959), as well as throughout the Yoknapatawpha stories.

As the Compson family moves swiftly toward its doom in *The Sound and the Fury,* it is Jason who presides over the dissolution. He robs his mother, drives his sister from the house, has his brother gelded and committed to a state institution. There is no remorse, no human sympathy, no pity for his victims.

The impotent Popeye of *Sanctuary,* who murders in cold blood and rapes by proxy, is admittedly a symbol of evil. With his tight clothes, his rubbery eyes, and damp hands, he projects the impression of some primal crawling thing, unfeeling, almost inhuman. His presence is everywhere in the novel; it informs every scene with a sense of the brooding presence of evil.

Throughout *Absalom, Absalom!,* the protagonist Sutpen is referred to as "the demon." He is "this Faustus, this demon, this Beelzebub fled hiding from some momentary flashy glare of his Creditor's outraged face . . . engaged in one final frenzy of evil and harm-doing before the Creditor overtook him next time for good and all" (p. 178). There is no question of Sutpen performing a good act; he is quite incapable of it.

If the Sartorises are the great sinners of Yoknapatawpha County, then Flem Snopes is their Satan. Indeed the whole Snopes clan, who begin their infiltration of Faulkner's county with Ab Snopes in *The Unvanquished,* stand in Faulkner's *symbolik* for "the putrescent within nature."[19] Under the leadership of Flem, the numerous members of the clan drift into the village of Frenchman's Bend where they form a pestilential band of malingerers, cheats, thieves, and double-dealers. Flem outwits the local peasantry and gentry at every turn, marries into money and becomes president of the Jefferson bank, while his relatives ooze up into analogous positions in town and village; later the Snopeses find their way to positions as administrators of wealthy Memphis brothels, and one named Cla'ence even finds his way into the Mississippi state legislature. They are for Faulkner the face of the "New South," which combines the worst elements of past and present. Snopesism is the inevitable reaping of the South's sowing of greed and injustice.

In *Light in August,* Faulkner lashes out in a violent attack on the harshness and pessimism of the Calvinist mystique, in the person of the grim-visaged Simon McEachern. Faulkner himself, however, is still caught fast in its toils. The same thing might be said of Faulkner that Parrington has said of Hawthorne, that the Calvinist attitude determines his art even when it does not command his loyalty. Just as Hawthorne and Melville tried to escape from the tradition that had nurtured them, so does Faulkner. Yet none of them found any great measure of success. Faulkner would like to assert man's freedom, but he cannot; he would like to assert man's goodness, but he can do so only rarely and hesitantly. The after-impression he leaves is one of corruption, like Addie Bundren's body which, after its six-day junket through the Mississippi countryside, gave off the smell of death.

Let there be no misunderstanding. There is no question here of denying that there is freedom to be found in Faulkner's work, that even the most doomed among his characters at times find strength to fight against their curse. Joe Christmas and Reverend Hightower, Charles Bon and Henry Sutpen, all fight back against the destiny they have not chosen. But in their very assertion of their own humanity, do they not fight with the strength of despair rather than of hope? Faulkner can no more keep man's free will from expressing itself in his writing than the American Puritan could keep himself from making free will acts in his daily life. It is in the nature of man. What we have been talking of here is a "bent of the imagination," a cast of mind, an attitude, a habitual way of looking at the world. Here, indeed, is a great part of the secret of Faulkner's power, as well as one reason for the constant violence of his dramatic movement: he is constantly expressing in artistic form the tension that actually exists between man's free will and the countless forces that thwart its exercise; between man's potential for goodness and his actual wickedness. Faulkner wants to assert goodness and freedom, but seems to have seen too much of guilt and, as he might put it, unfreedom.

The French critic Rabi, writing in 1951, said of Faulkner: "In Faulkner, there is no hope. Though the Redeemer has come, he has left no traces. He has given us only a sense of the irremediable, and the painful memory of our lost Paradise. The Faulknerian tragedy is a tragedy of exile."[20] But the story was not yet over. Two books were to be published which brought hope into the brooding magnificence of Faulkner's Calvinist world: *Requiem for a Nun* (1951) and *A Fable* (1954).

Requiem for a Nun stands as sequel to *Sanctuary*, the story of one of Faulkner's great sinners, Temple Drake. In this book, which was published exactly twenty years after *Sanctuary*, Faulkner approaches for the first time a possible solution for the problem of man's guilt. True, there had been fitful attempts at a solution from time to time, but these were more in the nature of a dying hero's bravado than of a true conviction of resolving a real problem: there is no expiation for sin, he seemed to be saying, but man can at least assert his humanity by bravery or violence or (rarely) love. Here for the first time, in *Requiem for a Nun*, Faulkner has caught a glimpse of the value of suffering in expiation for sin. It is theologically ungrounded in his work, to be sure, but his insight into the reality of the human situation has appreciably deepened.

Nancy Mannigoe, who has murdered Temple's child to keep it from evil influence, goes to her death in expiation for Temple's guilty life. Just before her execution, Nancy tells Temple: ". . . you got to trust Him. Maybe that's your pay for the suffering." And her lawyer Gavin Stevens asks:

> Whose suffering, and whose pay? Just each one's for his own?
>
> NANCY
>
> Everybody's. All suffering. All poor sinning man's.
>
> STEVENS
>
> The salvation of the world is in man's suffering.
> Is that it?
>
> NANCY
>
> Yes, sir.[21]

In the complex story called *A Fable,* the theme of salvation through suffering is carried through in greater detail. On the immediately obvious level, it is a re-creation of the narrative of Christ's Passion in the context of the mutiny, during World War I, of a group of pacifist soldiers. But a closer reading leaves one with the impression that the rich and complex symbolism can actually be reduced to a symbolic least common denominator which is far more simple in intent.

Once the numerous and multivalent symbols have been weighed and measured, the two most prominent figures, the Corporal and the old General, are found to carry the main burden of the inner structure of the book. In the last analysis, the two characters represent a kind of modern "everyman." They are, in a very real sense, two aspects of the reader, of Faulkner himself, of every man. Taken together, as Faulkner seems to intend them to be taken, they represent the dual polarity of the complete man: man is bound to earth, and yet he aspires to something higher. In the temptation scene, in which the General attempts to prevent his son (the Corporal) from submitting to martyrdom for the sake of peace, the General emphasizes this essential duality:

> ". . . we are two articulations, self-elected possibly, anyway elected, anyway postulated, not so much to defend as to test two inimical conditions which, through no fault of ours, but through the simple paucity and restrictions of the arena where they meet, must contend and—one of them —perish: I champion of this mundane earth which, whether I like it or not, is, and to which I did not ask to come, yet since I am here, not only must stop but intend to stop during my allotted while; you champion of an esoteric realm of man's baseless hopes and his infinite capacity—no: passion —for unfact."[22]

Yet even the General realizes that the two "articulations" are not contradictory, that man is somehow, by his very constitution, limited by the "restrictions of the arena" and at the same time endowed with an "infinite capacity" for something beyond. Even he must admit that these two drives of man can be brought into harmony with one another. For he continues: "No, they are not inimical really, there is no contest actually; they can even exist side by side together in this one restricted arena, and could and would, had yours not interfered with mine" (p. 348).

Beneath its complexity of symbol and structure, the central theme of *A Fable* seems clear: despite the materialism of those who yielded to the General's temptation to "take the earth" and use it for unworthy ends, mankind can still find peace. Earthbound man can, through suffering for the sake of his spiritual goals and his spiritual soul, reach the fulfillment of his higher self; he can suffer in the defense of principle. Hence Faulkner's central symbol here, the cross: man comes to peace through suffering.[23]

There is a pathetic note, to be sure, in Faulkner's belief that man by his own unaided powers can conquer evil and reach the fulfillment of his human dignity; the touch of Rousseau is unmistakable. At the same time, this glimpse of the meaning of suffering is a far cry from the desolate Calvinism of so much of his work. Human suffering, and hence human life, has finally been given positive significance. Faulkner has come closer to the redemptive nature of Christianity, and in so doing he has drawn nearer to humanity itself.

In a sense, the picaresque exuberance of *The Reivers,* published in 1962 just a few months before Faulkner's death, was a fitting conclusion to his work. In young Lucius and Everbe and Boon Hogganbeck there is a measure of guilt, to be sure, but there is also repentance and expiation; there is wickedness, but there is acceptance of responsibility for one's wickedness; and above all, there is joy. For Faulkner's final vision is one of hope: man sinful, but striving for the good; man shackled by bonds within and without him, but struggling to be free.

Commentary ═══════

Obviously, it is a risky business for a critic to try to link Faulkner —or any novelist, for that matter—too closely with any historical religious sect or tradition. It would also be dangerous to try to define too narrowly or too apodictically Faulkner's "religious beliefs." What was at issue in the preceding essay was nothing of the kind. Its aim was to delineate a cast of mind, a pervading attitude toward religious values.

The trouble is that one cannot simply say at any point in a novel, "Here is Faulkner speaking." One catches hints and glimpses of his attitude, always mediated through his characters—the personal ethos showing through the personae. The reader is constantly forced to be aware not only of his own judgment of a character or incident, but Faulkner's judgment of it as well. And Faulkner gives his judgment only by nuance and indirection, by context and juxtaposition, by sound, smell and color.

The result can only be disappointing to the theologian, who is accustomed to speaking with theological precision and in biblical and dogmatic terminology. There are moments when the theologian reading Faulkner must long for a clear affirmation of belief, or even for a precise statement of religious doubt. Faulkner does use biblical language and imagery, to be sure—what author writing in the Christian tradition can avoid it?—and he occasionally alludes directly even to Christian doctrines like sin, hell, and redemption. What is important, however, is not that he sometimes uses the traditional language of Christian belief but that the problems he is concerned with—whatever be the terms in which he expresses them—are often the same problems which face the theologian.

Of course, the theologian is a specialist. His particular task may be summed up in terms of the traditional Augustinian phrase *fides quaerens intellectum*—faith in search of an understanding of itself. He must study and reflect upon the data of revelation, both in Scripture and in the developing doctrine of the Christian tradition, and express it in terms understandable to the men of his own age. But the religious problems in terms of which he expresses the revelation are *human* problems—the same for the novelist as for the theologian.

Let it be said, too, that the theologian (and the philosopher and the moralist) is often a source of the novelist's attitudes—though in

32

hidden ways and from unseen springs. Matthew Arnold wrote in *The Function of Criticism at the Present Time* that "the elements with which the creative power works are ideas; the best ideas on every matter which literature touches, current at the time." The source of these ideas is commonly outside the artist himself, for "creative literary genius does not principally show itself in discovering new ideas." The gift of literary genius "lies in the faculty of being happily inspired by a certain intellectual and spiritual atmosphere, by a certain order of ideas, when it finds itself in them." One may not wholly agree with Arnold's virtual exclusion of the discovery of ideas from the imaginative writer's art—is not literature itself, among other things, a way of knowing?—but it is true enough that the artist, like any man of his time, is profoundly influenced by the ideas current around him. It need not surprise us, then, to find poets and novelists dealing with the same problems which exercise the philosophers and the theologians in their very different disciplines. Nor need we be surprised to find the attitudes of a novelist influenced by and similar to a particular "tradition," be it philosophical or theological. We may well expect to find that he has been inspired by a "certain order of ideas," if he has happened to "find himself" in their midst.

The religious themes discussed in the preceding essay are fundamentally human problems. Both of them—the problem of freedom and the problem of man's innate corruption—are obviously deeply bound up with Faulkner's vision of the nature of man, and perhaps, if only implicitly, the nature of God. We have seen that, in Faulkner's view, man is a guilty creature with an innate tendency toward evil; his freedom of action is severely limited by his chronic and essential weakness of will. And we have found that, at least in the later Faulkner, man can achieve some measure of redemption, usually through suffering—occasionally through vicarious suffering.

This is really all that has been asserted thus far, and perhaps it is little enough. Documentation has been offered, of course, but these assertions remain to be tested in greater detail throughout Faulkner's novels, as well as in terms of some of the more specific and detailed analyses of the succeeding essays. But besides these assertions, perhaps the essay has raised several other problems which it does not solve. One is that of Faulkner's conception of the nature of God, implicit in his view of the nature of man as we have sketched it. If man is predestined, who is the God who has predestined him? Does Faulkner really see him as a "cosmic joker," or as the "Player" who moves his pawns about on the great chessboard? If man is innately corrupt, evil by reasons of some hereditary guilt—whether of family or nation or race, or even of humanity itself —then is this an unjust God who has "set the children's teeth on edge" because of the sour grapes eaten by their parents? And if man is somehow saved through suffering, especially through vicarious suffering, what is God's role in this redemption? Is there a God somehow accepting this atonement of one man on behalf of another, or are men destined simply to atone for one another *to* one another —in simple love among men themselves? What is the name and nature of Faulkner's God, if there be one? What is the nature of Faulkner's "redemption"? Is this a religion of God, or a religion of humanity alone?

To ask these questions is only to bring home how much remains to be asked of Faulkner's novels. Most simply put, it is to ask whether there really is a God implicit in Faulkner's probing into the mysteries of evil and freedom and redemption. It is true, to be sure, that—whatever else it may be—Faulkner's Christianity is a "practical" religion. It has to do in the first instance not with metaphysics but with morality. The problems it raises and probes have to do with man's capacity for meaningful action, especially in his relationships with other men. These problems have been discussed in the essay—and they are the central problems of the Calvinist tradition, which is perhaps above all a religion of practice, a religious ethic. But once this has been said, the mind moves beyond, to ask what is not at all so clear in Faulkner's work: is there a God behind it all, and is he a God who saves? That, I think, remains to be seen.

3 ≣

Thus far Faulkner's Calvinist bent has been seen primarily as a problematic factor in his work, giving rise to difficulties that were only resolved (and that only partially or inchoately) by a movement away from Calvinism in his later writing. The following essay of Harold J. Douglas and Robert Daniel continues the discussion of Faulkner's Calvinism, taking a somewhat more positive view of the contribution of Calvinist thought to Faulkner's attitudes.

The authors are interested in the special turn Calvin's theology took in the American South, further specifying the view offered in the preceding essay. They go on to elucidate this particular kind of Calvinism by pointing out the striking resemblances between the Calvinist theology of Faulkner's South and that of Hawthorne's New England, with particular reference to *As I Lay Dying* and *The Scarlet Letter*. Finally, they insist on a note that is too often forgotten: that Faulkner's Calvinism is a source not only of problems and weaknesses, but of unquestionable strength.

This essay first appeared in and is published with permission from *Tennessee Studies in Literature*, Vol. II, edited by Alwin Thaler and Richard Beale Davis. Copyright © 1957 by the University of Tennessee Press.

Harold J. Douglas
and Robert Daniel

FAULKNER'S SOUTHERN PURITANISM

Calvin's system had great value in the history of Christian thought. It appealed to and evoked a high order of intelligence, and its insistence on personal individual salvation has borne worthy fruit. So also its insistence on the chief end of man, "to know and do the will of God," made for strenuous morality. Its effects are most clearly seen in Scotland, in Puritan England and in the New England States, but its influence was and is felt among peoples that have little desire or claim to be called Calvinist.

—Encyclopaedia Britannica

IT IS LIKELY THAT THE FICTION OF WILLIAM FAULKNER IS read less in the South than in any other region of the United States, and less in the United States than abroad. Certainly it first received significant recognition among foreign readers: not until after the European respect for it had culminated in the award of the Nobel Prize did an American prize-awarding committee seek it out, though Faulkner had previously published half-a-dozen novels more deserving of a prize than was *A Fable.* It may be that these books were disqualified because the committees thought they contained slanders on the American people. As to Faulkner's European reputation, that can hardly have been affected one way or the other by the question of his fidelity to Southern life. Yet books that are to be of permanent interest to readers in other times and places must be faithful in some sense to the real life of their own time and place. To ask, therefore, whether Faulkner's work gives a valid picture

37

of the recent South is a relevant enquiry, provided the enquirer does not hold that work to a naively realistic standard.

What, though, is the South really like? The answer to this question consists partly of what happens there, objectively considered, and partly of what Southerners think is happening there. Evidence of both is afforded by the news-stories and editorials in Southern newspapers. Of the two published in our town, one depicts a South that is strikingly different from what some Southerners and not a few outsiders like to imagine, and strikingly reminiscent of the South portrayed by Faulkner. To a much greater extent than is true of either its local competitor or even the American press generally, the front page of this newspaper is strewn with the remains of wrecked automobiles, knifed moonshiners, venal politicians, ruined girls, and other instances of the violence and corruption of our times. From these texts, the editorials draw appropriate morals—sometimes in sarcastic understatement, sometimes with only half-restrained fury. To more Jeffersonian readers—indeed, to the editors of the rival paper—the world also contains careful drivers, chaste women, honest public servants, etc. But many Southerners feel that if an accurate picture of human life is to be painted, the emphasis must fall upon the staggering amount of sloth, greed, and crime that life includes. Their scarcely latent Calvinism finds profound satisfaction in a newspaper whose front page offers the proof of human corruptedness, and whose editorials point the moral in the outraged tones of seventeenth-century pulpit eloquence. With perfect appropriateness, a different verse of the Bible appears each day at the top of the editorial page.

Such newspapers, not altogether rare in the middle and lower South, testify to the influence of Calvinism outside of Scotland, Puritan England, and the New England states. But to understand Southern Calvinism it is essential to recall the distinction between the teachings of Calvin himself and their modifications in the churches that he influenced—even the Presbyterian; for modification made possible the absorption of Calvin's psychology by sects that rebelled against the pristine rigor of his doctrines.

The most notorious doctrine, that through Adam's disobedience the race of man became deserving of damnation, though some are spared by God's election, should in logic lead to two others: that all human effort is vain, and that the corrupt state of society is always and everywhere the same. In practice, however, Calvinistic preachers exhort their listeners to repent and improve, so as to increase their chances of escaping God's wrath. Jonathan Edwards, who denied the freedom of the will explicitly, was perhaps the most powerful exhorter to penitence that this country has ever heard; and similarly, Puritan writers often depict society as having fallen from an earlier state of soundness and health. The sermon called "Degenerating New England," reprinted in Johnson and Miller's book *The Puritans*, typifies a theme that became prominent towards the close of the seventeenth century.

American Calvinism, then, conceives of man as bound to sin and threatened by damnation, but not *doomed* to it. The way to redemption, by an act of choice, remains open. In sermons that call upon their hearers to return to grace, the degeneracy of mankind—not only from the original state of perfection in the Garden but also from some previous age of relative goodness since the Fall—occurs often as proof both of the need for regeneration and of its possibility. Yet the knowledge that the majority of men are doomed not to receive the good tidings, along with descriptions of the punishments that await impenitent sinners, usually beclouds the message of hope and joy. Thus, a Calvinistic tinge is apt to infuse the utterances of such non-Calvinists, strictly speaking, as the Baptists and the Methodists. The influence of Calvin is to be detected not so much in a literal application of the doctrine of the elect and the damned, as in a serious and often gloomy view of man's fate, in an insistence upon strictness of behavior, particularly on the Sabbath, and in the belief, stated or implied, that sexuality is the chief sign of man's fallen nature. (Drunkenness, which also reduces man to the condition of a beast, comes close behind.)

Taking the term in this sense, the Calvinism of the South is easily accounted for. It came directly across the Atlantic with the Scottish and other settlers; it came also from New England, both before and after the war, in the teachings of Northern preachers and schoolmasters. It was propagated not only in the Presbyterian churches but also by the more numerous Methodists and Baptists; by Low-church Episcopalianism, which has exerted an influence on the South out of all proportion to its numerical weakness; by the sects that have splintered off from these others; and at revivals and tent-meetings. Calvinism is apt to turn up almost anywhere that religious belief impinges upon Southern life.[1]

From these facts it is evident that in novels giving a broad idea of Southern life the South's Calvinism must figure prominently. Faulkner's profound attention to the subject has been ably demonstrated by William Van O'Connor in his essay "Protestantism in Yoknapatawpha County," which he both modified and extended when making it a chapter in his *Tangled Fire of William Faulkner*.[2] The cruelly warping effect that Calvinism may have constitutes a significant part of the characterization in such novels as *The Wild Palms, Absalom, Absalom!*, and *As I Lay Dying*, and forms the very core, as O'Connor demonstrates, in *Light in August*, where we find the archetypal situation of Calvinism's impinging upon the main character, a Southerner, from both the native church groups and the transplanted New Englander Joanna Burden, whose grandfather's first name was Calvin. O'Connor was later to detect a similarity of temperament in Faulkner and Hawthorne, which implies that Faulkner's work, though it exposes the wickedness of Puritan bigots, is at the same time itself tinged with a Calvinistic point of view.[3] His earlier studies, however, were concerned largely with Faulkner's hostility to Calvinism; and this emphasis led him to such doubtful conclusions as his denial that there is "any aspect of the spirit of Protestantism at the center of *The Sound and the Fury*."[4] We shall return later to this statement; at present, taking a hint from one of O'Connor's footnotes, we suggest that Faulkner's relation to Calvinism resembles that of Joe Christmas in *Light in August*, who detests his stern Presbyterian stepfather, yet prefers his harsh morality to Mrs. McEachern's softness and weakness—though not so much because he "wants to live inside a system of rules and sanctions,"[5] as because he believes that McEachern evaluates man truly. Faulkner's plots tend to emphasize the same kind of incident as the front page of our Puritan newspaper; his bootlegging and maniacal drivers, his Snopeses and Temple Drakes, furnish the proof of man's fallen condition. And by man's condition Faulkner is appalled.

O'Connor's reason for ignoring Faulkner's Calvinism may have been that other writers, some of whom have been Faulkner's harshest critics, had already pointed it out. As long ago as 1934 Wyndham Lewis satirized it in an article called "A Moralist with a Corn-Cob"—reprinted, *horresco referens*, in his book

entitled *Men Without Art*.[6] Eighteen years later an article by
Edith Hamilton treats Faulkner's work even more contemptu-
ously; but the ground of her hostility is the same—Faulkner
is a "violently twisted Puritan."[7] It is not clear whether this
means that Faulkner, being a Puritan, is violently twisted, or
that he has perverted the original sanity of Puritanism; but so
many readers of the *Saturday Review* have found Miss Hamilton's depreciations logical and persuasive that they must detain
us for a paragraph or two.

Like many critics before her, Miss Hamilton objects to Faulkner's work because the world that it creates is unlovely. Even
his landscapes, she asserts, are composed of loathsome images.
Likewise he hates his female characters, and slanders them as
being snares for men. In his novels before *Sanctuary* none of
the characters is individualized or "alive," for "Power of choice,
the great individualizer, Mr. Faulkner will not allow them.
They are all volitionless servants of fatality, and thereby unim-
portant, even to their creator." Above all, she ridicules Faulkner's plots, as being full of "preposterous circumstance . . .
violence, cruelty, and all manner of sexual doings."[8]

Any critic who takes seriously the relation of literature to life
may be forgiven or even commended for resenting the misogyny
that is indeed present in Faulkner's writing; and if Miss Hamilton rejects his plots, then for her it can be no defense of his
landscapes that they are the emotional concomitants of his
action. Her inability to feel the life in Faulkner's characters
cannot be argued about, though it must be lamented; it seems
safe to say that not even the severest critic before her has found
Faulkner lacking in the power of characterization. Moreover,
as we have shown, one must be cautious in stating that Puritanism in practice denies the freedom of the will; and this caveat
is related to an even more pointed answer to Miss Hamilton's
splenetic article. She is also the author of an admirable book
called *The Greek Way*, which eulogizes the life and literature
of ancient Athens. Well . . . preposterous circumstance? freedom of the will? Suppose we set any of Faulkner's plots beside
that of *Oedipus the King*—not to mention some of the more
horrendous Greek tragedies, *Medea* or *Electra*, say—and what
is there to choose?[9] The fact that Sophocles, Euripides, and
Faulkner share a fondness for doomed characters, violence,
cruelty, and all manner of sexual doings can only lead to one
conclusion, which is that the presence or absence of these ele-

ments of plot has never determined what the world will consider a masterpiece. And if the example of Sophocles does not make the point eloquently enough, then let us remember *Hamlet*.

Critics who have remarked on the Calvinistic strain in Faulkner's work and consider it a source of strength, not weakness, have usually likened it to the work of the greatest Calvinistic American novelist before him. (A middle term such as *Calvinic* is needed, corresponding to *Hellenic*. Calvinistic would then correspond to *Hellenistic*—though not Greek, colored by Hellenism—and would obviate the possible implication that either Hawthorne or Faulkner professes the faith of Calvin.) Both George Marion O'Donnell and Malcolm Cowley mention the affinity between Faulkner and Hawthorne; and an article on the subject by Randall Stewart, which in many ways anticipates O'Connor's latest study, sets up a striking parallel between Faulkner's South and Hawthorne's New England. Both regions, in the process of being industrialized, are changing from traditional societies into progressive, materialistic ones, their mania for money being reflected in such characters as Jason Compson and Judge Pyncheon. Stewart, however, is wary of asserting that Hawthorne influenced Faulkner; he sees in their work only "a common view of the human condition." Setting them both in the orthodox Christian tradition, he concludes somewhat imprecisely, "It doesn't much matter, perhaps, whether the tradition is called Protestant or Catholic, Calvinist or Augustinian. . . ."[10]

That Hawthorne would have consented to this merger may be doubted, and a summary of the six main elements in Faulkner's work that stem from his Calvinism will enable the reader to judge of his orthodoxy. These elements are the saturnine tone that characterizes it except when it is grotesquely humorous; its misogyny, which recalls Milton's revision of Genesis so that Eve succumbed to the serpent whereas Adam succumbed only to Eve; the sense of doom that lies heavy upon many of the characters, together with their *limited* power of choice; incidents of violence that symbolize the degeneracy of modern man; an ambivalent attitude towards slavery and the Negro; and Faulkner's certainty about the will of God, who expects mankind to live in a right relation to the world he created.

These strains, of course, can be separated only artificially: Faulkner's melancholy, for instance, originates in his brooding over the double degeneration of his people—from the natural life of the early settlers to the sophisticated society of the Old South, and from that to the modern world possessed by Popeye and the Snopeses. Yet such analysis is necessary to an understanding of his Calvinism, which in turn accounts for many of those otherwise inexplicable elements that have long been under fire from his unfriendly critics, and culminate in the explicit religiosity of his later writing: for example, *Requiem for a Nun,* the commencement speech "Faith or Fear," and *A Fable.*

The similarity between the work of Faulkner and of Hawthorne extends beyond the general likenesses noticed by George Marion O'Donnell and Malcolm Cowley—the pervasively sombre tone arising from an awareness of degeneration, the sense of doom, the absolute moral certainty. The substructure of Faulkner's early masterpiece, *As I Lay Dying,* resembles *The Scarlet Letter* in ways that virtually establish a direct influence. By "substructure" we mean those recollections of the characters which inform the reader of the love-affair between Addie Bundren, the "I" of the title, and her minister, the Reverend Whitfield, which results in the birth of Jewel, Addie's third child, and her estrangement from her husband. Addie's infidelity, like Hester Prynne's, stems from the earlier sin of marrying without love—a point that is reinforced in each novel by the husband's deformity. Prynne, alias Chillingworth, has a twisted shoulder; Anse Bundren is humpbacked. In both novels the sin is aggravated by the sacred profession of the lover; Addie is a member of Whitfield's congregation, as Hester is of Dimmesdale's. To Addie, the act seems "more utter and terrible since he was the instrument ordained by God who created the sin, to sanctify that sin He had created. . . . I would think of him as dressed in sin. I would think of him as thinking of me as dressed also in sin, he the more beautiful since the garment which he had exchanged for sin was sanctified."[11] The metaphor of the garment, though a traditional one, probably derives from *The Scarlet Letter;* for Dimmesdale, appalled at the hypocrisy of his position, replies to Hester's attempt at consolation by saying, "I should long ago have thrown off these garments of mock holiness, and shown myself to mankind as they will see me at the judgment seat." Addie only thinks of herself and Whitfield as clad in the beautiful garments of sin; Hester's embroidery literally makes beautiful her symbol of sin, the scarlet letter, and Pearl is clothed in a crimson splendor that reflects the flame of Hester's passion.

The adulteries of both Hester and Addie produce children, and the two children, Pearl and Jewel, are given remarkably similar names that testify to the intensity of their mothers' loves. Both children are passionate, impulsive, mercurial, and exotic; Jewel, like Pearl, is undemonstrative towards his mother and often torments her—indeed, is sometimes almost demonic in his deliberate cruelty. Like Pearl, he is forever "flinging into tantrums or sulking spells, inventing devilment to devil her. . ." (p. 352). In each relationship of mother and child there is a continual attraction and repulsion; and each child serves as his mother's sole link with humanity. Yet neither is accepted by other children. Pearl, though mocked and taunted by the other little Puritans until she realizes that she is a child apart, does not suffer. Jewel feels no kinship with his half-brothers and his half-sister, and Darl reminds him constantly that he stands isolated from the family circle; yet, like Pearl, he is content in his separateness.

Even more than their children, Hester and Addie are cut off from the common stream of humanity. Hester is forced to dwell in a lonely cottage on the outskirts of the settlement; Addie "lived, a lonely woman, lonely with her pride" (p. 353). Hester, who is not lacking in pride herself, sees other women draw their skirts away from contact with her. Addie's pride, along with her mute acceptance of what she considers her immutable doom, keeps her from communion with family or friend. She resents the violation of her aloneness by Anse's children, but afterwards is made whole again. Accepting her lot, Hester declines, by pointing to her scarlet badge, to have her isolation violated.

Hester's badge proclaims her guilt; and as the A gradually changes its meaning from Adulteress to Able, or even Angel, it becomes a symbol of expiation. Addie says, "My daily life is an acknowledgement and expiation of my sin" (p. 459). Although she does not confess, she teaches her children that "deceit was such that, in a world where it was, nothing else could be very bad or very important, not even poverty" (p. 429) —a belief that may be considered an echo of the principal didactic burden of *The Scarlet Letter*. Addie considers truth the greatest of virtues, and though she practises deceit in order to protect Whitfield, according to Darl she hates herself in consequence. Hester finds herself in the same dilemma: "Truth is the one virtue," she tells Dimmesdale, "which I might have held fast, and did hold fast, through all extremity; save when thy good,—thy life,—thy fame,—were put in question! Then I consented to a deception. But a lie is never good, even though death threaten on the other side!"

When we consider Faulkner's treatment of Whitfield alongside of Hawthorne's treatment of Dimmesdale, the resemblance between the two novels becomes even more marked. Whitfield, it is true, suffers no remorse over concealing his guilt; but like Dimmesdale he takes refuge in concealment because confession would ruin him in his profession. Like Dimmesdale he is weak and unworthy of his partner in sin; he eventually resolves to confess, but circumstances never bring him, as they do Dimmesdale, to keep his resolution. Both Dimmesdale and Whitfield, as ministers, single out their partners for special exhortations; both, ironically, are considered by their congregations to be of a particular godliness. Of Dimmesdale Hawthorne writes: "They deemed the young clergyman a miracle of holiness. They fancied him the mouthpiece of Heaven's messages of wisdom, and rebuke, and love. In their eyes, the very ground on which he trod was sanctified." And Cora, who reflects community opinion in *As I Lay Dying*, says to Addie: "Brother Whitfield, a godly man if ever one breathed God's breath, prayed for you and strove as never a man could except him" (p. 460).

The substructure of *As I Lay Dying* exhibits other resemblances to *The Scarlet Letter*—minor resemblances that may be coincidental. Enough has been said, we hope, to demonstrate specifically the fundamental affinity between Hawthorne's mind and Faulkner's. Both must be considered Calvinistic novelists, but with the same important qualification: that both hate the excesses of Calvinism. Hawthorne, while rejecting the gloominess of New England life and the cruelty that marred its early history, participated in the seriousness with which the Puritans regarded the fact of human depravity; and similarly, to say that Faulkner is Calvinistic is not to deny O'Connor's thesis that much of his work consists of savage satire upon the monsters sired by Protestantism. It would be inexplicable, indeed, if Faulkner did not detest those of his characters who represent distortions of that tradition which has endowed him with his own profoundest intuitions of life. His work belongs to the same stream of American fiction as that of Hawthorne, the stream which perhaps Parrington was wrong in not regarding as the main current.

Two objections may arise from a comparison of *As I Lay Dying* to *The Scarlet Letter,* even though the evidence for the likeness seems incontrovertible. In the first place, some may find the implication incongruous that a general kinship exists between Faulkner's violent, often indecent stories and the work of the gentler Hawthorne. The similarity of *The Sound and the Fury,* say, and *The House of the Seven Gables* is virtually limited to the general situation: the degeneracy of once-powerful families. Faulkner is often accused of being preoccupied with sex; in Hawthorne's work one cannot say that sexual passion plays the leading part. Yet when Hawthorne came to write his masterpiece he chose adultery as the basis of that "tale of human frailty and sorrow," and as Yvor Winters observes, "by selecting sexual sin as the type of all sin, he was true alike to the exigencies of drama and of history."[12] An adulteress was both the epitome of human weakness to the historical Puritans, and the epitome of the human dilemma to everyone. Any writer of the stature of Hawthorne or Faulkner is liable to be accused of a preoccupation with sex; a century ago *The Scarlet Letter* was attacked from many pulpits for its immorality.

A second objection must also be forestalled: that in thus stressing the story of Addie Bundren and the Reverend Whitfield we are upsetting the relation between the two plots of *As I Lay Dying,* which is primarily about the journey of the Bundrens, through all kinds of obstacles, to bury Addie's body in the graveyard at Jefferson. Even though the title emphasizes the importance of the dying woman's memories of her married life and infidelity, the principal emotion in the novel is admiration for the heroic efforts of her survivors to comply with her last wish, despite their often ludicrous weaknesses and the humiliating accidents of the journey. This emotion, however, is immeasurably strengthened by the presence of the contrasting substructure—for there can be no doubt that Addie and Whitfield are presented as having acted "naturally," with all the pejorative meaning that the word can have. Her survivors act ritualistically.

Such a double, contrasting structure typifies many of Faulkner's best novels; and, though it lies beyond the subject of Hawthorne's influence on them, it must be further analyzed if their Calvinistic bent is to be fully shown. As Faulkner employs it, it divides his characters into two groups: the Elect and the Damned. *The Sound and the Fury* exemplifies it in the contrast between Dilsey and her employers: notwithstanding O'Connor's denial that Protestantism is important in that novel, its climactic scene concerns Dilsey's emotions just after she has listened to a sermon on sin and redemption. Her face suffused with tears, she thinks of the plight of humanity, and in her view humanity is the Compson family: Jason, with his monomaniac greed; Candace, who acts naturally as Addie Bundren would understand the word; Quentin, of a twisted and ineffectual goodness like that of Horace Benbow in *Sanctuary;* and the rest whose damnation the preacher's words have made Dilsey understand. The same sort of structural contrast exists in *Light in August,* between the action centered on Lena Grove and the main one, centered on Joe Christmas; and in *The Wild Palms* the two stories are narrated in alternating chapters. O'Connor, who notices Faulkner's propensity for such double structures, suggests that the double plots of Elizabethan drama were his models. A more plausible suggestion would be the novels of Leo Tolstoy, for the Elizabethan plots are not necessarily related to each other through contrast—or, when they are, it is not often a contrast of right and wrong. Tolstoy, however, sets in opposition the societies of Moscow and St. Petersburg— Holy Moscow versus artificial St. Petersburg—or St. Petersburg and the countryside, as when the sophistication of Anna Karenina and Vronsky is opposed to Kitty and Levin's immersion in the life of the peasants, even to Levin's participation in the ritual act of reaping the grain. Whether influenced by Calvinism or not, Tolstoy clearly regards characters like Anna, Vronsky, and Anatole Kuragin in *War and Peace,* as being among the Damned. Faulkner's Bundren family in *As I Lay Dying,* excepting Addie, correspond to Tolstoy's peasants; Addie and Whitfield embody a kind of sophistication—she being a former schoolteacher and he a preacher—which makes them reason that what is natural is right. In fulfilling their obligation to convey the coffin to Jefferson, the Bundrens display the same kind of simplicity as Levin, the kind that expresses itself in a complex ritual. It is a simplicity that both Tolstoy and Faulkner revere.

We have already mentioned several articles, some of which appeared many years ago, that point out Faulkner's involvement in the tradition that stems from the teachings of Calvin. It may be asked why we think it necessary to canvass the matter again. The question must receive two answers: first, we do not find that the point has really registered upon many critics of Faulkner's work. Irving Howe's *William Faulkner,* for instance, a perceptive and on the whole sympathetic study, does not mention it once, although surely an understanding of the religious values in *The Sound and the Fury* would have restrained Howe from disparaging the characterization of Dilsey.[13] Second, when critics do take notice of Faulkner's religious feelings, they are likely to stigmatize them as "puritanism"—a thing that in our age is liable to be either reprobated or tactfully ignored. If we can acknowledge that far from being a weakness, the sternness of Faulkner's Calvinism is a vital source of that power which is now widely recognized in his work (just as Calvinism is acknowledged to be a source of power to Hawthorne), we shall cease to be distracted by some of his apparent eccentricities, and hence arrive at a better understanding of his towering position among contemporary writers.

Evaluating Faulkner is one of the most puzzling tasks that face contemporary criticism; but once his religious position has been properly understood, two problems at least that have perplexed his critics will vanish. One concerns the attitudes expressed in his work, the other its fidelity to actual life. Faulkner's attitudes are never contradictory, though they are not often simple and sometimes appear ambiguous. What one thinks of their validity depends upon one's own relation to Calvinism.

Let us consider two examples: his attitude towards women and his attitude towards Negroes. The decidedly masculine morality of Calvinism regards a man's sexuality as the predominant symbol of his fallen nature; woman is thought of not as his equal partner, like him inhibited from salvation, but rather as the means whereby he is kept from redeeming himself. We may therefore be distressed but hardly surprised that Faulkner should treat his Temple Drakes and Joanna Burdens and Eula Varners as mantraps.

Faulkner's attitude towards Negroes has an equally venerable history. There were few Abolitionists among the Puritans; the Abolition Movement had to wait upon the liberalizing influ-

ences of the Quakers and the Unitarians. The Puritan, even
if he did not deal in slaves himself, was anything but outraged
at those who did. (We may compare Hawthorne on John
Brown: "Never was a man more justly hanged!") In the first
place, slaves were not Puritans, and second, the slaves' sufferings were as nothing compared with those that all mankind
deserves. At the same time, the cruelty shown by the masters
might be considered typical of what the Puritan thought
human nature was like. Faulkner's attitude is modified by his
compassion, as well as by the facts that he lives in a more
humane time and writes not about slaves but about Negroes in
an inferior social position; nevertheless, it is Calvinism that
explains the apparent contradiction between siding with such
a character as Mr. Coldfield in *Absalom, Absalom!* who refuses
to fight on the side of the slaveholders, and accepting the position of Dilsey in the Compson household. If Faulkner looks
back to the Old South as a nobler age while tracing its ruin to
the sin of slavery, or (through Quentin) protests almost too
much that he does not hate it, his liberal critics should not
charge him with a confusion of values. To Faulkner the relationship of the races in the South symbolizes the human situation, for pride, cruelty, suffering, pity, and endurance are its
components.

When we come to the question of Faulkner's realism, we
must again speak of the symbolic aspect of his work. In fiction
that abounds with flooding rivers, country stores, barbershops,
plantation-houses, and other settings so faithfully and vividly
described that the reader has an almost painful sense of being
there, it is strange to encounter a concentration of actions and
characters that seems not at all typical of the real society which
is presumably being represented. Granted that the South contains sluts, idiots, suicides, and misers, probability is outraged
when all four of the Compson children are drawn from these
categories. But to condemn *The Sound and the Fury* for this
concentration of undesirables is to judge it from the standpoint
of a statistician. It no more corresponds to a photograph of a
real Southern family than our Puritan newspaper gives a balanced account of a real Southern city. The writers of the newspaper and the novel have both selected symbols of the corruption with which they believe society is afflicted. Perhaps the
newspaper should be more faithful to statistics, but no such
obligation rests upon a body of imaginative work that expresses

its author's vision of damnation and judgment. The progeny of Faulkner's imagination, his plots and characters, hold an enduring interest for his readers because of the simple fact that they adequately express his vision of life.

Finally, we may speculate a little on why a Calvinistic inheritance should so enhance a writer's power. In Robert Cantwell's introduction to *Sartoris* we read: "By some intensity of telling, rather than by their actions or their words, we are made to feel that the Sartoris destiny is truly tragic."[14] If we set this sentence beside our quotation from the *Encyclopaedia,* does the latter not suggest that the intensity of Faulkner's telling is related to the influence on him of Calvinism? The quotation reminds us first that, far from hindering the portrayal of character, Calvinism's "insistence on personal individual salvation" may be expected to aid it; and equally does a writer benefit from an influence that "evoked a high order of intelligence, and . . . made for strenuous morality." Consequently, the Calvinistic writer, though prone to be gloomy and stern, sees human life as perpetually meaningful and interesting. Our best liberal critic, Lionel Trilling, begins his first book of essays by asserting that liberalism is America's only intellectual tradition. He ends it with the rueful admission that modern literature "to which we can have an active, reciprocal relationship, which is the right relationship to have, has been written by men who are indifferent to, or even hostile to, the tradition of democratic liberalism."[15] He does not say why. Perhaps the reason is that for a novelist or a poet the idea of progress is ultimately meaningless. The example of Faulkner shows, at any rate, that even in a positivistic age the human experience may be charged with supernatural meaning; and it is possible that Faulkner's position is now established partly because his religious beliefs are both deeply felt and true. Remove from Calvinism the specific points of doctrine that are not serviceable for literature, and its vision of man remains: a creature alienated from his creator by his own choice. Though this is not peculiar to Calvin, no writers have expressed it more energetically than those of the Calvinistic order. It provides the conditions for tragedy; and as Yeats wrote, "We begin to live when we have conceived life as tragedy."

It is the province of the critic to point out that Faulkner's work is steeped in Calvinism, not to explain precisely how that came about. The future biographer of Faulkner will doubtless discover the extent of his exposure to churchgoing in his childhood. But the basis of much of his work is said to be the stories that he heard from the farmers of Lafayette County, with whom he would squat on the steps of the Oxford courthouse when they came to town on Saturdays. A better source of Calvinistic attitudes would be hard to find.

Commentary

One of the most helpful contributions of the preceding essay is its insistence on the special character of American Calvinism, namely, that it had to some extent grown away from its roots in John Calvin. Surely Douglas and Daniel are right to insist that Calvinism in the American South, like American Calvinism generally, was influenced profoundly by what might be called the "American experience." They might in fact have gone on to investigate—as literary historians like Perry Miller and, more recently, Alan Heimert have done—the extent to which Calvinism was liberalized by the new political freedom of the American situation. In any case, they are surely right to generalize that American Calvinism["conceives of man as bound to sin and threatened by damnation, but not *doomed* to it. The way to redemption, by an act of choice, remains open."]

At the same time, the impression should not be given that either American Calvinism or Southern Calvinism is all of a piece. The authors themselves point to the ambiguity latent in the American Calvinist theology between the doctrine of predestination and the practical acceptance of man's power of free choice. They properly point out that many Calvinist preachers ignored the logical contradiction, and urged their flocks to repentance and improvement. If this ambiguity is inherent in the tradition, then, the way is clear—in American Calvinism and in Faulkner—for very different attitudes toward religious values. Depending on his cast of mind, one might insist primarily on the wrath of God and man's helplessness before him; or he might focus above all on man's need for repentance and an upright life. Another, perhaps more scholastic tradition might be able to reconcile the two to some extent in terms of the mystery of God's work and man's work in the process of salvation. The American Calvinist seems to have been content to move from one to the other, depending on the spiritual need of the moment, or simply to remain tied fast to one or the other.

Some of this ambivalence is reflected in Faulkner. The problem of predestination and free will was not brought sufficiently into focus to allow it to be seen as a "mystery," as a two-sided truth both of whose sides must be accepted and lived with. His insight, deep as it is, does not seem—at least through most of his career—to have pierced beyond his realization of the anguish of the contradiction. The result is that although Douglas and Daniel are correct, of

course, in linking Faulkner with the liberalized American tradition
which allowed man in some measure a practical freedom of repentance, we must learn to expect to find in Faulkner that the pendulum
sometimes swings so far to the side of doom that some of his characters no longer have even this "practical" freedom of repentance.
The "way to redemption, by an act of choice" may have been open
at some time to the Reverend Hightower, for example, but can we
say that it was ever really open to Joe Christmas? It may conceivably
have been open once to Jason Compson, before he himself closed it,
but was it ever open to Quentin? ⌈Many of Faulkner's most memo-
rable characters seem to belong to a kind of limbo of unfreedom,
where they can only exist or, at best, struggle in agonized frustration against their particular doom⌋.

Perhaps some of this difficulty might be obviated, however, by
recurring to the realization that there is a chronological development in Faulkner's work. His Calvinist attitudes should not be
taken as a fixed and immutable body of truths. There is in Calvinist
theology not only predestination, man's degeneracy, limited power
of choice, hell-fire and damnation; there is also grace and redemption. While it is true that it is only in his later writing that Faulkner
came to reflect at all strongly the redemptive aspects of Christianity
—though one must not forget Dilsey and the "ricklickshun en de
blood of de Lamb"—he did come to it at last. With this develop-
mental aspect of Faulkner's religious attitudes in mind, the essay
of Douglas and Daniel might profitably be read in tandem with the
essay which precedes it. It is clear, as Douglas and Daniel point out
very well, that through most of his corpus of novels Faulkner, like
Hawthorne, hated the excesses of Calvinism. However, it is also true
that later—for example, in *Requiem for a Nun* and *A Fable*—he
came to see that there may have been a reason for the excesses: the
neglect of redemptive suffering and love, which are as essential to
Christianity as is the sense of sin.

This essay has righted the balance upset by some who have written of ⌈Calvinism too exclusively as a source of weakness in Faulkner's work.⌋ Chief among the "strengths" afforded Faulkner by
Calvinism, the authors assert, is that the vision of man as "a creature
alienated from his creator by his own choice" provides "the conditions for tragedy." Two questions should be raised, I think, about
this assertion: first, whether this alienation of man from his creator
is in fact generally represented by Faulkner in his characters as by
the character's "own choice"; and secondly, whether, if the "Calvinist" vision is reduced to such generic terms, it is any longer meaningful to refer to it as Calvinist rather than simply as Christian.
More importantly, though, this essay has focused very well the
problem of tragedy, perhaps even that much-vexed question of

"Christian tragedy." One can only rejoice to see the suggestion raised that here, in this "tragic vision," is the distinctive contribution of Christianity to Faulkner's religious insight. There is room here for almost endless discussion—articulating, defining, questioning the nature of Faulkner's tragic sense and his conception of tragedy —but happily the question has been raised.

4 ≡≡≡

The preceding essays have attempted to show Faulkner's relationship to a particular tradition of Christianity—Calvinism, and more specifically, the Calvinism of the American South. Now Cleanth Brooks, whose volume *William Faulkner: The Yoknapatawpha Country* (1963) contains some of the most perceptive studies yet written of Faulkner's major novels, tries to define the nature of Faulkner's religious ideals in broader terms than the sectarian. In particular, he works toward definitions of good, of evil, and of holiness as Faulkner conceives them. For closer study of these definitions he singles out *Sanctuary*, the story "An Odor of Verbena" from *The Unvanquished, Light in August,* and *The Sound and the Fury*.

This essay was first published as a chapter in Brooks's *The Hidden God* (New Haven: Yale University Press, © 1963), pp. 22–43, and is used with permission.

Cleanth Brooks

FAULKNER'S VISION OF
GOOD AND EVIL

PROFESSOR RANDALL STEWART, IN HIS VERY STIMULATING
little book *American Literature and Christian Doctrine,* asserts
that

> Faulkner embodies and dramatizes the basic Christian
> concepts so effectively that he can with justice be regarded
> as one of the most profoundly Christian writers in our
> time. There is everywhere in his writings the basic premise
> of Original Sin: everywhere the conflict between the flesh
> and the spirit. One finds also the necessity of discipline, of
> trial by fire in the furnace of affliction, of sacrifice and the
> sacrificial death, of redemption through sacrifice. Man in
> Faulkner is a heroic, tragic figure.[1]

This is a view with which I am in basic sympathy. I agree
heartily with Professor Stewart on the matter of Faulkner's concern with what he calls "Original Sin," and with Faulkner's
emphasis upon discipline, sacrifice, and redemption. But to call
Faulkner "one of the most profoundly Christian writers in our
time" seems somewhat incautious. Perhaps it would be safer
to say that Faulkner is a profoundly religious writer; that his
characters come out of a Christian environment, and represent,
whatever their shortcomings and whatever their theological
heresies, Christian concerns; and that they are finally to be
understood only by reference to Christian premises.

Probably the best place to start is with the term "original
sin." The point of reference might very well be T. E. Hulme,
one of the profoundly seminal influences on our time, though
a critic and philosopher whom Faulkner probably never read.

In "Humanism and the Religious Attitude," Hulme argued for a return to orthodox doctrine. His concern with religion, however, had nothing to do with recapturing what he called "the sentiment of Fra Angelico." Rather, "What is important," he asserted,

> is what nobody seems to realize—the dogmas like that of Original Sin, which are the closest expression of the categories of the religious attitude. That man is in no sense perfect, but a wretched creature, who can apprehend perfection. It is not, then, that I put up with the dogma for the sake of the sentiment, but that I may possibly swallow the sentiment for the sake of the dogma.[2]

Hulme's position as stated here would seem to smack of scholastic Calvinism rather than of the tradition of Catholic Christianity. His emphasis at least suggests that nature is radically evil and not merely gone wrong somehow—corrupted by a fall. But if Hulme's passage is so tinged, that very fact may make it the more relevant to Faulkner, who shows, in some aspects, the influence of Southern Puritanism.

Be that as it may, Hulme's is not a didactic theory of literature, which stresses some direct preachment to be made. On the contrary, his "classicism" derives from a clear distinction between religious doctrine and poetic structure. It is romantic poetry which blurs that distinction, competing with religion by trying to drag in the infinite. With romaticism we enter the area of "split religion," and romantic "damp and fugginess." For Hulme, the classic attitude involves a recognition of man's limitations—his finitude. Since the classical view of man recognizes his limitations and does not presume upon them, the classical attitude, Hulme argues, is a religious attitude. For Hulme is quite convinced that man, though capable of recognizing goodness, is not naturally good. It is only by discipline that he can achieve something of value.

The whole point is an important one, for Faulkner's positive beliefs are often identified with some kind of romantic primitivism. Thus his concern with idiots and children and uneducated rural people, both white and Negro, is sometimes interpreted to mean that man is made evil only by his environment with its corrupting restrictions and inhibitions, and that if man could only realize his deeper impulses, he would be good.[3]

Allied to this misconception is another, namely, that Faulkner's characters have no power of choice, being merely the creatures of their drives and needs, and that they are determined by their environment and are helplessly adrift upon the tides of circumstance. It is true that many of his characters are obsessed creatures or badly warped by traumatic experiences, or that they are presented by Faulkner as acting under some kind of compulsion. But his characters are not mere products of an environment. They have the power of choice, they make decisions, and they win their goodness through effort and discipline.

If Faulkner does not believe that man is naturally good and needs only to realize his natural impulses, and if he does believe that man has free will and must act responsibly and discipline himself, then these beliefs are indeed worth stressing, for they are calculated to separate him sharply from writers of a more naturalistic and secularistic temper. But I grant that to attribute to Faulkner a belief in original sin or in man's need for discipline would not necessarily prove him a Christian. The concept of grace, for example, is either lacking or at least not clearly evident in Faulkner's work.

Let us begin, then, by examining Faulkner's criticism of secularism and rationalism. A very important theme in his earlier work is the discovery of evil, which is part of man's initiation into the nature of reality. That brilliant and horrifying early novel *Sanctuary* is, it seems to me, to be understood primarily in terms of such an initiation. Horace Benbow is the sentimental idealist, the man of academic temper, who finds out that the world is not a place of moral tidiness or even of justice. He discovers with increasing horror that evil is rooted in the very nature of things. As an intellectual, he likes to ponder meanings and events, he has a great capacity for belief in ideas, and a great confidence in the efficacy of reason. What he comes to discover is the horrifying presence of evil, its insidiousness, and its penetration of every kind of rational or civilized order.

.There is in this story, to be sure, the unnatural rape of the seventeen-year-old girl by the gangster Popeye, and the story of Popeye's wanton murder of Tommy, but Horace Benbow might conceivably accept both of these things as the kinds of cruel accidents to which human life is subject. What crumples him up is the moral corruption of the girl, which follows on her rape: she actually accepts her life in the brothel and testifies at the trial in favor of the man who had abducted her. What Horace also discovers is that the forces of law and order are also corruptible. His opponent in the trial, the district attorney, plays fast and loose with the evidence and actually ensures that the innocent man will not only be convicted but burned to death by a mob. And what perhaps Horace himself does not discover (but it is made plainly evident to the reader) is that Horace's betrayal at the trial is finally a bosom betrayal: Horace's own sister gives the district attorney the tip-off that will allow him to defeat her brother and make a mockery of justice. Indeed, Horace's sister, the calm and serene Narcissa, is, next to Popeye, the most terrifying person in the novel. She simply does not want her brother associated with people like the accused man, Lee Goodwin, the bootlegger, and his common-law wife. She exclaims to her brother, "I dont see that it makes any difference who [committed the murder]. The question is, are you going to stay mixed up with it?"[4] And she sees to it with quiet and efficient ruthlessness that the trial ends at the first possible date, even though this costs an innocent man's life.

Sanctuary is clearly Faulkner's bitterest novel. It is a novel in which the initiation which every male must undergo is experienced in its most shattering and disillusioning form. Horace not only discovers the existence of evil: he experiences it, not as an abstract idea but as an integral portion of reality. After he has had his interview with Temple Drake in the brothel, he thinks: "Perhaps it is upon the instant that we realize, admit, that there is a logical pattern to evil, that we die," and he thinks of the expression he had once seen in the eyes of a dead child and in the eyes of the other dead: "the cooling indignation, the shocked despair fading, leaving two empty globes in which the motionless world lurked profoundly in miniature" (pp. 265–266).

One of the most important connections has already been touched upon in what I have said earlier. Horace Benbow's initiation into the nature of reality and the nature of evil is intimately associated with his discovery of the true nature of woman. His discovery is quite typical of Faulkner's male characters. In the Faulknerian notion of things, men' have to lose their innocence, confront the hard choice, and through a process of initiation discover reality. The women are already in possession of this knowledge, naturally and instinctively. That is why in moments of bitterness Faulkner's male characters—Mr. Compson in *The Sound and the Fury*, for example—assert that women are not innocent. Mr. Compson tells his son Quentin: "Women are like that[;] they dont acquire knowledge of people[. Men] are for that[. Women] are just born with a practical fertility of suspicion. . . . they have an affinity for evil[—]for supplying whatever the evil lacks in itself[—]for drawing it about them instinctively as you do bed clothing in slumber. . . ."[5] Again, "Women only use other people's codes of honor" (p. 193).

I suppose that we need not take these Schopenhauerian profundities of the bourbon-soaked Mr. Compson too seriously. It might on the whole be more accurate to say that Faulkner's women lack the callow idealism of the men, have fewer illusions about human nature, and are less trammeled by legalistic distinctions and niceties of any code of conduct.

Faulkner's view of women, then, is radically old-fashioned—even medieval. Woman is the source and sustainer of virtue and also a prime source of evil. She can be either, because she is, as man is not, always a little beyond good and evil. With her powerful natural drives and her instinct for the concrete and personal, she does not need to agonize over her decisions. There is no code for her to master—no initiation for her to undergo. For this reason she has access to a wisdom which is veiled from man; and man's codes, good or bad, are always, in their formal abstraction, a little absurd in her eyes. Women are close to nature; the feminine principle is closely related to the instinctive and natural: woman typically manifests pathos rather than ethos.

A little later I shall have something more to say about Faulkner's characters in confrontation with nature. At this point, however, I want to go back and refer to another aspect of *Sanctuary*. The worst villains in Faulkner are cut off from nature. They have in some profound way denied their nature, like Flem Snopes in *The Hamlet,* who has no natural vices, only the unnatural vice of a pure lust for power and money. In *Sanctuary* Popeye is depicted as a sort of *ludus naturae*. Everybody has noticed the way in which he is described, as if he were a kind of automaton, with eyes like "two knobs of soft black rubber" (p. 2). As Horace watches him across the spring, Popeye's "face had a queer, bloodless color, as though seen by electric light; against the sunny silence, in his slanted straw hat and his slightly akimbo arms, he had that vicious depthless quality of stamped tin" (p. 2). Faulkner's two figures of speech are brilliantly used here. They serve to rob Popeye of substance and to turn him into a sinister black silhouette against the spring landscape. The phrase "as though seen by electric light" justifies the description of his queer, bloodless color, but it does more than this. Juxtaposed as it is to the phrase "against the sunny silence," it stresses the sense of the contrived, the artificial, as though Popeye constituted a kind of monstrous affront to the natural scene. These suggestions of a shadowy lack of substance are confirmed at the end of the sentence with the closing phrase: "depthless quality of stamped tin." Faulkner relentlessly forces this notion of the unnatural: Popeye deliberately spits into the spring, he cringes in terror from the low swooping owl, he is afraid of the dark.

Popeye has no natural vices either. He cannot drink. Since he is impotent, he is forced to use unnatural means in his rape of Temple. As a consequence, some readers take Popeye to be a kind of allegorical figure, a representation of the inhumanly mechanistic forces of our society. We may say that Popeye is quite literally a monster, remembering that the Latin *monstrum* signifies something that lies outside the ordinary course of nature.

Though Popeye represents an extreme case, in this matter he is typical of all of Faulkner's villains. For example, Thomas Sutpen, in *Absalom, Absalom!*,[6] is a man of great courage and heroic stature, who challenges the role of a tragic protagonist. Yet he has about him this same rigid and mechanical quality. Sutpen, as an acquaintance observes, believes "that the ingredients of morality were like the ingredients of pie or cake and once you had measured them and balanced them and mixed them and put them into the oven it was all finished and nothing but pie or cake could come out."

Sutpen has a great plan in mind, his "design," he calls it—which involves his building a great plantation house and setting up a dynasty. As he tells General Compson, "I had a design. To accomplish it I should require money, a house, and a plantation, slaves, a family—incidentally, of course, a wife" (p. 263). But when he finds later that his wife has a trace of Negro blood, he puts her aside, and he does it with an air of honest grievance. He says "[Her parents] deliberately withheld from me the one fact which I have reason to know they

were aware would have caused me to decline the entire matter,
otherwise they would not have withheld it from me—a fact
which I did not learn until after my son was born. And even
then I did not act hastily. I could have reminded them of these
wasted years, these years which would now leave me behind
with my schedule. . ." (p. 264). (The last term is significant:
Sutpen, modern man that he is, works in accordance with a
timetable.) He tells General Compson that when he put aside
his wife and child, "his conscience had bothered him somewhat
at first but that he had argued calmly and logically with his
conscience until it was settled" (p. 262). General Compson is
aghast at this revelation of moral myopia. He calls it "innocence" (p. 220), and by the term he means a blindness to the
nature of reality. And since the writer is Faulkner, the blindness involves a blindness to the nature of woman. For Sutpen
has actually believed that by providing a more than just prop-
erty settlement he could reconcile his wife to his abandoning
her. General Compson had thrown up his hands and exclaimed:
"Good God, man . . . what kind of conscience [did you have]
to trade with which would have warranted you in the belief
that you could have bought immunity from her for no other
coin but justice?—" (p. 265).

Evil for Faulkner, then, involves a violation of nature and
runs counter to the natural appetites and affections. And yet,
as we have seen, the converse is not true; Faulkner does not
consider the natural and instinctive and impulsive as automatically and necessarily good. Here I think rests the best warrant
for maintaining that Faulkner holds an orthodox view of man
and reality. For his men, at least, cannot be content merely with
being natural. They cannot live merely by their instincts and
natural appetites. They must confront the fact of evil. They are
constrained to moral choices. They have to undergo a test of
their courage, in making and abiding by the choice. They
achieve goodness by discipline and effort. This proposition is
perhaps most fully and brilliantly illustrated in Faulkner's
story "The Bear." Isaac McCaslin, when he comes of age,
decides to repudiate his inheritance. He refuses to accept his
father's plantation and chooses to earn his living as a carpenter
and to live in a rented room. There are two powerful motives
that shape this decision: the sacramental view of nature which
he has been taught by the old hunter, Sam Fathers, and the discovery of his grandfather's guilt in his treatment of one of his

slaves: the grandfather had incestuously begotten a child upon his own half-Negro daughter.

"The Bear" is thus a story of penance and expiation, as also of a difficult moral decision made and maintained, but since it is so well known and has received so much commentary, I want to illustrate Faulkner's characteristic drama of moral choice from a less familiar story, "An Odor of Verbena," which is the concluding section of Faulkner's too little appreciated but brilliant novel *The Unvanquished*.[7] As this episode opens, word has come to Bayard Sartoris, a young man of twenty-four off at law school, that his father has been assassinated by a political enemy. Ringo, the young Negro man of his own age and his boyhood companion, has ridden to the little town where Bayard is at law school to bring the news. Bayard knows what is expected of him—the date is 1874, the tradition of the code of honor still lingers, the devastating Civil War and the Reconstruction have contorted the land with violence, and Bayard knows that the community expects him to call his father's assassin to account. Even the quiet and gentle Judge Wilkins with whom he is studying law expects him to do so, and though he speaks to the boy with pity ("Bayard, my son, my dear son"),[7] he offers him not only his horse but his pistol as well. Certainly also Bayard's father's Civil War troop expect him to avenge his father. Bayard's young stepmother, eight years older than he, expects it. Speaking in a "silvery ecstatic voice" (p. 272) like the priestess of a rite wrought up to a point of hysteria, she offers Bayard the pistols when he returns to the family home. Even Ringo expects it.

Some years before, when Bayard and Ringo were sixteen, at the very end of the Civil War, when the region had become a no-man's land terrorized by bushwhackers, Bayard's grandmother had been killed by a ruffian named Grumby, and Bayard and Ringo had followed him for weeks until finally they had run him down and killed him. Bayard had loved his grandmother, and was resolved that her murderer should be punished. But there was no law and order in this troubled time to which he could appeal; the two sixteen-year-old boys had to undertake the punishment themselves.

Now as the two young men ride back to Jefferson, Ringo says to Bayard, "We could bushwhack him. . . . Like we done Grumby that day. But I reckon that wouldn't suit that white

skin you walks around in" (p. 251). Bayard in fact has resolved
that he will not kill again.

The motive for this decision is complex. For one thing, he
realizes that his father had become a proud and abstracted and
ruthless man. Bayard had loved his father but is well aware that
his father had pressed his opponent, Redmond, far too hard.
George Wyatt, the countryman who had served under his
father, earlier had in fact come to Bayard to ask him to restrain
his father:

> "Right or wrong, us boys and most of the other folks in
> this county know John's right. But he ought to let Red-
> mond alone. I know what's wrong: he's had to kill too
> many folks, and that's bad for a man. We all know Colonel's
> brave as a lion, but Redmond ain't no coward either and
> they ain't any use in making a brave man that made one
> mistake eat crow all the time. Can't you talk to him?"
> (p. 260)

Another powerful motive is evidently the psychic wound that
Bayard has suffered in the killing of Grumby. He has executed
vengeance once, and in that instance there were extenuating
circumstances to justify his taking the law into his own hands.
But this case is different, and as he says to himself before he
begins his journey home, "If there [is] anything at all in the
Book, anything of hope and peace for [God's] blind and be-
wildered spawn, the command *'Thou Shalt not kill'* must be
it" (p. 249). Finally, there is the example of his own father.
Even his father had decided that there had been too much killing. Two months before, he had told Bayard: "Now I shall do
a little moral house cleaning. I am tired of killing men, no
matter what the necessity or the end" (p. 266). Thus Bayard,
in resolving not to avenge his father, may be said to be following his father's own resolve.

But Bayard, as a member of a tightly knit community, does
not want to be branded as a coward; he respects his community's opinion, and he feels compelled to live up to what the
community expects of him. And so he resolves, though the
reader does not learn of it until late in the story, to face Redmond, but to face him unarmed.

There is one person who understands his dilemma and can

support him in his decision. It is his Aunt Jenny, who tells him
when he arrives home that night:

> "Yes. All right. Don't let it be Drusilla, poor hysterical
> young woman. And don't let it be [your father], Bayard,
> because he's dead now. And don't let it be George Wyatt
> and those others who will be waiting for you tomorrow
> morning. I know you are not afraid." "But what good will
> that do?" I said. "What good will that do?" . . . "I must
> live with myself, you see." "Then it's not just Drusilla?
> Not just him? Not just George Wyatt and Jefferson?"
> "No," I said." (p. 276)

It is indeed not just Drusilla and George Wyatt and the other
outsiders that are forcing Bayard to take his proposed course
of action. As he tells his aunt, it is not enough that *she* knows
that he is not afraid. He must prove it to himself. "I must live
with myself," he says. This is the situation of many a Faulkner
character. He must live with himself. He must prove to himself
that he possesses the requisite courage.

Bayard is fortunate. The man that he goes to meet is also
brave, also decent. He has decided that, having killed the
father, he will not kill the young son. Thus, when Bayard walks
up the stairs past the small faded sign *"B. J. Redmond. Atty
at Law"* and opens the door, he sees Redmond sitting

> behind the desk, not much taller than Father, but thicker
> as a man gets that spends most of his time sitting and listen-
> ing to people, freshly shaven and with fresh linen; a lawyer
> yet it was not a lawyer's face—a face much thinner than
> the body would indicate, strained (and yes, tragic; I know
> that now) and exhausted beneath the neat recent steady
> strokes of the razor, holding a pistol flat on the desk before
> him, loose beneath his hand and aimed at nothing. (pp.
> 285–286)

Redmond fires twice but Bayard can see that the gun was not
aimed at him and that the misses are deliberate. Then Redmond gets up from his desk, blunders down the stairs and
walks on out past George Wyatt and the six other members of
Colonel Sartoris' old troop. He

walked through the middle of them with his hat on and his head up (they told me how someone shouted at him: "Have you killed that boy too?") saying no word, staring straight ahead and with his back to them, on to the station where the south-bound train was just in and got on it with no baggage, nothing, and went away from Jefferson and from Mississippi and never came back. (pp. 287–288)

George Wyatt rushes up to Bayard, mistakenly thinking that he had taken Redmond's pistol away from him and then missed him, missed him twice. "Then he answered himself . . . 'No; wait. You walked in here without even a pocket knife and let him miss you twice. My God in heaven.'" But he adds, "'You ain't done anything to be ashamed of. I wouldn't have done it that way, myself. I'd a shot at him once, anyway. But that's your way or you wouldn't have done it" (pp. 288–289). And even Drusilla, the wrought-up priestess of violence, before she leaves the house forever to go back to her kinsfolk in Alabama, leaves on Bayard's pillow a sprig of verbena because it is the odor of courage, "that odor which she said you could smell alone above the smell of horses" (p. 293), as a token that she too has accepted his act as brave and honorable.

One further observation: as I have already remarked, it is the men who have to be initiated into the meaning of reality, who have to observe a code of conduct, who have to prove themselves worthy. Aunt Jenny, as a woman, is outside the code. Indeed she sees the code as absurd and quixotic, though she knows that Bayard as a man will have to observe it. And what shall we say of Drusilla, who is a woman, and yet is the very high priestess of the code? Drusilla is the masculinized woman, who as a type occurs more than once in Faulkner. Drusilla's story is that she has lost her fiancé early in the war and finally in her boredom and despair has actually ridden with the Confederate cavalry. She is brave and Faulkner gives her her due, but he is not celebrating her as a kind of Confederate Joan of Arc. Her action exacts its penalty and she ends a warped and twisted woman, truly a victim of the war.

I realize that I am risking oversimplification in pressing some of these issues so hard—for example, the contrast between man and woman, in their relation to nature and to their characteristic roles as active and passive. One may be disposed to doubt that even a traditional writer writing about a traditional society would stylize these relationships as much as I have suggested Faulkner has. Yet I am very anxious to sketch in, even at the risk of over-bold strokes, the general nature of Faulkner's conception of good and evil, and so I mean to stand by this summary: Faulkner sees the role of man as active; man makes choices and lives up to the choices. Faulkner sees the role of woman as characteristically fostering and sustaining. She undergirds society, upholding the family and community mores, sending her men out into battle, including the ethical battle. This generalization I believe, is, if oversimplified, basically true. And I should like to relate it to Faulkner's "Calvinistic" Protestantism. Insofar as his Calvinism represents a violent repression and constriction of natural impulse, a denial of nature itself, Faulkner tends to regard it as a terrible and evil thing. And the natural foil to characters who have so hardened their hearts in accordance with their notion of a harsh and vindictive God is the feminine principle as exemplified by a person like Lena Grove, the heroine of *Light in August*. Lena has a childlike confidence in herself and in mankind. She is a creature of warm natural sympathies and a deep instinctive commitment to her natural function.

But Faulkner has still another relation to Calvinistic Protestantism. Insofar as the tradition insists that man must be brought up to the urgency of decision, must be set tests of courage and endurance, must have his sinews strung tight for some moral leap or his back braced so as to stand firm against the push of circumstance, Faulkner evidently derives from this tradition. From it may be derived the very necessity that compels his male characters to undergo an initiation. The required initiation may be analogous to the crisis of conversion and the character's successful entrance into knowledge of himself, analogous to the sinner's experiencing salvation.

On the conscious level, Faulkner is obviously a Protestant anticleric, fascinated, but also infuriated, by some of the more violently repressive features of the religion that dominates his country. This matter is easily illustrated. One of his masterpieces, *Light in August,* provides a stinging criticism of the harsher aspects of Protestantism. Indeed a basic theme in *Light in August* is man's strained attempt to hold himself up in a rigid aloofness above the relaxed female world. The struggle to do so is, as Faulkner portrays it in this novel, at once monstrous, comic, and heroic, as the various characters take up their special postures.

In a character like old Doc Hines, there is a definite distortion and perversion. His fury at "bitchery and abomination" is the fury of a crazed man. In her conversation with Bunch and Hightower, Mrs. Hines states quite precisely what has happened to her husband: he began "then to take God's name in vain and in pride to justify and excuse the devil that was in him."[8] His attribution of his furies to God is quite literally a taking of God's name in vain, blasphemy. The tendency to call one's own hates the vengeance of a just God is a sin to which Protestantism has always been prone. But not merely Southern Protestantism and, of course, not merely Protestantism as such.

Calvin Burden represents another instance of the militant Protestant, but this man's heartiness and boisterous energy have something of the quality of comedy. He is the son of a Unitarian minister; but when he runs away to the West, he becomes a Roman Catholic and lives for a year in a monastery. Then, on his marriage, he repudiates the Catholic Church, choosing for the scene of his formal repudiation "a saloon, insisting that every one present listen to him and state their objections" (p. 211). Then, though he cannot read the English Bible—he had learned from the priests in California to read Spanish—he begins to instruct his child in the true religion, interspersing his readings to the child in Spanish with "extemporised dissertations composed half of the bleak and bloodless logic which he remembered from his father on interminable New England Sundays and half of immediate hellfire and tangible brimstone." Perhaps he differs from the bulk of doctrinaire hellfire and brimstone Protestants in not being a "proselyter" or a "missionary." But everything else marks him as truly of the breed: his intensity, his stern authoritarianism, and his violence. He has killed a man in an argument over slavery and he threatens to "frail the tar" out of his children if they do not learn to hate what he hates—hell and slaveholders (p. 212).

The case of the Rev. Gail Hightower is one of the most interesting of·all. He is the only one of these Protestants who has had formal theological training. Because of that fact one might expect him to be the most doctrinaire. He is not. He seems at the beginning of the book the most tolerant and pitying of all the characters, the one who recoils in horror at man's capacity for evil and man's propensity to crucify his fellows: he is a man whose only defense against violence is nonresistance. One may be inclined to say that Hightower had rebelled against his Calvinist training and repudiated the jealous and repressive God. Certainly, there is truth in this notion. Hightower is a disillusioned man and a man who has learned something from his sufferings. But there is a sense in which he has never broken out of the mold: he still stresses a God of justice rather than of mercy, for his sincerest belief is that he has somehow "bought immunity." He exclaims: "I have paid. I have paid" (p. 429)— in confidence that God is an honest merchant who has receipted his bill and will honor his title to the precious merchandise he has purchased at such cost.

Lastly there is the case of Joe Christmas, the violent rebel against hellfire Protestantism. His detachment from any kind of human community is shocking. Here is a man who has no family ties, no continuity with the past, no place in any community whatsoever. He is a man who has literally tried to kick the earth out from under his feet. Yet his very alienation and his insistence upon his own individual integrity are touched with the tragically heroic. As a child he is conscious that he is being hounded by old Doc Hines; he resists stubbornly the discipline imposed by his foster father McEachern, whom he finally brains with a chair; and when his paramour, Joanna Burden, threatens him with hell and insists that he kneel with her and pray for forgiveness, he decapitates her. Yet there is a most important sense in which Joe Christmas is the sternest and most doctrinaire Calvinist in the book.

He imbibes more from the training of his foster father than he realizes. For all that he strains in fierce resistance against him, he "could depend" on "the hard, just, ruthless man" (p. 144). It is the "soft kindness" (p. 147) of the woman, his foster mother, that he abominates. If one mark of the Calvinists in this novel is their fear and distrust of women and their hatred of the female principle, then Joe Christmas is eminently qualified to take a place among them. He even has affinities with his old childhood ogre, Doc Hines, and Hines' fury at the bitchery of women and the abomination of Negro blood. Joe, hearing the "fecundmellow" voices of Negro women, feels that he and "all other manshaped life about him" had been returned to the "lightless hot wet primogenitive Female" (p. 100) and runs from the scene in a kind of panic.

Christmas too wants not mercy but justice, is afraid of the

claims of love and its obligations, and yearns only for a vindication of his identity and integrity—a vindication made the more difficult by his not really knowing precisely what he would vindicate. When he puts aside the temptation to marry Joanna and win ease and security, he does it by saying: "If I give in now, I will deny all the thirty years that I have lived to make me what I chose to be" (p. 232). Finally, Joe is something of a fatalist, and his fatalism is a kind of perversion of Calvinist determinism. On his way to murder Joanna, "he believed with calm paradox that he was the volitionless servant of the fatality in which he believed that he did not believe." But so "fated" (p. 244) is his act of murder that he keeps saying to himself "I had to do it" (p. 245)—using the past tense, as if the act had already been performed.

Lena (along with Eula of *The Hamlet*) has sometimes been called an earth goddess. The description does have a certain aptness when applied to Eula, especially in some of the more rhapsodic passages of *The Hamlet*. But it is a little highfalutin for Lena. It is more accurate to say that Lena is one of Faulkner's several embodiments of the female principle—indeed one of the purest and least complicated of his embodiments. Her rapport with nature is close. She is never baffled as to what course of action to take. She is never torn by doubts and indecisions. There is no painful introspection. This serene composure has frequently been put down to sheer mindlessness, and Lena, to be sure, is a very simple young woman. But Faulkner himself undoubtedly attributes most of Lena's quiet force to her female nature. In this novel the principal male characters suffer alienation. They are separated from the community, are in rebellion against it—and against nature. But Lena moves serenely into the community, and it gathers itself about her with protective gestures. Its response to her, of course, is rooted in a deep and sound instinct: Lena embodies the principle upon which any human community is founded. She is the carrier of life and she has to be protected and nurtured if there is to be any human community at all.

I have said that *Light in August* depicts man's strained attempt to hold himself up in rigid aloofness above the relaxed female world. In terms of the plot, Lena is the direct means by which Byron Bunch and the indirect means by which Hightower are redeemed from their pallid half lives and brought back into the community. This coming back into the community is an essential part of the redemption. Unless the controlling purposes of the individuals are related to those that other men share, and in which the individual can participate, he is indeed isolated, and is forced to fall back upon his personal values, with all the risk of fanaticism and distortion to which such isolation is liable.

The community is at once the field for man's action and the norm by which his action is judged and regulated. It sometimes seems that the sense of an organic community has all but disappeared from modern fiction, and the disappearance accounts for the terrifying self-consciousness and subjectivity of a great deal of modern writing. That Faulkner has some sense of an organic community still behind him is among his most important resources as a writer.

In *Light in August* Faulkner uses Lena to confirm an ideal of integrity and wholeness in the light of which the alienated characters are judged; and this is essentially the function of Dilsey, the Negro servant in *The Sound and the Fury*, regarded by many people as Faulkner's masterpiece. Dilsey's role, to be sure, is more positive than Lena's. She has affinities not with the pagan goddess but with the Christian saint. She is not the young woman and young mother that Lena is. She is an older woman and an older mother, and she is the sustaining force— the only possible sustaining force of a broken and corrupted family.

Yet Dilsey's primary role is generally similar to Lena's: she affirms the ideal of wholeness in a family which shows in every other member splintering and disintegration. *The Sound and the Fury* can be regarded as a study in the fragmentation of modern man. There is Benjy, the idiot brother who represents the life of the instincts and the unreflective emotions; there is Quentin, the intellectual and artistic brother, who is conscious of his own weakness and failure and yet so hagridden by impossible ideals that he finally turns away from life altogether and commits suicide; and there is Jason, the brother who represents an aggressive and destructive rationalism that dissolves all family and community loyalties and attachments. There has been a somewhat strained attempt to portray the brothers in Freudian terms: Benjy as the *id,* Quentin as the tortured *ego,* and Jason as the tyrannical and cruel *super-ego.* Faulkner's own way of regarding the three brothers (as implied in the appendix he supplied for the Modern Library edition) is interesting.

Benjy is an idiot, of course; Quentin, in his obsession, is obviously half-mad; and Jason is perfectly sane, the first "sane" Compson for generations. Faulkner's mocking choice of the term "sane" to characterize Jason's coldly monstrous self-serving (all of Faulkner's villains, let me repeat, are characterized by this devouring and destructive rationalism) is highly significant. It is as if Faulkner argued that mere sanity were not enough—indeed that pure sanity was inhuman. The good man has to transcend his mere intellect with some overflow of generosity and love.

But we ought not to confine ourselves to the three brothers, for Dilsey is being contrasted not merely with them but with the whole of the family. There is Mr. Compson, who has been defeated by life and has sunk into whisky and fatalism. There Mrs. Compson, the mother, whom Faulkner calls a "cold, weak" person. She is the whining, self-centered hypochondriac who has poisoned the whole family relationship. She is evidently a primary cause of her husband's cynicism; she has spoiled and corrupted her favorite son, Jason; and she has withheld her love from the other children. Quentin, on the day of his suicide, can say to himself bitterly, "If I only had a mother." Mrs. Compson is all that Dilsey is not. It is the mother role that she has abandoned that Dilsey is compelled to assume. There is lastly the daughter of the family, Candace, who in her own way also represents the dissolution of the family. Candace has become a wanton. Sex is her particular escape from an unsatisfactory home, and she is subject to her own kind of specialization, the semiprofessionalism of a sexual adventuress.

In contrast with this splintered family, Dilsey maintains a wholeness. Indeed, Dilsey's wholeness constitutes her holiness. (It is well to remember that *whole* and *holy* are related and come from the same root.) In Dilsey the life of the instincts, including the sex drive, the life of the emotions, and the life of ideal values and of rationality are related meaningfully to one another. To say this is to say, of course, that Dilsey is a profoundly religious person. Her life with its round of daily tasks and responsibilities is related to the larger life of eternity and eternal values. Dilsey does not have to strain to make meaningful some particular desire or dream or need. Her world is a solid and meaningful world. It is filled with pain, toil, and difficulty, but it is not wrenched by agonizing doubts and perplexities.

I said a moment ago that Dilsey was sometimes compared to the saint and in what I am going to say I do not mean to deprive her of her properly deserved halo. But we must not allow the term to sentimentalize her. If she treats with compassion the idiot Benjy, saying "You's de Lawd's chile, anyway" (p. 333), she is quite capable of dealing summarily with her own child, Luster, when he needs a rebuke: "Lemme tell you somethin, nigger boy, you got jes es much Compson devilment in you es any of em. Is you right sho you never broke dat window?" (p. 292). Dilsey's earthiness and her human exasperations are very much in evidence in this novel. Because they are, Dilsey's "saintliness" is altogether credible and convincing.

One may say in general of Faulkner's Negroes that they remain close to a concrete world of values—less perverted by abstraction—more honest in recognizing what is essential and elemental than are most of the white people. Faulkner certainly does not assume any inherent virtue in the Negro race. But he does find among his Negro characters less false pride, less false idealism, more seasoned discipline in the elemental human relationships. The Negro virtues which Faulkner praises in "The Bear" are endurance, patience, honesty, courage, and the love of children—white or black. Dilsey, then, is not a primitive figure who through some mystique of race or healthiness of natural impulses is good. Dilsey is unsophisticated and warm-hearted, but she is no noble savage. Her role is in its general dimensions comparable to that of her white sisters such as the matriarchs Aunt Jenny and Mrs. Rosa Millard, fostering and sustaining forces. If she goes beyond them in exemplifying the feminine principle at its best, still hers is no mere goodness by and of nature, if one means by this a goodness that justifies a faith in man as man. Dilsey does not believe in man; she believes in God.

To try for a summary of a very difficult and complicated topic: Evil for Faulkner involves the violation of the natural and the denial of the human. As Isaac's older kinsman says in "The Bear," "Courage and honor and pride, and pity and love of justice and of liberty. They all touch the heart, and what the heart holds to become truth, as far as we know truth."[9] A meanness of spirit and coldness of calculation which would deny the virtues that touch the heart is by that very fact proven false. Yet Faulkner is no disciple of Jean-Jacques Rousseau. He has no illusions that man is naturally good or that he can safely trust to his instincts and emotions. Man is capable of evil, and this means that goodness has to be achieved by struggle and discipline and effort. Like T. S. Eliot, Faulkner has small faith in social arrangements so perfectly organized that nobody has to take the trouble to be good. Finally, Faulkner's noblest characters are willing to face the fact that most men can learn the deepest truths about themselves and about reality only through suffering. Hurt and pain and loss are not mere accidents to which the human being is subject; nor are they mere punishments incurred by human error; they can be the means to the deeper knowledge and to the more abundant life.

Commentary ━━━━

The brilliance of Brooks's achievement will become clear only when recognized as an achievement in definition. He has drawn with clarity lines which others have only hinted at or sketched out warily.

His first important achievement is the strong insistence on the two distinct and very different principles operative in Faulkner's novels, the male and the female. Others have had glimpses of this dichotomy in Faulkner, but its crucial importance has not before been expressed so clearly. It would be interesting and perhaps extremely rewarding to apply this definition more in detail to, for example, Eula Varner of the Snopes trilogy (whom Brooks has time only to mention in passing), as well as to other novels whose women have fairly prominent roles, such as *Pylon* and *A Fable*. One might also suggest the need to consider instances where Faulkner seems to move somewhat away from this dichotomizing approach, such as in *Requiem for a Nun*, where Temple Drake herself enters the arena of moral decision. And finally, it is tantalizing to conjecture whether Faulkner might not have had the scriptural prototype at least dimly in mind: Eve, the eternal woman, to whom Brooks's definition may be applied *par excellence*—woman as at once "the carrier of life," a "source and sustainer of virtue," and "a prime source of evil."

Brooks's outline of the process of male asceticism—by which a man has "sinews strung tight for some moral leap or his back braced so as to stand firm against the push of circumstance"—will also bear application to other novels and other characters. Too often in the past this asceticism has been discussed only in terms of obvious ritualistic initiations like "The Bear." It is Brooks's special contribution to see this asceticism in terms of the progress toward moral choice necessary for any man, whether it be Ike McCaslin or Thomas Sutpen or Rev. Gail Hightower; or, one might add, even for such seeming "onlookers" as Gavin Stevens or V. K. Ratliff.

The essay's basic definitions of Faulknerian good and evil in terms of their relationship to nature—evil as the denial of nature, good as its acceptance—are unassailable. They seem to be reinforced, too, by being linked with the male/female principles, which are defined precisely in terms of nature. Woman is commonly not "torn by doubts and indecisions," because she has an instinctive rapport with nature—whether this be in terms of the simple goodness of

76

Lena Grove or the total amorality of Eula Varner. ⌈Man, on the other hand, must involve himself in the agony of moral choice because he is alienated from nature. But then must not the question arise, in what sense can either Lena or Eula be said to be morally good or evil? Neither makes a moral choice; neither seems even to be capable of it. Lena does what is right instinctively, seemingly quite without reflection. Eula does the opposite, equally without reflection. Can either one of them be praised or blamed?

Brooks's expression of the role of the community in Faulkner's redemptive process is admirable, particularly in what he says of the need for men to draw strength from one another in achieving clarity and assurance in their "controlling purposes." Again, however, one must ask—and in this I am not disagreeing with Brooks but only underscoring him—does Faulkner see the community as the complete solution to the problem of making right moral choices, or merely as a necessary step? Men, even in community, may conceivably be (in T. S. Eliot's words) only "hollow men . . . leaning together, headpiece filled with straw." A community of Snopeses may have common "controlling purposes," and yet one would hardly call them redeemed. One must add, as Brooks does, that this "coming back into the community" is only an "essential part" of redemption. Other essential parts are personal and individual "struggle and discipline and effort," with, it may be hoped—as in the case of Dilsey, the holy woman—a perception of the relationship of all these to "the larger life of eternity and eternal values."

There is one qualification I feel obliged to make. Excellent though Brooks's definition and analysis of the process of moral choice may be as Faulkner's ideal, the question remains: how many of his characters are actually able to achieve it? Early in his essay Brooks insisted that Faulkner's men "have the power of choice, they make decisions, and they win their goodness through effort and discipline." Ideally, yes. Faulkner has conceived the process very much as Brooks has described it. But this is not to say that all, or even very many, of ⌈Faulkner's characters—limited and bound in by environment, by heredity, by human nature's innate selfishness—ever achieve personal freedom sufficient to make a moral decision.⌉ For I think it might be questioned whether freedom of choice in Faulkner's view is simply a "given" attribute common to, and the same in, all men. Faulkner does hold, of course, as Brooks says, that men "cannot live merely by their instincts and natural appetites," that they must "confront the fact of evil," that they are "constrained to moral choices." But that very many of them actually do go on by discipline and effort to "achieve goodness" may well be questioned.

Examples are given, of course, of two men who do so "achieve goodness": Ike McCaslin in "The Bear" and Bayard Sartoris in "An

Odor of Verbena." Undoubtedly others may be found, but I have the feeling that their ranks would be depressingly thin. Their opposite numbers, on the other hand, seem to abound: Popeye, the Compsons (Jason, Quentin, Benjy—all of them), Thomas Sutpen, Joe Christmas, Harry Wilbourne in *The Wild Palms*, the Sartorises (almost the whole doomed and disastrous clan of them), to say nothing of a whole mountain of Snopeses. And if it is true that so many, perhaps the majority, of Faulkner's men fail to achieve goodness— seem indeed to be incapable of achieving it—what can it mean to say that Faulkner's men have in any real sense "freedom of choice"? Faulkner sees men rather as laboring under varying degrees of freedom of moral choice. Some, like most of the Snopeses, are devoid of moral vision and are therefore incapable of moral choice. Others, like the Sartorises, may once have been capable of such choice, but now, for whatever reason—guilt for their rape of the land, family dishonor, an "Original Sin"—they no longer have the strength of "discipline and effort." Still others, like Quentin Compson, try and fail. Some few others, like young Chick Mallison in *Intruder in the Dust*, try and succeed in making a personal moral choice. In this last category one is hard put to find examples, for in most of the few truly free men in Faulkner, like Byron Bunch in *Light in August*, their good choices give the impression of being made instinctively, without effort or anguish. There seems to be almost as little need for Byron to "brace his back against the push of circumstance" as there is for Lena. Both suffer, it is true, and Byron toils, but he seems not to exercise "discipline and effort" in making moral decisions. He is as naturally, as instinctively good as Lena.

This last qualification obviously in no way detracts from the remarkable achievement of the preceding essay. The paradigm Cleanth Brooks has given of the moral structure of good and evil in Faulkner's world is not only clear but also very strong. It remains for the reader to test his understanding of Faulkner's characters against this excellent matrix.

5⎓

Besides the strongly Christian elements in Faulkner's novels, there are clear strains of other cultures and value-structures as well. John W. Hunt sees Faulkner's "theological center" to be in fact a tension between Christianity and Stoicism. In the following essay he defines this tension in Faulkner's work. Later, in another essay, we shall see him apply his insight in detail to *Absalom, Absalom!*

The following excerpt is taken from Hunt's *William Faulkner: Art in Theological Tension* (Syracuse: Syracuse University Press, 1965), pp. 25–33; it is here used with permission.

John W. Hunt

THE THEOLOGICAL COMPLEXITY
OF FAULKNER'S FICTION

FAULKNER SEES THE WORLD AS AT ONCE FALLEN AND
redeemed: he looks at one world. Because he is characteristically modern in his literary method he looks at the world
through character, and at any one time it is the character's
vision before the reader, or, in many cases, the vision of a composite character-author-reader. Consequently, if one is not careful to read Faulkner's works as imaginative productions, he is
apt to judge Faulkner's vision as fragmentary.

The unity of Faulkner's vision does not depend upon the fact
that it is, after all, one writer who is presenting various worlds.
In his total theological vision, Dilsey [in *The Sound and the
Fury*] does not live in one world and Quentin in another. Both
share the same objective reality. Dilsey is not a stranger to the
facts of Quentin's experience, although she does not participate
in his response. Caroline Compson's querulous self-pity and
Jason's cunning meanness are facts of experience to her. But
Dilsey has resources the others do not tap. She observes the
violence and decadence of the unredeemed world of those who
have only the past as their present, but takes her own stance
at the center of a redemptive present which comprehends a
view of the beginning and the end.

Faulkner's ability to give a full rendering of a world at once
fallen and redeemed can be seen easily by contrasting Quentin's
and Dilsey's views of the resurrection. For Quentin, Christ is
an inanimate doll with "sawdust flowing from what wound in
what side that not for me died not."[1] Christ does not speak to
his condition. Quentin contemplates the resurrection of his
body which will occur after he has carried out his plan to
drown himself in the Charles River by weighting his body with

81

some flatirons. He thinks: "And maybe when He says Rise the eyes will come floating up too, out of the deep quiet and the sleep, to look on glory. And after awhile the flat irons would come floating up" (p. 135). Dilsey's vision of the power and the glory is generically different. In church during Shegog's Easter sermon, "Dilsey sat bolt upright . . . crying rigidly and quietly in the annealment and the blood of the remembered Lamb" (p. 313). As she leaves church, she is able to place the Compson history in the comprehensive context of a Christian view of time:

> "I've seed de first en de last," Dilsey said. . . .
> "First en last whut?" Frony said.
> "Never you mind," Dilsey said. "I seed de beginnin, en now I sees de endin." (p. 313)

Dilsey furnishes an easy case for the positive content of the Christian faith even as Quentin exhibits the despair familiar to its pessimistic side. But the Christian faith does not provide the only frame of reference in terms of which Faulkner renders positive and negative responses to modern experience.

We should not dwell upon the fallen character of Faulkner's world in the second place, then, because the meaning and truth of his religious center is as much Stoic as it is Christian. To interpret his vision as simply skeptical is to diagnose the symptom as the disease. Faulkner's religious center, as revealed by his entire imaginative performance—theme, character, action, the total structure of his individual fictions—is best described as a tension between Stoic and Christian visions. The tension is not a dualism, not mere strain, not a contradiction. His is a religious center *of* tension. This is another way of describing the unity of his theological core; the world in Christian terms is at once fallen and redeemed, and in Stoic terms it is hostile, inhuman, thoughtless, alien, and hopeless on the one hand and the locus of possible human meaning on the other. Except for a few instances, the theological assumptions (unarticulated and for the most part unknown) underlying his characters' vision—negative or positive—can be identified as either Stoic or Christian.

One may, of course, take this central theological tension as evidence of an irresolution on Faulkner's part: he is trying to have it both ways. But such a conclusion assumes Faulkner to be engaged directly in a theological task in which he has attempted but failed to reach a resolution. If we assume Faulkner's task to be primarily aesthetic and judge by the mimetic achievement of his fiction, we can at the most claim only that he has given lyrical validity to both alternatives, that he is able *where the fictive logic demands it* to make each aesthetically valid.

Because the history of Christian thought is so complex, so eclectic, there is not a thoroughgoing difference between orthodox Christianity and classical Stoicism. Stoic rationalism, especially in the doctrine of the Logos, contributed to the Christian understanding of the relation of God to nature; the Stoic emphasis upon human brotherhood and the attendant imperative upon duty became part of the Christian ethic. And Stoicism itself is not single and unambiguous; it has its own phases, its own sidelines of thought, and its own inner contradictions, and its modern expressions do not derive in a clear line from its classical forms. Nevertheless, as Paul Tillich documents so well in *The Courage to Be,* Stoic religiousness is fundamentally different from the Christian and is, in fact, the classical religious alternative to it.[2] For example, in the realm of ethics, in which the valuation of a human act is considered, the notion that human brotherhood roots in love is definitely antithetical to the Stoic doctrine of *eudaimonia,* tranquillity. Edwyn Bevan's classic study of Stoicism makes clear that the Stoic "was not to *concern* himself with his brethren . . . he was only to serve them."[3] Bevan sees a central difference between Stoicism and Christianity to lie in their incompatible ideals of detachment and love:

> The Stoics, I think, saw with perfect truth that if you were going to allow any least entrance of love and pity into the breast, you admitted something whose measure you could not control, and might just as well give up the idea of inner tranquillity at once. Where love is, action cannot be without desire; the action of love has eminently regard to fruit, in the sense of some result beyond itself—the one thing that seems to matter is whether the loved person really is helped by your action. Of course you run the risk of frustrated desire and disappointment. The Stoic sage was never frustrated and never disappointed. Gethsemane,

looked at from his point of view, was a signal break-down. The Christian's Ideal Figure could never be accepted by the Stoic as an example of his typical Wise Man.[4]

In the realm of metaphysics or ontology, especially that area of it which verges upon a theological doctrine of man, there is also a fundamental difference between the Stoic and the Christian. The Stoic doctrine of man, which identifies man's reason, his ruling principle, as a detached spark of the divine reason, could not admit the notion of guilt or guilty existence. The concept of guilt would contradict the rationality of man, disallow his essential identity with the divine, the universal, the natural. Yet, though guilt or guilty existence is a concept alien to the Stoic mind, evil is not. The undeniable presence of evil in experience can be explained only as a defection of reason and will or as dire fate. The proper response to it is courageous resignation, assent. A modern Stoic, Bertrand Russell, has described the Stoic vision and the strategy of Stoic courage: "only on the firm foundation of unyielding despair, can the soul's habitation . . . be safely built."[5] For him,

> to defy with Promethean constancy a hostile universe, to keep its evil always in view, always actively hated, to refuse no pain that the malice of Power can invent, appears to be the duty of all who will not bow before the inevitable. . . . there is a kind of self-assertion which it is necessary for the wise to overcome. . . . the Stoic freedom in which wisdom consists is found in the submission of our desires, but not of our thoughts. From the submission of our desires springs the virtue of resignation. . . . Freedom comes only to those who no longer ask of life that it shall yield them any of those personal goods that are subject to the mutations of Time.[6]

In his essay *On Providence,* Seneca encourages his friend Lucilius to bear evil and bad fortune with fortitude because "in this you may outstrip God; he is exempt from enduring evil, while you are superior to it" (VI. 6).[7] As C. M. Bowra puts it, "in their divine security [the gods] . . . lack something of the dignity which man gains from the short time at his disposal."[8] The ideal Stoic does suffer, says Seneca: "I do not mean to say that the brave man is insensible to these [externals which cause suffering], but that he overcomes them" (*On Providence,* II. 2); yet, he is able to endure because in the most dire fate "it is nothing of our own that perishes" (*On Providence,* V. 8). What is "our own," he tells Lucilius in his letter "On the Happy Life," is our soul, our rational being derived from divine reason, which provides the good (Stoic) man with "peace of mind, and lasting tranquillity" (*Epistles,* XCII. 2, 3). Neither suffering nor death can reach the soul, one's rational being: Anytus and Meletus, Epictetus likes to repeat, can kill Socrates, but they cannot harm him.

The Stoic's refusal to recognize guilt dictates that his adjustment to experience be one of active renunciation. He affirms himself in the face of fate and death and sickness. "It is the part of courage, when misfortune comes, to bear without repining the ruin of our hopes," says Russell (pp. 49–50), and Seneca and Epictetus, like Camus, would add that one does not fear if one does not hope. But the vision of a world fallen "from essential rationality to existential foolishness as a matter of responsibility and as a problem of guilt," is foreign to the Stoic; it could not be otherwise, says Tillich, "for the courage to face one's own guilt leads to the question of salvation instead of renunciation."[9] Human failure in Stoicism is a failure of nerve, an error in judgment, or a result of ignorance rather than sin; it is a failure because of finitude rather than guilt. Like Kierkegaard's "knight of infinite renunciation," the Stoic responds to the human condition by heroic or courageous resignation. By virtue of his will, a surrogate for faith, he is capable of a complete renunciation of all that is not soul. He "can become a tragic hero by his own powers" because he can will to act in harmony with a universal principle.[10] This means that he can therefore "rejoice in the security of the universal" (p. 86), says Kierkegaard, and find the peace it provides. The Stoic thus by his own act of will and reason puts meaning into experience, manufacures a truth which is *there* only so long as it receives his assent.

The Christian's diagnosis of the human problem in terms of sin and guilt means that the solution must come by a reconciliation with the God from whom man is estranged. Sin, as the condition of existence, means that man's very will and reason—so crucial in the Stoic scheme of "salvation by acquiescence," an act of the will in harmony with reason—are unable to save him

for they *are* the problem. The Christian claims to have discovered meaning *in* reality, a God-given and guaranteed meaning always there and available to him who will receive it in
humility. Stoic courage is heroic, while Christian courage is
humble; Stoic endurance is a human achievement, while Christian endurance is a gift of forgiving love.

The touchstone for judging the *kind* of religious meaning in
Faulkner's vision is his understanding of the origin and nature
of evil and the resources for dealing with it. Specifically, this
question is raised by asking what went wrong with the tradition. Where is it, or why is it, that the Sartorises failed? Was
their failure a result of a wrong assessment of the nature of
things, or was it a failure of nerve? How is man to live in the
face of all the violence, chaos, and decadence so apparent in
modern experience? The question for theological anthro-
pology is whether man's basic problem is finitude or sin and the
related question for soteriology is how, *qua* human and only
finite or *qua* human and guilty before his creator, the resources
for overcoming evil or sin are made available. Finally, the question can be raised another way: do Faulkner's bedrock virtues
of courage, endurance, pride, and love ultimately have a Christian or a Stoic reference?

Answers to these questions can be found only in an analysis
of the texts before us, and I have possibly already said too
much. For the present, I need make only two further observa-
tions. In the first place, it is apparent that the more comprehensive vision—be it Christian or Stoic—of a Dilsey must be thought
of as closely representative of Faulkner's vision. The perception
involved is like a one-way street. Faulkner can see what a Dilsey
can see and Dilsey can see what a Quentin can see, but Quentin
cannot share Dilsey's vision—he is too preoccupied in looking
back.

In the second place, it is apparent that Faulkner's religious
center has from the beginning been more complex, his private
vision has been more constant, than those who emphasize his
pilgrimage would imply. The Stoic and Christian assessments,
with him from the beginning, have formed the poles of a theological tension. If they saw anything religious at all in Faulkner, the early critics could see little else beside his Stoicism. But
we do not have to wait until the appearance of *Go Down,
Moses*, in 1942, in order to find a balance between the visions
of a fallen world and a redeemed world. *The Sound and the*

Fury of 1929 is a celebration of Easter's victory as well as a rendering of Good Friday's despair; it is an aesthetic demonstration that man can live meaningfully in the midst of a hopeless condition. In what is often called his most skeptical period, Faulkner is capable of a Benjy, a Dilsey, an Addie Bundren, or a Lena Grove. For this reason, I would claim that Faulkner's religious center has not undergone any fundamental change.

Commentary

Hunt's addition of the Stoic elements of Faulkner to a consideration of his religious stance is obviously an important one. Charles Anderson, writing in *Études Anglaises* in 1954 (VII, 48–58) on "Faulkner's Moral Center," had already noted some of these elements, contending that Faulkner's moral values derive primarily from Latin moralists like Cicero, Horace and Seneca. He summarizes these values as *virtus, gloria, pietas* and *integritas*. Anderson suggests that novels like *The Sound and the Fury, Absalom, Absalom!* and *The Unvanquished* are primarily concerned with the South's loss of these virtues, which constituted the moral structure of its heritage. The suggestion is a useful one, because it brings into focus the role in Faulkner of certain positive Stoic attitudes and values. It could be misleading, however, were it not brought within the larger context of a treatment like Hunt's, which sees the Stoic elements as only part, though an important part, of a complex theological tension in Faulkner's work.

Contributions of other religious cultures to Faulkner's work have also been studied elsewhere, notably the influence on Faulkner of the ethical values of the Greek tragedies. Lennart Björk, in a 1963 essay in *American Literature* (XXXV, 196–204) on "Ancient Myths and the Moral Framework of Faulkner's *Absalom, Absalom!*," sees in Faulkner's tragic portrayal of Sutpen "the *fusion* of the three major Western cultures—the Greek, the Hebrew, and the Christian" (p. 196). Old and New Testament echoes are evident, as they are throughout much of Faulkner's work, and Björk points particularly to analogies between Sutpen's story and that of King David, referred to in the book's very title. The Greek conceptions which operate strongly in the novel are the sense of doom (which, we have seen, pervades many of Faulkner's novels), and the "hamartia," the flaw of character which brings a curse upon Sutpen and his offspring, as it did upon Agamemnon and his. In speaking of predestination in Faulkner it is helpful to remember that its roots are not in Calvin alone but in Aeschylus as well.

One of Hunt's most significant contributions is his insistence that Faulkner's basic theological stance may be more constant than has often been realized. One may, I think, still contend (as I have contended in Chapter 2) that there is a certain movement in Faulkner's theological viewpoint from beginning to end, in particular that his sense of man's capacity for redemption becomes more acute in his later work. At the same time Hunt argues effectively that the element of redemption was present in tension from the beginning, that Faulkner's world was always both a fallen and a redeemed world. And after following through Hunt's detailed analyses of this tension in *The Sound and the Fury, Absalom, Absalom!*, and "The Bear" (in his book *William Faulkner: Art in Theological Tension*), the reader is likely to find the argument a convincing one.

The question might remain open, however, whether the redemption of the early work is not in part a merely "potential" redemption, only theoretically available to all men. It is easy enough to speak of Dilsey in terms of this redemption; as Faulkner has created her, we cannot think of her other than as "redeemed." But is there a real possibility of redemption for Jason, for Caddy, for Benjy, even for Quentin? Often there seem to be simply "the redeemed" and "the damned." The reader ought, then, to bear in mind this question: within Faulkner's at once fallen and redeemed world (at least of the earlier works) are we simply presented with men who are already "saved" or "damned," the elect and the non-elect, or is it really possible for a man to *achieve* redemption?

Later in Faulkner's work it may be that this redemption becomes a more real possibility for those who need it most. There is then at least one notable instance of an "unredeemed" person finding a real possibility of redemption: Temple Drake in *Requiem for a Nun*. Other examples are distressingly difficult to find, however, though the process of growing to moral maturity (and hence redemption)—such as we find in Ike McCaslin in "The Bear" and Chick Mallison in *Intruder in the Dust*—may be an analogous counterpart.

Be that as it may, the basic tension Hunt affirms in Faulkner seems validly conceived. It may not always be possible to know with certainty whether this or that element is to be attributed to Christianity or to Stoicism. But perhaps this is something less than crucial to our understanding of Faulkner, once we realize that the two cultures as they appear in his work feed on and often draw strength from one another. This is precisely why Faulkner's religious center is, in Hunt's phrase, "a religious center of tension."

6 ▬▬▬

Amos N. Wilder of the Harvard Divinity School has been one of the most articulate defenders and definers of the growing dialogue between the theologian and the literary critic. His discussion of *The Sound and the Fury* offers a good example of the kind of "theological" problem which the theologian finds treated meaningfully and well by the literary artist. The ones he highlights here—the problem of community and alienation and the problem of time—may not seem at first to be particularly theological in nature. They are, after all, common human problems. And yet this is perhaps why they are particularly susceptible of successful treatment by the poet or novelist; they are not only fraught with profound theological implications, but they are at the same time part of man's— particularly modern man's—common experience. And this "common experience" is precisely the stuff of which art is made.

The following excerpt is taken from Dr. Wilder's book *Theology and Modern Literature* (Cambridge, Mass.: Harvard University Press, © 1958), pp. 116–131. It is used here with permission.

Amos N. Wilder

VESTIGIAL MORALITIES IN
THE SOUND AND THE FURY

IN A PERIOD OF CULTURAL CHANGE LIKE THAT IN THE midst of which we stand, the great task is that of a reconception of the Christian ethic. But a prior problem is that of the lag of outworn moralities, the stubbornness of inherited and indurated attitudes which are no longer relevant, and which have often themselves become baneful rather than healthy. We may think, for example, of certain aspects of the New England Puritan tradition, or of the Southern cultural tradition. Even those who are intellectually emancipated are often still unconsciously motivated and ruled by such patterns: by mechanisms which are stronger than they are; by legacies of a sound tradition which have become destructive rather than helpful, negative rather than positive. There is a puritan granite which strengthens, but there can be a Puritan granite which crushes. There is a Southern way of life which nourishes, and there is one which strangles.

William Faulkner sees these issues, the problem of a decadent or otiose order—the curse of a vestigial code. His exploration of such themes has its favoring setting in the Southern scene, and other Southern writers have wrestled with it from this point of vantage. But the issues raised have a universal bearing. The codes in question are, at the same time, social and religious, and so far as religious codes are involved, there is no separation of ethic from sanction; that is, theology itself is involved as well as behavior.

Among the many charges brought against modern writers, including Faulkner, by their critics is the charge that they avidly scent out extreme aspects of human corruption and dredge up such instances of depravity and violence as may lend their work a spurious shock appeal, or pander to men's secret urge toward cruelty. There are such writers and they should be condemned. But such criticism may arise from an unduly fastidious or genteel habit of mind, one that cloaks a deep fear of reality. Art must relate itself to the whole compass of life. It must not drape reality, though it should clothe it, in the sense of seeing it in context. So far as the unflinching portrayal of evil goes, we have to make distinctions among modern writers. We may note that the best of them are in good company under this head if we look back at the world's classics, that the important test is not one of the kind of subject matter but the way it is treated—and by *proper way* here we do not mean a shallow, moralizing one. We may add that much of the most significant theology today speaks of the "boundary situation" in life as the necessary focus of revelation and redemption. The boundary situation is no mere abstract point of tangency between creature and creator, but that locus of freedom where the diabolical and the divine are joined in dramatic conflict. Unsavory episodes and situations are the outcome of private complacencies and passions, and they afford unique opportunity for the scrutiny of life as a whole. As Karl Barth has said, "Life emerges at the point of mortification." And Yeats: "Test act, morality, custom, thought in Thermopylae."

But we are concerned here with a special aspect of this charge that modern writers revel in evil. It is pointed out that figures like Proust, Joyce, Kafka, Eliot are preoccupied with subjectivity, with psychologism. Modern literature and art represent a kind of psychoanalytic activity, and what is more, they are actuated by an impulse to unmask human nature and disparage it. The public man, the civic man, is no longer interesting. In a mass society he has lost his freedom and responsibility. Only the Marxist artist has been interested in social man, and this for reasons of propaganda. Indeed, we hear it said that it is not only literature and the arts today that are dominated by psychologism. The same is true of philosophy and religion. Existentialism in particular starts out with man, the individual or generic man, and has only a secondary interest, if any, in the world or the public order.

Now the present moral situation may go far to explain this obsession with inwardness, but our special interest here is to note that accusations of psychologism and denigration of man are not in order so far as Faulkner is concerned. With whatever finesse he scrutinizes the human heart, it is always with a full awareness of the historical and social context. He is not only an analyst, but a moralist and a social moralist. He is interested not only in a locale, but in a region, the South; not only in a region, but in a "Way of life," and in ways of life; and not only in one generation, but in many generations in their interlocking continuity. And instead of denigration or reveling in evil, what we have is rather—along with a Brueghel-like gift for satire and the grotesque—a persistent, urgent, and delicate scrutiny of the moral forces by which men endure, and the transcendent factors by which men endure, and the transcendent factors by which they are saved.

We propose now to examine in some detail Faulkner's novel *The Sound and the Fury,* giving attention especially to the portrayal here of the breakdown of an inherited order, the decline and fall of the Compson family—a rotting family in a rotting house—all representative of a wider cultural fatality. We are interested especially in the implicit critique of Christian elements in the society presented. We shall find supplementary clues in other writings of the author. Since we are dealing with novels, we do not assume that we hear Faulkner speaking in the voice of his characters. None the less, we identify intimations and values in the fable which he has ordered, and we identify laws in the drama he has conceived. It is the myth that speaks to us through Faulkner, not Faulkner who preaches to us through a contrived tale.

In this fable we find ourselves part of a run-down Southern family, all of whose members are, it is said, "poisoned." The action takes place, for the most part, in the first quarter of this century, but the incubus of the past is formidable. The cast is well-known: the dipsomaniac father; the querulous mother, an invalid; the several children, including the idiot Benjy, whose phantasmagoric stream of consciousness gives us part of the story. Then there are the Negro servants, including Dilsey: drudge, cook, nurse, who keeps two sinking families afloat, the one white and the other her own.[1] We see the meager and irremediably injured early years of the children, the prenatal history, as it were, of later giant traumas and obsessions; the inculcation of social and racial distortions; the inbreeding of desiccated, feudal-Christian survivals in the son Quentin. We see the blasting from the start of the delicate filaments of adolescent bloom in his doomed sister, Candace (or Caddy), whose later dereliction represents sheer despair rather than rebellion. We see this theme repeated in *her* daughter, who, as she flees from the family to her lover, cries: "Whatever I do, is your fault. If I am bad, it's because I had to be. You made me. I wish I was dead. I wish we were all dead."[2] Incidentally, let us note here that Faulkner does not finally see his doomed characters as mere puppets. In the case of the similar heroine, Temple Drake, in *Requiem for a Nun,* she herself asserts over and over again her own complicity, "because," as she says, "Temple Drake liked evil."[3]

But to return to *The Sound and the Fury:* the story moves on to the suicide of Quentin, and to the later period when his brother Jason becomes the head of the family and the agent of its final extinction and dispersion.

But our interest is especially in the son Quentin, in whose monologue in the hours preceding his suicide as a Harvard student, we find the best documentation on the deeper, tangled roots of the family calamity. We find in this section the same agonized, sardonic interior monologue which we have come to recognize in *The Waste Land,* in parts of *Ulysses,* and in other revealing transcripts of the modern consciousness. Windows are opened for us upon radical alienation and estrangement, upon a private inferno. Excruciating reminiscences alternate with even more tormenting echoes of vanished felicity (moments of childhood—hunting episodes—lines of great poetry). Reveries of nostalgic beatitudes are punctuated by motifs of horror and putrefaction; re-enacted shame is accompanied by blasphemies and maledictions. We look into a landscape of molten lava and fumes, the purlieus of dissolution. Yet evident throughout the monologue, as an ultimate sounding board, is an imprescriptible moral order or criterion, without which there would be no spiritual torment, no revulsion, and no flight from time. Yet this valid order is confused with false authorities, with a usurping superego or tyrannical social code, so that valid and invalid claims are hopelessly intertwined.

The consummate art and wisdom of Faulkner appear here, above all, in his success in making the self-destruction of the student convincing, and in lending verisimilitude to the act and its motives and antecedents, and to the extended monologue which accompanies it. This means that the author must show us convincingly both the personal, psychic derangement and the relation of this to the family history, as well as the more general cultural determinants. These factors can be distinguished as the role of his father, his intimate relation to his sister Caddy, and the ghostly social and religious patterns he was bred to.

When Quentin graduated from high school, his father gave him the watch which he himself had received from his own father:

> "Quentin, I give you the mausoleum of all hope and desire, I give it to you not that you may remember time, but that you might forget it now and then for a moment, and not spend all your breath trying to conquer it. Because no battle is ever won, they are not even fought. The field only reveals to man his own folly and despair and victory is an illusion of philosophers and fools." (*The Sound and the Fury*, p. 95)

When the son got up on the morning of the day in which he would take his own life, he broke the glass of the watch and twisted off the hands—but, even so, he could not help hearing the ticking. Another thing he remembered his father saying was that "Christ was not crucified: he was worn away by a minute clicking of little wheels." The preoccupation with mechanical time, which runs all through Quentin's long monologue, is highly significant. It exalts by contrast what Faulkner often recurs to: the health associated with intuitive, natural, organic, uncorrupted rhythms.

Two critics have dealt in interesting ways with the concept of time in this novel. Peter Swiggart[4] sees Quentin as a victim of the false romantic attitude of a decadent South to its past. On this view, the present is cut off from the past, the past is unredeemable. Clock time only reinforces this despair. Swiggart appeals to Allen Tate, who contrasts duration measured by a "logical series" with a more responsible view of time, in which life is accepted "as from a religious or atemporal perspective." Such a view characterized the Christian South at its best, and by such a view of time and life Quentin was hopelessly haunted. On such a view, the past, whether of the group or of the individual, is redeemable. We may say that Faulkner himself is to be identified with such a Christian view of time. The whole positive meaning of the sequence of novels, *Sanctu-*

ary and *Requiem for a Nun,* is expressed in the words of Gavin Stevens, "The past is never dead. It's not even past."[5]

Jean-Paul Sartre has an interesting paper on our present topic.[6] He notes that for Quentin, as it is said: "time is your misfortune"—in the sense of past time. Quentin knows no living presence of freedom, and therefore no future. Even his imminent suicide is presented as already accomplished. Sartre cites the lines: "I am not is, I was." The order of the past is the order of the heart—hence the absurdity of clocks. A man is defined as the "sum of his past" and nothing more, and the past is an accumulation of fortuitous rubbish. As Quentin's father put it: "Man, the sum of what have you. A problem in impure properties carried tediously to an unvarying nill: statement of dust and desire" (*The Sound and the Fury,* pp. 142–143).

Sartre rightly objects to this view of time. He holds to the idea of real freedom and real future in his familiar existentialist terms, but he wrongly identifies Faulkner's views with those of Quentin. He contrasts Faulkner and Proust. With regard to the past, Proust would remember it all; Faulkner would forget it—in favor of mystical, ecstatic escapes. Sartre ascribes a thorough-going doctrine of despair to Faulkner, but prefers his own version of this. But Sartre has entirely misconstrued Faulkner, and that through the ingenuous error of identifying the author with one or more of his characters. The whole fable of *The Sound and the Fury* points toward a healthful order of values which has been violated.

Quentin's relation to his sister Caddy is the decisive factor in his disarray and self-destruction. In her corruption the doom of the family and his own impotence to help are brought home to him most intolerably. She was the only human creature from whom he had received any sustenance throughout his meager and blocked childhood. This meant that his relationship with her was inevitably intense and obsessive, and that he was vulnerable to incestuous fantasies, at least in retrospect—fantasies which served as a pretext for guilt. He could persuade himself that he had initiated his sister's demoralization. His feeble attempts to drive off her lovers or to convince her that they were scoundrels had no effect; but, as Faulkner makes clear, he did not really love her. Like all the children, he had been rendered all but incapable of love. He loved "the idea of chastity in her," as Faulkner tells us, "some concept of Compson honor." And so far as Caddy loved him, what she loved in him—again, as Faulkner explains in his appendix—was "the bitter prophet and inflexible, corruptless judge of what he considered the family's honor and its doom" (p. 10).

But the inherited religious criterion played a significant part here too—a religious legacy so denatured that it operated for destruction. Quentin so far warped the idea of guilt and penalty as to seek damnation for his sister and himself, dramatizing his suicide as a retribution for both. As Faulkner states it, he

> loved not the idea of incest, which he would not commit, but some Presbyterian concept of eternal punishment: he, not God, could by that means cast himself and his sister both into Hell, where he would guard her forever and keep her forevermore intact amid the eternal fires. (p. 9)

This meant that in his own fatal solitude Quentin had to take her with him into the negative salvation of his own suicide and escape from time. But the whole drama in his mind was clothed about with a borrowed or vestigial Christian crime-and-punishment ideology.

All this is not so strange as may at first appear. We are aware of the fact that there are people whose lives are undernourished and who are impelled to punish themselves or to flout their own best opportunities for a better life—to court persecution or ascetic poverty or ugliness—as perhaps the only way open to them to feel important or to gain identity, or achieve some intensity of personal consciousness. And all this can be cloaked under religious sanctions, and carried out in Christian terms of pseudo-martyrdom, re-enactments of the Cross, orgiastic or refined.

The tragedy of Quentin Compson is conditioned on the one hand by a social code of Southern chivalrous honor and womanhood, and by a truncated Christian conception of guilt and retribution, severed from all ideas of grace: law without grace. We have an inverted vestigial nobility or chivalry—ultimately a Christian order—which is powerful for destruction rather than for ·health, and it is powerful for destruction because it is fed by the main taproot of biological vitality. The cables carrying the powerful life-impulse, as in all men, provide here in reverse the strength of the death-wish.

Thus Faulkner as moralist is exposing all the mechanisms, social as well as psychological, which represent the destructive element in his society, and in other forms in all societies. We find a warning against inveterate social tyrannies, the incubus of inherited and desiccated cultural ideals and patterns: obsessive vestigial codes and rigidities, whether associated with ideas of honor or caste, with social authority, status, or manners, with sexual deportment or economic activity. We find also a warning against fossilized religious sanctions, conceptions, or rituals, which, detached from their healthful or vital sources, become malign tools of social control, thus lending a specious absolute authority to inhuman usages. And such religious axioms and norms are all the more dangerous because they are bred into the unconscious life of new generations. One of the most obstinate elements in social evil is represented by its inverted Christian components: inverted guilt conceptions, inverted asceticisms, inverted sacrificial impulses.

We have in this area a good illustration of the considerations which lead many perceptive moderns to withhold allegiance from some forms of institutional religion and religion generally. They have had personal experience of a negative or an ambiguous operation of religiosity in persons or groups that they have known. When pseudo-Christian attitudes and codes are part of the malign social stream in which individuals have lost their freedom to impersonal group authorities, we can understand the bitter ejaculation of Quentin, citing his father:

> "All men are just accumulations, dolls, stuffed with sawdust, swept up from the trash-heaps where all the previous dolls had been thrown away. The sawdust-flowing from what wound in what side that not for me died not." (p. 194)

Quentin says that men are puppets and that the death of Christ for such men and for himself makes no sense to him. Quentin, in this situation and with his acquaintance with Christianity, could say this, just as Joyce could say something like it in *The Portrait of the Artist as a Young Man,* out of the same truncated experience with another Christian tradition.

The kind of diagnosis of culture and religion which occurs in fiction like that of Faulkner is far more searching and illuminating than is possible in other media. The form of the modern novel encourages presentation of many dimensions and levels and facets of reality. Sociological analysis, with all its advantages, confines itself to particular tools and methods. The social prophet or revolutionary—a Saint-Simon, a Proudhon, or a Marx—combining moral vision with acute discernment, forfeits one great advantage: that of presenting social reality in terms of living persons and their interrelations. The novelist can carry his portrayal of human life down into the deeper roots of motive and action, and deal with the hidden jungle in ways not open even to the psychologist.

One can illustrate this in connection with the history of modern anti-Christian polemic. The critics of Christianity from the time of Celsus have often been severe on the church; even when their own position has been heretical, they have nonetheless made it sensitive to its errors. But the value of such criticism depends upon its cogency. Compared with such analysis in depth as the one that Faulkner affords, the older, familiar charges against secularized Christianity are superficial. By such older charges I refer to the orthodox Marxist reproach against it, that it is escapist and other-worldly—that it lulls the exploited into acceptance of their lot, and discharges the conscience of the powerful classes of their real responsibility. Or the Nietzschian reproach against Christianity, that it condones and flatters the unheroic and fosters a slave morality. Such polemics have had their validity and have had fateful historical influence. But such analyses of Christianity have been ideological rather than dramatic, and their impact has been correspondingly limited. A disclosure in dramatic terms of attenuated Christian society, such as we find in novels like those of Faulkner or Dostoievsky or Gide, brings the issue home to us in a far more urgent manner.

No doubt the Freudian challenge to Christianity is more subtle and pressing than those of Marx and Nietzsche. But even here, the probing of the artist and the novelist gives a greater sense of reality and due complexity than the approach of the scientific analyst. The scientist is more limited in his field of operation. He works from a confessedly partial perspective, with tools adapted to a selective observation. Faulkner, like many other creative writers of our time, is immeasurably indebted to modern psychology. But the total picture of man which emerges in his novels offers more inclusive insights than one finds in the clinic.

We have given primary attention to the exposure of perverted and festering moralities in Faulkner—moralities that had formerly been healthful: "Lilies that fester smell far worse than weeds." But Faulkner can also present the other side of the shield of Christianity. In *The Sound and the Fury*, we find this significantly in the last section, in the account of the church service of the Negroes, and of the sermon of the colored preacher from St. Louis, the Rev'un Shegog. This whole episode stands out in the novel like the corresponding sermon in the whalemen's chapel in *Moby Dick*. Faulkner sets forth the life-giving mystery of the Christian faith here among the poor in spirit over against the riddle or even curse which religion may represent for most of the more cultured whites.

The meaning of the Negro service emerges especially in the person of the old, enduring servant of the Compsons, Dilsey. This colored slavey, nurse, confidant, and foster-mother—battered and buffeted—has, as we have said, kept the swamping raft of the household afloat, has absorbed in herself the grievances and hostilities of all through the daily wear and tear and throughout periodic disasters. The religious service discloses to us where she gets what she calls "de comfort en de unburdenin," and the meaning to her of what the Rev. Shegog appeals to as "de recklickshun en de blood of de Lamb." We have a good example here of how the dangerous theme of blood and atonement can be understood in a healthy and not a masochistic way, even in an uncultured group.

The preacher evokes "de blastin, blindin, sight" of Calvary, and "de turnt away face of God," and warns the rapt congregation that God can turn his face away from men: "I can see de widowed God shet His do'; I sees de whelmin flood roll between; I sees de darkness an de death everlastin upon de generations" (p. 312). One could almost say that these words of the preacher sum up the landscape of evil which Faulkner presents throughout the changing scenes of the novel: "I see de darkness an de death everlastin upon de generations." But the preacher goes on:

> "Den, lo! Breddren! Yes, breddren! Whut I see? Whut I see, Oh sinner? I sees de resurrection en de light; sees de meek Jesus saying Dey kilt Me dat ye shall live again; I died dat dem whut sees en believes shall never die. Breddren, oh breddren! I sees de doom crack, en hears de golden horns shoutin down to glory, en de arisin dead whut

got de blood en de recklickshun of de Lamb!" (pp. 312–313)

As Dilsey is walking away from the service, her daughter bids her stop weeping.

> "Why'nt you quit dat, mammy?" Frony said, "Wid all dese people lookin. We be passin white folks soon."
> "I've seed de first en de last," Dilsey said, "Never you mind me."
> "First en de last whut?" Frony said.
> "Never you mind," Dilsey said, "I seed de beginnin en now I sees de endin." (p. 313)

Dilsey has seen the beginning and the ending in two senses: the beginning and the ending, the first and the last, in the sense of Christ as Alpha and Omega; but also the beginning and the ending of the long tragedy of the last generation of the Compsons. For just that morning the granddaughter, Quentin, had run away with the concealed wealth of her uncle Jason, and this act entails the disasters that follow, the death of the mother, the incarceration of Benjy, and dispersal of the family.

Christianity in its uncorrupted aspects appears in other novels of Faulkner, and is not only identified with the lowly Negro, or, as in *A Fable,* with a disesteemed element from the lower strata of society. In *Requiem for a Nun,* the sequel of *Sanctuary,* we have one of the most authentic and searching Christian dramas in modern literature. Its focus on husband, wife, and family and the agony of the modern household sets it beside Eliot's *Family Reunion*. It offers us a study in pride and contrition, in vicarious sacrifice and forgiveness; and includes the Negro slavey, the "demon nun," but also the college-trained lawyer, Gavin Stevens, as witnesses of the Christian claim and hope. The pride of a Southern belle, Temple Drake, is inexorably probed and sifted by God and the devil—we are reminded of Kipling's Tomlinson—in a long scene which represents no less than the threshing out of a naked soul before the divine throne. The paradox appears in the fact that the instrument of redemption is a Negro Magdalen, drug addict, and household drudge. The import of the whole spiritual transaction is connected with the unlikely human instruments involved. Grace takes on authenticity when its power is manifested among the lost, when daemons are exorcised and hell is harrowed. As Yeats says,

> out of rock,
> Out of a desolate source,
> Love leaps upon its course.[7]

and again,

> Love has pitched his mansion in
> The place of excrement:
> For nothing can be sole or whole
> That has not been rent.[8]

We learn here to recognize the incognitos of God. Faulkner seems to be saying that there are many nuns not in habits, and many apostles who have not been ordained, and who would not presume. He knows how to present the baneful legacy of a fossilized religion and of a secularized Christian society, but he also can demonstrate the perennial vigor of the faith in redeeming those very ills.

Commentary

The problem of "radical alienation and estrangement" which is brought to the fore in Wilder's discussion is clearly one of the most pressing concerns of the modern artist, and Faulkner is no exception. With this in mind it might be well to broaden the consideration of this problem by referring back to Cleanth Brooks's insistence, in Chapter 4, on the role of the "return to the community" in Faulkner's view of man's redemption. He wrote that "unless the controlling purposes of the individuals are related to those that other men share, and in which the individual can participate, he is indeed isolated, and is forced to fall back upon his personal values, with all the risk of fanaticism and distortion to which such isolation is liable." Quentin Compson was forced back upon his personal values, and the resulting fanaticism and distortion involved daydreams of hell, imagined incest, and ultimately suicide. In Brooks's view, since Faulkner has a "sense of an organic community," one may expect to find in his work not only those who are alienated from one another, but some symbol or representative of the sustaining community itself, an "ideal of integrity and wholeness in the light of which the alienated characters are judged." In *Light in August* such an ideal is Lena Grove; in *The Sound and the Fury* it is Dilsey. Dilsey "affirms the ideal of wholeness in a family which shows in every other member splintering and disintegration."

This theme of alienation and the concomitant theme of the return to the community is a constant one in Faulkner. It may take the form we have already described, that is, primarily a "judgment" on those who are thus alienated. It may, on the other hand, emphasize the aspect of the return to the community, in which an individual finds himself either making his way back to the "controlled purposes" of his fellow men or even establishing his relationship to the community for the first time. Temple Drake, for example, seems to make this return to the community in *Requiem for a Nun*, as perhaps does Gowan Stevens in the same book. Ike McCaslin in "The Bear," under the tutelage of Sam Fathers, learns his relationship to the human community for the first time, as Chick Mallison does in *Intruder in the Dust;* they are much in the tradition of the *Bildungsroman*. Many others—like the Compsons, like Charlotte in *The Wild Palms*, like Joe Christmas—remain alienated; and in

103

novels where there is an ideal of wholeness—like Dilsey or Lena—the alienated ones are simply judged in the light of that ideal.

An equally important issue raised by Wilder's essay is Faulkner's attitude toward time. He is right, first of all, to begin with the premise of Jean-Paul Sartre that the primary theme of *The Sound and the Fury* is time. As Sartre wrote in the brilliant essay already referred to, "Faulkner's is a metaphysic of time." Wilder is right, too, to disagree with Sartre's identification of Quentin's view of time with that of Faulkner. What Sartre seems not to realize is that Quentin himself is being judged, and clearly he is found wanting.

For Quentin man is simply "the sum of his past." He carries his past about with him like a burden, without being able to divest himself of it and without being able to change it. For him, as Wilder pointed out, "the past is unredeemable." If this is true, we can understand why for Quentin it makes no sense to say that Christ was crucified for him. The past is unredeemable; what is done cannot be undone. Nor does Quentin have freedom even in the present. He is so obsessed with the influence of past time on the present that his present is no longer free. "I am not is, I was." For Quentin there can be only one solution: to escape from time. He tries, symbolically, when he breaks the hands from the watch his father had given him. "I went to the dresser and took up the watch, with the face still down. I tapped the crystal on the corner of the dresser and caught the fragments of glass in my hand and put them into the ashtray and twisted the hands off and put them in the tray. The watch ticked on" (*The Sound and the Fury*, p. 99). His escape from time can come only with death.

What may not be quite clear from Wilder's discussion is how the other view of time, the "Christian view of time" with which he identifies Faulkner, functions in the novel. It functions primarily, I think, in terms of Dilsey and the realm of grace she represents. Her life is accepted "as from a religious or atemporal perspective." There is a world outside of time, an atemporal, eternal world, which impinges, in terms of Christianity and the incarnation, on the world of time. The life of that other world is not bound down to the limitations of time and space, and thus God can act to redeem time-bound man. In this Christian view of time the past is, after all, redeemable. The view of time which contrasts strikingly with that of Quentin, therefore, is that of Dilsey. And this is nowhere more powerfully portrayed than in the sermon sequence of *The Sound and the Fury*. For Dilsey, as for the Rev'un Shegog and his congregation, the blood of the Lamb and his glory are not past. They are present realities, and can be so precisely because they not only took place in time but are also outside of time, and thus eternally present. "I sees de resurrection en de light; sees de meek Jesus saying Dey kilt Me dat ye shall live again; I died dat dem whut sees en believes shall never die." And Dilsey, too, sees this present reality, this present source of her redemption.

Ultimately, the perverted view of time represented by Quentin is the reason for the "vestigial moralities" Wilder speaks of. The sense of law remains—with its sense of guilt and of punishment for the past—while the sense of present redemption is no longer felt. "The past is unredeemable." As Wilder says, the tragedy of Quentin Compson stems from "a truncated Christian conception of guilt and retribution, severed from all ideas of grace."

Happily, though, Faulkner gives us a matrix of salvation: Dilsey. Tears of joy streaming down her face, she has seen, in her own present time, "de power en de glory," "de first en de last." She has felt "the annealment and the blood" of the Lamb of God.

Here perhaps the themes of alienation and time may be brought together, since an essential part of Dilsey's "wholeness" against which the alienated Compsons are judged is her Christian view of time—time related to the eternal—a context within which grace and redemption are possible.

7 ═══

Much of what has been written on the religious aspects of Faulkner's fiction has dealt with their properly Christian elements, and it is these that have provided the major focus of our essays thus far. It must not be forgotten, however, that Faulkner's Old Testament echoes are (at least in some of his works) almost equally as important as his resonances of the New Testament. We have noted in Chapter 5, for instance, that the Old Testament comes rather prominently into play in *Absalom, Absalom!,* and we shall have occasion to discuss this matter further (in Chapter 9) in terms of that novel. In the essay which follows, Philip C. Rule, former literary editor of *America,* argues that the Old Testament is not only an important element in *As I Lay Dying* but actually determines its inner structure of attitudes and values.

Father Rule's essay was written especially for the present volume.

Philip C. Rule, S. J.

THE OLD TESTAMENT VISION IN
AS I LAY DYING

IN SEARCHING OUT THE RELIGIOUS VALUES THAT UNDER-
lie *As I Lay Dying,* critics have suggested Greek and Roman
influences, Calvinism, and the Christian message in general.
However, nothing so permeates the tone and texture of the
story as does the spirit of the Old Testament. The themes, the
attitudes, and frequently the very words and prose rhythms
derive from the written account of the "pre-Christian" experience. Specifically, the story as a whole has strong overtones of
the Book of Job. Salvation, religiosity, tribal solidarity, the
importance of sex as an almost religious act—these and other
Old Testament themes assert themselves. Where we might also
expect a patriarchal society, Faulkner with typical irony gives
us a matriarchal one. Above all, there is the brooding Old
Testament spirit of despair, hope, endurance—tensions as old
as mankind—with which man faces the darkness and mystery
of the world around him.

The plot is deceptively simple: A woman dies and her family
fulfills its promise to take her body back to her own family
burial ground. At the outset we are reminded of the patriarch
Jacob's charge to his sons: "I am to be gathered to my people:
bury me with my fathers in the cave that is in the field of
Ephron the Hittite" (Genesis, 49:29). And as, no doubt, the
patriarch's sons could handle personal errands while carrying
out this sacred obligation, we find the Bundrens capitalizing on
the lugubrious trip to Jefferson: Dewey Dell to seek an abor-
tion; Cash to buy a graphophone; Anse to get a new set of teeth
—and a new wife. Those familiar with the Old Testament know
that its characters were quite capable of very human motivation. Holy King David, for example, was inspired by more than

religious zeal in bringing the ark of the covenant to Jerusalem. His dance before the ark probably owed much of its enthusiasm to the fact that the ark's presence helped make the city a stronger military and political center.

Faulkner himself said the novel was "a *tour de force*. I took this family and subjected them to the two greatest catastrophes a man can suffer—flood and fire, that's all. That was a simple *tour de force*. That was written in six weeks without changing a word because I knew from the first where I was going."[1] Yet, around this simple journey, this "abracadabrante Odyssée," as one writer calls it, wind at least a half dozen major themes. The book is in fact a poetic meditation on the mysteries to which the human mind inevitably turns.[2] Life and death, success and failure, loneliness and solidarity confront us in rhythmic patterns. Here we find the bitter-sweet of human life, in which the dignity of man is asserted only to be overshadowed by the awe-inspiring immensity of the Infinite. Faulkner's world is a grim demanding valley of tears where the struggle to eke out an existence from the soil is seen as "man's puny gnawing at the immemorial flank."[3]

The very structure of *As I Lay Dying* manifests Faulkner's acceptance of the principle of human solidarity that holds the human race together. The fifteen characters who speak out during the course of the story exist primarily in their relationship to one another. Addie Bundren's death and funeral trip become the focal point, the historical event in which all these persons participate at differing levels of psychological involvement. As the Exodus is a type of everyman's wandering toward an elusive but ever-present God, so too the little world of the Bundrens is a paradigm of man's struggle to prevail.

Even in death Addie gives meaning to the actions of the other characters. Darl, Vardaman, Cash, Jewel, Dewey Dell, and Anse stand next to that inner circle which is Addie's alone. Around this family group stand the other characters, choruslike in their function. Tull, Armstid, and Samson respond with actions to Anse's empty words; while Peabody interprets key actions and relates them to the outside world. Cora and Whitfield react to Addie's death with ethical words and phrases that border on the Pharisaical. Only two characters are set outside the central action, entering the plot because of Dewey Dell's plight: Moseley, who responds to her with outraged morality and self-righteousness, and MacGowan, who responds by taking advantage of the pregnant girl.

The basic supposition that makes such an intense interrelation of these personalities possible is the solidarity of all men. Theologically this solidarity arises from the doctrine found in *Genesis* and in St. Paul's *Epistle to the Romans* (a Christian commentary on this section of *Genesis*). Adam as head of the race has sinned, and subsequent generations have ratified Adam's sin in themselves by their personal sins—thus sin, the power of darkness, reigns in the world. All men are in Paul's words *tekna orgēs,* children of wrath. [Jewel explicitly symbolizes the child born in sin (like his namesake Pearl in *The Scarlet Letter*);] but he may also stand as an unconscious symbol of that sinfulness in which all men are born. It is not the sin of the person but the sin of the race, of which the psalmist reminds us when he sings: "Against thee, thee only have I sinned, and done that which is evil in thy sight, so that thou art justified in thy sense, and blameless in thy judgment. Behold I was brought forth in iniquity, and in sin did my mother conceive me" (Ps. 51:4–5). The words remind us that within man continues to rage the endless battle between the desire for salvation and an almost primitive sense of guilt and sinfulness—something born into us simply because we are men.

This sense of guilt is closely bound up with the sense of solidarity and community because the impersonal guilt is passed on through the sexual process. Hence Faulkner finds it easy to link human solidarity with the mystery of woman and sexuality. In *Absalom, Absalom!* Quentin speaks of "that massy five-foot thick maggot-cheesy solidarity which overlays the earth, in which men and women in couples are ranked and racked like ninepins; thanks to whatever Gods for that masculine hipless tapering peg which fits light and glib to move where the cartridge chambered hips of women hold them fast."[4] The Old Testament parallels are striking: Adam's sin is passed on through the sex act; the lives of the great patriarchs turn around sexual experiences; the begetting of children is a religious duty and yet a contaminated process. The first book of the Bible, we might recall, is *Genesis:* the narration of God's creating and man's procreating.

As in the Old Testament accounts of the patriarchs, the life cycle pervades *As I Lay Dying.* Even though Addie Bundren lies on her death bed, her own flesh and blood, Dewey Dell, carries within her womb the extension of Addie into space and time. Dewey Dell's own involvement in the story frequently manifests itself in rich sensual imagery, imagery that suggests the "womanliness" of nature: the hot sweet cow breath on her thighs, the cool night air drifting suggestively across her naked legs. As the pregnant girl climbs into the wagon Darl reflects on "her leg coming long from beneath her tightening dress: that lever which moves the world; one of that caliper which measures the length and breadth of life."[5]

Again as in the Old Testament, the female and her sexuality play a large role in Faulkner's world view. Of all his characters women seem most representative of that sense of inevitability tempered by hope: Addie and Dewey Dell in *As I Lay Dying;* Lena Grove in *Light in August;* Charlotte in *Wild Palms.* Women symbolize the quiet, immemorial, life-giving quality of the earth.

Furthermore, sex has traditionally been the basic concupiscence, and historically Eve has borne more than her share of the blame for the Fall. Faulkner has committed himself to this theological tradition. This tension between man and woman flows in the background of *As I Lay Dying,* especially in Addie's treatment of Anse not as a subject but only as an object, a means whereby she tries to penetrate her loneliness. Twice she describes their courtship by saying, "so I took Anse."

For Faulkner, life depends on the fundamental experiences which can be reduced to man's struggle with the earth; the hatred, fear, and love which prove a man in his relationship with a woman are paralleled by the hatred, fear, and love born of his struggle with the thorn and thistle-infested soil. The world of Yoknapatawpha differs little from the desert home of the biblical patriarchs, where life centers on tribal solidarity, sex, the search for food and water, and (not always clearly distinct from these for the patriarchs) salvation. Perhaps it is this fundamental parallel of man against the elements that makes the central action of *As I Lay Dying* appear so thoroughly biblical. Faulkner said he subjected this family to "the two greatest catastrophes man can suffer—flood and fire." Addie says that Jewel will save her from "the water and the fire" (not knowing how literally this would be fulfilled). This is also the psalmist's boast: "We went through fire and through water; but thou brought us forth to a spacious place" (Ps. 66:12).

In sharp contrast to the strong sense of tribal solidarity that we find in the Old Testament runs the parallel biblical theme of man's rejection and loneliness. Throughout scripture we find such laments as: "Turn unto me and have mercy on me, for I am lonely and afflicted" (Ps. 25:16). From the dark loneliness of her home-made coffin Addie could well cry out with the psalmist: "They surround me like a flood all day long: and they close in upon me together. Thou hast caused lover and friend to shun me; my companions are in darkness" (Ps. 88:17–18). Ironically, man finds himself alone amid the community. Like the chosen people of God who wandered for forty years through the desert, the Bundrens would make their journey trying to be "beholden to no man."

The very act which carries on the tribe in space and time has a dual aspect. Biologically speaking, it carries out its purpose with an impersonal relentlessness—pregnant women abound in the pages of Faulkner's stories. Humanly speaking, it should also be the "act of love," something personal that draws two people into a circle of mutual awareness. To the extent that it is not personal, another avenue of violating one's aloneness is sealed off. Addie Bundren represents the human desire to understand and be understood, to love and be loved in this act of love.

From the opening pages of the book the reader is led deeper and deeper into the spirit of this lonely woman. Her husband says, "she was ever a private woman." The intense conflict between her independence and her desire for involvement permeate the story. Even in death Addie cannot break through her core of loneliness. Anse tells Cash—superficial though it may be coming from him—"We would be beholden to no man . . . me and her. We have never yet been, and she will rest quieter for knowing it and that it was her own blood sawed out the boards and drove the nails. She was ever one to clean up after herself" (pp. 350–351).

In a desperate attempt to communicate with those outside herself Addie had resorted to physical violence against her young students. Words proved meaningless for Addie: only actions could begin to penetrate the invisible barriers of loneliness that surround each human being. With each lash of the switch Addie felt some sense of communication: "When the switch fell I could feel it upon my flesh; when it welted and ridged it was my blood that ran, and I would think with each blow of the switch: Now you are aware of me! Now I am something in your secret and selfish life, who have marked your blood with my own for ever and ever" (pp. 461–462).

Even Addie's marriage to Anse, her ultimate attempt to surrender her aloneness, proved a failure. The surrender of the sex act, which nature intends in man as a balance for the inward pulling egocentricity, cannot satisfy Addie's thirst for awareness—for love, which was only a word to Anse. Her aloneness, she says, "had never been violated until Cash came. Not even by Anse in the night." She continues, "my aloneness had been violated and then made whole again by the violation: time, Anse, love, what you will, outside the circle" (p. 464).

This sense of alienation infects the whole Bundren clan. Jewel purchases the horse, an act symbolizing his alienation from the family of which he is only a partial member. Darl, chapter by chapter, fades into the twilight world of his brooding utterances about space, time, and existence.

Dewey Dell shares in this terrible conflict between aloneness and self-surrender: "It's because I am alone. If I could just feel it, it would be different, because I would not be alone. But if I were not alone, everybody would know it. And he [Peabody] could do so much for me, and then I would not be alone. Then I could be all right alone" (pp. 379–380). This feeling mounts until she cries, "I feel my body, my bones and flesh beginning to part and open upon the alone, and the process of coming unalone is terrible" (p. 382).

Closely related, for example, to the theme of isolation and alienation is that of the worthlessness of mere words. This in turn opens out onto the constant rejection of hypocritical religious attitudes against which the Old Testament prophets preached for centuries. Thus, God through Jeremiah warned the people: "Amend your ways and your doings, and I will let you dwell in this place. Do not trust in these deceptive words: 'This is the temple of the Lord, the temple of the Lord, the temple of the Lord'" (Jer. 7:3–4). Of course, the prophet's reward for destroying the people's hope in mere words is alienation and rejection—loneliness in the midst of the tribe. Actions, not words will save Israel, just as actions, not words, will save Addie Bundren. Apart from such stray references as "a fallen sparrow, a log rising up like Christ walking on the waters, or Addie's statement that Jewel is her cross, there are few specifically Christian allusions in the story. These fragments are few in comparison to the many quotations and near quotations from the Old Testament. Ironically, most of this biblical language is spoken by the three most superficial and hypocritical characters in the book: Cora Tull, Whitfield, and Anse.

The book which comes most obviously to mind is the Book of Job. Even in structure the two stories are alike. Addie, like Job, rests in the center surrounded by her friends. Addie, like Job, finally rejects the words of those who do not really know what suffering is all about. The verbal parallels are striking. Several times, as we shall see, there are variations on Job's utterance: "Naked I came from my mother's womb, and naked shall I return; the Lord gave, and the Lord has taken away; blessed is the name of the Lord" (1:21). Anse frequently, and be it added hypocritically, assumes a Job-like pose. Twice, to Tull's "the Lord giveth," he laconically replies, "the Lord giveth." Three times he says, "if ever was such a misfortunate man." "It's a trial," he sighs, "but I don't begrudge her it" (pp. 457–458). Knowing Jewel is outraged over his selling the horse, Anse laments, "I do the best I can. 'Fore God, if there were ere a man in the living world suffered the trials and floutings I have suffered" (p. 477).

Cora Tull is conventional religion incarnate. She has a tidbit of scripture to wrap around every one of her neighborly condemnations and rash judgments. Dewey Dell calls her "old turkey-buzzard Tull coming to watch her die" (p. 356). Jewel sees her joining with "them others [the women] sitting there like buzzards" (p. 347)—like Job's friends gathering around him. Anse, too, is infected with this meaningless spirit, a belief without any seeming personal commitment or involvement. When Addie dies there rises from his soul the anguished cry: "God's will be done. . . . Now I can get them teeth" (p. 375).

However, no character in the story presents a more pathetic picture of religiosity and the emptiness of words than does Whitfield. We first see him after he has safely crossed the river on his way to pray over the dying Addie. His prayer, it might be noted in passing, is a perfect imitation of the repetitive structure of the psalms: "It was His hand that bore me safely above the flood, that fended from me the dangers of the waters" (p. 469). Like Dimmesdale in *The Scarlet Letter,* he feels the pangs of remorse over his hidden guilt; unlike Dimmesdale, however, Whitfield never gets beyond words. The news that Addie is dying arouses him to contrition. With cruel mockery Faulkner describes Whitfield's rationalizing as his momentary sorrow cools at the news of Addie's death: "I have sinned, O Lord, Thou knowest the extent of my remorse and the will of my spirit. But he is merciful; He will accept the word for the deed" (p. 469).

Through the persons of Vernon Tull and Addie Bundren Faulkner rejects this religious posing. Tull at one point challenges Cora's "theologizing" and shows her to be ironically contradicting herself: " 'I don't know what you want, then,' I said. 'One breath you say they were daring the hand of God to try it, and the next breath you jump on Anse because he wasn't with them.' Then she begun to sing again, working at the wash-tub, with that singing look in her face like she had done give up folks and all their foolishness and had done went on ahead of them, marching up the sky, singing" (p. 449).

Addie, more deeply involved in the central movement of the story, has an even more telling criticism of such religiosity: "One day I was talking to Cora. She prayed for me because she believed I was blind to sin, wanting me to kneel and pray too, because people to whom sin is just a matter of words, to them salvation is just words too" (p. 468). Like Job, Addie is surrounded by her friends—people who talk much of sin and suffering and salvation; yet their hearts are unexperienced, untried. Her only chapter in the novel is preceded by one of Cora's and immediately followed by Whitfield's only chapter. Job, hemmed in and thoroughly tired of his advisers, dourly remarks: "Worthless physicians are you all . . . . Your maxims are proverbs of ashes" (13:4, 12). In the same spirit Addie says:

> "And so when Cora Tull would tell me I was not a true mother, I would think how words go straight up in a thin line, quick and harmless, and how terribly doing goes along the earth, clinging to it, so that after a while the two lines are too far apart for the same person to straddle from one to the other; and that sin and love and fear are just sounds that people who never sinned nor loved have for what they never had and cannot have until they forget the words. Like Cora, who could never even cook." (p. 465)

This comes close to being the principal theme of *As I Lay Dying*.

Addie is concerned about her salvation—she is concerned

about love and belonging—and it seems to be the salvation through endurance and suffering that runs throughout Faulkner's other stories. Addie sees her redemption bound up in some confused way with her relationship with Whitfield. When Cora, unaware of Jewel's true father, tells Addie "Jewel is your punishment. But where is your salvation?" Addie replies, "he is my cross and he will be my salvation. He will save me from the water and from the fire. Even though I have laid down my life, he will save me" (p. 460).

The vision is not clear, at least theologically speaking; but Addie herself says, in trying to explain her terrible sense of aloneness, "I learned that words are no good; that words don't ever fit even what they are trying to say at" (p. 463). Yet how closely, even verbally, her retort to Cora matches Job's cry of hope in the face of the seemingly unjust trials inflicted upon him: "For I know that my Redeemer lives, and at last he will stand upon the earth; And after my skin has been thus destroyed, then from my flesh I shall see God" (19:25–26). The full Christian vision does not enter the picture. Just as Faulkner does not resolve the paradox of aloneness in the face of solidarity, so he does not offer a solution to the problem of salvation. The human heart aches in *As I Lay Dying* and later novels, but its yearning is not calmed by the clear promise of intimate union with a personal redeemer. The hope is vague and distant—as it is in the Old Testament. His message is the Old Testament message of Job: "Naked I came from my mother's womb, and naked shall I return."

Even when tempered by irony and hope and folk-humor the feeling is still present that man must face the mystery of life alone—naked before God and his fellow men. Darl speaks of this nakedness: "It was like we had all—and by a kind of telepathic agreement of admitted fear—flung the whole thing back like covers on the bed and we all sitting bolt upright in our nakedness, staring at one another and saying, 'Now is the truth'" (p. 433). Riding to Jefferson, Dewey Dell says, "I sit naked on the seat above the unhurrying mules, above the travail" (p. 422). Finally, Peabody looks at the dying Addie and reflects—in what is almost a modern paraphrase of Job's utterance—"That's what they mean by the love that passeth understanding: that pride, that furious desire to hide that abject nakedness which we bring here with us, carry with us into the operating rooms, carry stubbornly and furiously into the earth again" (p. 370).

The vision is troubled and strained, because it is man's lot to be caught up in an enigmatic existence: both spirit and matter, man is destined to suffer in the midst of plenty, to be lonely in the multitude of his relationships, to achieve life through death. For Faulkner it is a world in which life is predominantly a struggle, but a struggle in which victory is at least a possibility and not a mere velleity.

One feels at journey's end that the battered contingent sitting on the wagon eating bananas may yet survive: Cash will have a graphophone to listen to; Dewey Dell in her sullen way will have the child; shrewd old Anse has his new teeth and a new Mrs. Bundren; even Darl, Cash reflects, will be better off: "It is better so for him. This world is not his world; this life his life" (p. 532).

Twenty years after writing *As I Lay Dying* Faulkner could still sound the note of hope that flows through his books: "I believe that man will not merely endure: he will prevail. He is immortal, not because he alone among creatures has an inexhaustible voice, but because he has a soul, a spirit capable of compassion and sacrifice and endurance."[6]

Commentary ====

Philip Rule's essay has argued that the basic attitudes which inform *As I Lay Dying* are founded upon the values, insights, and attitudes of the Old Testament. In this view the relatively few echoes of the New Testament are incidental references or images, which do not change in any important way the pre-Christian biblical tone of the whole.

If this is the case, a further question suggests itself: Why is this so? How does it happen that the basic values of a people in a supposedly Christian environment are so little touched by the values inherent in Christianity? Probably there is no simple answer, but at least a partial response (or better, a direction for investigation) might be found by referring back to our earlier chapters, where several authors touched upon the particular kind of Protestantism which served as background for Faulkner's work. In other words, I am suggesting that to ask this particular "why?" is only to ask how Calvinist Protestantism can be historically characterized. Calvinism has tended to stress the ways in which man is under the governance of an all-powerful God; it has emphasized the sterner, Old Testament attitudes, with but little of the sense of Christian joy in redemption. Reading some of the American Calvinist fire-and-brimstone preachers, one sometimes has the uncomfortable feeling that for the mass of men the redemption of Christ is, as it was for the people of the Old Covenant, only a dim hope. And, whatever it may be elsewhere in Faulkner, this seems to be very much the tone of *As I Lay Dying*.

There are those, of course, who would disagree with the premise of this argument. Hyatt Waggoner, for instance, in his *William Faulkner: From Jefferson to the World* (Lexington, Kentucky: University of Kentucky Press, 1966, pp. 62–87), lays much more emphasis on the importance of the few Christian images in *As I Lay Dying*. In particular he singles out the Vardaman sections of the novel. "In Vardaman's chapters the religious theme is at once most precisely defined and most hidden from casual reading" (p. 65). For Waggoner it is the symbol of the fish—a traditional early Christian symbol for Christ—which focuses and gives meaning to much of the novel. The chopped-up fish, "laying in the kitchen in the bleeding pan, waiting to be cooked and et," is a parallel to "Christ killed and ritualistically eaten and drunk to prevent the death of the believer" (p. 66). What

117

this means for Vardaman, Waggoner argues, is that he "does not accept his mother's 'change' as final. . . . She has somehow *become* the fish: when the fish is eaten she will live on hidden away 'from the sight of man' " (p. 66). In Vardaman's words, "My mother is a fish." Waggoner goes on to analyze Addie's character in some detail, and ultimately concludes—as do many critics—that she is a profoundly ambivalent character. Rule was speaking of the same ambivalence when he wrote in his essay of "the conflict between aloneness and self-surrender." In Waggoner's view it is this in fact that makes her a "redemptive" figure: "She is a redemptive character—Vardaman's fish—because she recognizes both the difficulty and the necessity of love" (p. 81).

If Waggoner's analysis is not compelling, it is at any rate highly suggestive. And in any case, Waggoner's interpretation and Rule's come together to some extent in their conclusions about the general "tone" of the novel. Taking the outlook of Cash the "artist" as normative for the world of *As I Lay Dying*, Waggoner concludes: "What his approach to life would seem to imply is a sacramental view of nature—all nature—without a specific historical incarnation: a religious view of life but not one that, in the historic sense of the word, can be called Christian" (p. 84).

This brilliant novel was not Faulkner's final word about religion, of course. Nor was it his final word about mankind. If the hope held out for fallen man in *As I Lay Dying* is only a dim one, the flickering light of the Old Testament, it may help to make us more aware of what is perhaps a brighter light and a stronger hope in some of the later novels.

8 ▬▬▬▬

The religious elements of *Light in August* are strikingly obvious: the excoriation of puritanic excesses, the deliberate parallels of Joe Christmas and Christ, the tortured questionings of Hightower. There have been a few attempts, with varying degrees of success, to come to terms with them. Too often, however, at least some of these elements have been dismissed or minimized as unnecessary and unwise accretions on an otherwise powerful story. The following essay by Hyatt H. Waggoner sees these religious elements as a carefully articulated depiction of the nature of true Christianity in the modern world.

Waggoner's essay first appeared in his book *William Faulkner: From Jefferson to the World* (Lexington, Kentucky: University of Kentucky Press, 1959), pp. 100–120. It is here used with permission.

Hyatt H. Waggoner

LIGHT IN AUGUST: OUTRAGE AND COMPASSION

IN ONE OF GAIL HIGHTOWER'S FINAL MEDITATIONS [IN *Light in August*], he pronounces an often quoted judgment on Southern Protestant Christianity. The music he hears coming from the church seems to him to have "a quality stern and implacable, deliberate and without passion so much as immolation, pleading, asking, for not love, not life, forbidding it to others, demanding in sonorous tones death, as though death were the boon, like all Protestant music."[1] "Puritanism," or punitive religious moralism, is perhaps the chief intended antagonist in *Light in August,* as it is the immediate antagonist in *Sanctuary.*

"Pleasure, ecstasy," Hightower thinks, "they cannot seem to bear" (p. 322). Hines and McEachern could be his illustrations, the two most obviously pious people in the story and the two most responsible for the fate of Joe Christmas. He does not think of them because he does not know what we know about Christmas' past, but we, reading, supply them for him. And when we have finished the novel we feel that events have proved Hightower right when he pictures a crucifixion inflicted not despite, but because of, the religion of his fellow townsmen:

> *And so why should not their religion drive them to crucifixion of themselves and one another?* . . . It seems to him that the past week has rushed like a torrent and that the week to come, which will begin tomorrow, is the abyss, and that now on the brink of the cataract the stream has raised a single blended and sonorous and austere cry, not for justification but as a dying salute before its own plunge,

121

and not to any god but to the doomed man in the barred cell within hearing of them and of the two other churches, and in whose crucifixion they too will raise a cross. 'And they will do it gladly,' he says, in the dark window. (p. 322)

Hightower's thoughts constitute a terrible indictment of Southern Christianity, charging that it has become so distorted that it leads men toward hatred and destruction and death, crucifying Christ all over again, and "gladly." A great deal of the substance of the book has the effect of leading us to accept this judgment, and *Light in August* is Faulkner's most fully documented statement on what he sees as the religious errors and the racist guilt of his region. The grim fanatical fundamentalism of McEachern and the mad fundamentalist racism of Hines are judged in negative terms and without any shadow of qualification.

But a recognition of this theme of the book, necessary as it is, will not alone take us to an understanding of the whole novel. We may get at a further meaning by going on with Hightower's meditation to a passage which, unlike the negative judgment of the Southern Protestant churches, has not been quoted by the critics. Hightower has thought that the people would crucify "gladly." Now he thinks why they will have to do it gladly: "Since to pity him would be to admit self-doubt and to hope for and need pity themselves. They will do it gladly, gladly. That's why it is so terrible . . ." (p. 322). They will do it as Percy Grimm commits his murder and mutilation, secure in the confidence that they are doing their duty, without the least shadow of self-doubt, with perfect confidence in their own rectitude; like Percy Grimm, whose face "above the blunt, cold rake of the automatic . . . had that serene, unearthly luminousness of angels in church windows" (pp. 404–405).

But the whole strategy of the book is designed to prevent the reader not only from sharing their sense of their rectitude—this would be easy—but from resting confident in his sense of his own rectitude, his superiority to Joe Christmas, the warped sadist and murderer, and to Christmas's bigoted and cruel tormentors. Faulkner has said that a writer should be judged partly in terms of the difficulty of what he attempts, and that those writers who lack courage and so continue to do only what they know they can do well perhaps have earned less of our respect than those who attempt more and fail. In *Light in*

August Faulkner attempts a task difficult enough to be a challenge to any novelist, too difficult perhaps to be perfectly accomplished. He attempts to make us pity, identify ourselves with and even, in the religious sense of the word, love, a man who would be rejected not only by Southern mores with their racial bias but by any humane standard. He tries to awaken compassion for "one of the least of these" based on a recognition of universal guilt and mutual responsibility, not so that we may suspend judgment entirely but so that we may judge with love. *Light in August* is addressed not only to the conscience of the South but to the conscience of all readers anywhere. It has never to my knowledge been called a tract, but if it were not so powerful as a work of art it might well justify that designation. The moral feeling in it is intense. It demands nothing less than a withholding of self-righteous negative moral judgments and a substitution of unlimited compassion. If it shows us how and why "faith without deeds is dead," it shows us equally why we must "repent" before we "believe."

The novel moves toward this end the hard way, aesthetically and morally. It never makes Joe Christmas attractive. With the exception of a few passages on which I shall comment later, it does not picture him as "good at heart," forced into bad actions by circumstances. It shows us a man of whom we might say that it is surprising not that he commits one murder but that he has not committed more, a man apparently capable of any violent and repulsive deed, a man who hates not *even* those who love him but *especially* those who love him. It asks us to consider this man's death as parallel to the crucifixion of Christ.

The Joe Christmas-Jesus Christ analogy is prominent and consistent throughout the novel, and not simply, as the introduction to the Modern Library edition would have it, begun and then forgotten. It has nothing to do with any resemblance in character or outlook between Christmas and Jesus: indeed, this is precisely the point, that we are asked to see Christmas's death as a crucifixion despite the fact that Christmas is in every imaginable way different from Jesus. To make us pity a Christ-like figure would be easy, but the novel never attempts to do this. It asks pity for Christmas by making us see that the terrible things we do and become are all finally in self-defense. We are asked to feel not that Christmas is really good or nice but that he epitomizes the human situation. To do this is difficult for precisely the reason given by Hightower: it must be preceded by a personal confession of sin and a felt need for pity, forgiveness.

When we first see Joe Christmas it is through Byron Bunch. Bunch refuses to judge him but we are not likely to make the same refusal. Christmas's hat is "cocked at an angle arrogant and baleful above his still face" (p. 27). And there is nothing superficial or deceptive about the appearance of arrogance. All the men in the mill note his "air of cold and quiet contempt." The foreman speaks the general mind when he says "We ought to run him through the planer. Maybe that will take that look off his face" (p. 28). Christmas is later run through a planer of suffering, but "that look" comes off his face only at the moment of his death. The foreman is right, in a way, but his judgment is that of the reader at this point, lacking compassion.

After we have seen Christmas at his baleful and repellent worst we are taken back into the childhood that produced the man. The homicidal maniac who now thinks in fantasy "God loves me too" (p. 91) is the product of a complete absence of love in his earliest formative years. The experiences in the orphanage beyond present conscious memory were the formative ones in Christmas's life, and they all lead to one multiple impression: rejection, self-hatred, hatred of others.

> Memory believes before knowing remembers. Believes longer than recollects, longer than knowing even wonders. Knows remembers believes a corridor in a big long garbled cold echoing building of dark red brick sootbleakened by more chimneys than its own . . . the bleak windows where in rain soot from the yearly adjacenting chimneys streaked like black tears. (p. 104)

By the time the McEacherns take the boy he is already shaped to reject love and respond only to hatred. It is unnecessary to qualify the description of McEachern as a "ruthless and bigoted man" (p. 144), a man cold, hard, and cruel, to recognize that he was faced with a virtually hopeless task in his efforts to transform Joe into an acceptable Presbyterian foster-son. We learn that though the man beat him and the wife attempted to be kind and was unfailingly sympathetic, the boy hated the woman more than the man: "It was the woman: that soft kindness which he believed himself doomed to be forever victim of and which he hated worse than he did the hard and ruthless justice of men" (p. 147).

When we remember his response to Mrs. McEachern's attempts to befriend him and his kicking of the Negro girl in the shed, we see that his finally murdering the woman who had loved him and was trying to help him was predictable, in character, true to form psychologically. Unable to accept himself, Joe Christmas seeks punishment and death throughout his life as, earlier, he had forced McEachern to beat him. Psychologists might describe his character as "sadomasochistic." His aggressiveness is turned in upon himself as well as out toward others: he seeks to hurt and be hurt. Only when he has suffered the final pain and outrage inflicted by Percy Grimm does a look of peace come into his eyes. He had been waiting for this since the dietician offered him fifty cents instead of beating him.

Joe Christmas wants justice, not kindness—law, not mercy. The dietician should have punished him to preserve life's moral clarity. Christmas would be justified by keeping the law, not by declaring himself a sinner and throwing himself on the grace of God. To be able to accept kindness is implicitly to acknowledge one's self in need of it: Christmas is like his persecutors in having no humility, for all his "inferiority complex." He is like them too, even like mad old Doc Hines, in being an absolutist and a legalist. This is the quality which creates the curious kinship between him and McEachern even while they oppose each other with all their strength. For both of them right and wrong must be clear and definite; only so may a system of rewards and punishments ensure justice. McEachern seeks to enforce his, and God's, commandments, Christmas to violate them. The two are more alike than different.

All his life Christmas demands to know whether he is black or white. What he feels he cannot endure and will not accept is the not knowing, the ambiguity of his situation. Like many another Faulkner character, he is Ahab-like in his scorn of all petty satisfactions and his determination to "strike through the mask" to get at absolute truth, ultimate certainty and clarity, for good or for ill. He must know the truth, and for truth kindness is no substitute. In this sense his very "idealism" drives him to every degradation and finally to his destruction.

But there is still another light in which we may look at him. We have seen him as doubly victimized, first by circumstance and a loveless society, which together have made him what he is, second by his own need for the kind of justice and certainty not to be found (the novel implies) in life. But now, as we think of the final events of his life, we see him becoming society's victim in still a further sense—its scapegoat. Society heaps on him all the sins which it cannot, will not, see in itself. Hightower has understood this too: "to pity him would be to admit self-doubt and to hope for and need pity themselves" (p. 322). A scapegoat is needed not by the innocent but by the guilty. Joe Christmas makes it possible for his persecutors never to recognize their guilt. Hines, McEachern, and Grimm are all, in their several ways, "believers," but they have never repented and their actions are unconsciously calculated to protect them from the need to repent. To concentrate on this aspect of the portrait of Christmas leads one to feel the religious profundity of *Light in August,* and to realize that the work is deeply Christian in its meaning, despite its excoriation of the exemplars of piety.

This is the man, then—debased murderer, victim, scapegoat —whom we are forced, by the frequent symbolic pointers, to think of in terms of Christ. Readers have generally taken the parallel either as pure irony—everything so much the same, and yet the two figures so utterly different as to be quite incomparable—or as an ironically expressed insight into a likeness that remains real despite the irony. For the latter reading, which seems much better able to account for all the facts of a highly complex portrait than the former, a passage of Scripture is helpful:

> Then shall they also answer him, saying, Lord, when saw we thee an hungered, or athirst, or a stranger, or naked, or sick, or in prison, and did not minister unto thee?
> Then shall he answer them, saying, Verily I say unto you, Inasmuch as ye did it not to one of the least of these, ye did it not to me. (Matt. 25:44–45)

Joe Christmas is surely "one of the least of these." When the novel opens he is soon to be captured and put in prison; early in the book we see him naked beside the road; during his flight he suffers from hunger and thirst and is sick: every item in the catalogue of the unfortunate is paralleled in the book. The irony lies partly in the fact that he rejects or strikes down those who do try to "minister unto" him—Mrs. McEachern, Miss

Burden, Gail Hightower. But we are invited to believe that by the time these attempts to help him came he was beyond being able to respond to them except with rejection.

The motif of Christmas's adult life takes its pattern in part from the *Agnus Dei* of the service of Holy Communion. In the *Agnus Dei* the worshipper calls upon the "lamb of God" first to have mercy and then, in culmination, to "grant us thy peace." "All I wanted was peace" (p. 97), Christmas thinks during his reverie about his killing of Miss Burden; and on another occasion, though the word used here is the close synonym "quiet": "That was all I wanted . . . That was all, for thirty years" (p. 289). In his boyhood he had slain a sheep and dipped his hands in the blood, thus in fantasy and symbol being "washed in the blood of the lamb." When he is killed and his own blood flows he seems to find peace at last.

> For a long moment he looked up at them with peaceful and unfathomable and unbearable eyes. Then his face, body, all, seemed to collapse, to fall in upon itself and from out the slashed garments about his hips and loins the pent black blood seemed to rush like a released breath. It seemed to rush out of his pale body like the rush of sparks from a rising rocket; upon that black blast the man seemed to rise soaring into their memories forever and ever. (p. 407)

It is perhaps the last irony of Joe Christmas's life that at his death there is a kind of metaphoric ascension. There is a sense in which he himself has become "the slain sheep, the price paid for immunity" (p. 164), to use a phrase applied earlier to his taking Bobbie Allen into the fields. Those who witnessed his death, into whose memories his blood has "ascended," are never to lose this memory

> in whatever peaceful valleys, beside whatever placid and reassuring streams of old age, in the mirroring faces of whatever children they will contemplate old disasters and newer hopes. It will be there, musing, quiet, steadfast, not fading and not particularly threatful, but of itself alone serene, of itself alone triumphant. (p. 407)

The career of Joe Christmas constitutes a rebuke to the community, a measure of its sin of racial arrogance and of its corruption of Christianity from a religion of love and life to one of hatred and death, from Jesus to Doc Hines and Mc-Eachern. But Christmas is not the only source of the rebuke. The novel opens with Lena, an "unconscious Christian"; it moves, except in the sections on Christmas's childhood, largely through the minds of Byron Bunch and Gail Hightower, Christians of two different kinds; and it closes with Byron and Lena. The story of Christmas is thus framed and illuminated by the stories of several kinds of praticing Christians. McEachern and Hines, it would appear, do not give us the whole picture. Each is true to those aspects of religion under condemnation, but taken alone they would constitute a caricature. The force of the criticism comes from the recognition that they are so typical, their errors of practice or doctrine so widespread.

Meanwhile there is Lena to suggest a Christianity different from that of McEachern or Hines. She is not only a kind of nature or fertility goddess, but also a witness to the efficacy of the three theological virtues, faith, hope, and love. Her trust is in the Lord, as Armstid recognizes when he recalls how "she told Martha last night about how the Lord will see that what is right will get done" (p. 22). She may have been created with a passage from St. Paul in mind; at any rate she suffers long, and is kind, does not envy and is not (like Joe Christmas) too proud to accept help, is never unseemly in her conduct, and (to shift to the Revised Standard Version) "is not irritable or resentful"; she "bears all things, believes all things, hopes all things, endures all things." Considering that she is so saintly an image, it is remarkable that she seems so real to us. Novelists have seldom been successful in portraying saints. No wonder there is what has been called a "pastoral" quality in the Lena episodes. No wonder she moves "with the untroubled unhaste of a change of season." Unlike Christmas she is not in flight.

And Byron Bunch. He is the portrait of the unlettered practicing Christian. He works alone at the mill on Saturday afternoon to avoid any occasion of sin, thus following good Catholic precept. (He finds that even so he cannot avoid temptation.) Only Hightower knows that he "rides thirty miles into the country and spends Sunday leading the choir in a country church—a service which lasts all day long" (p. 42). He immediately offers Christmas a part of his lunch when they first meet (the reply is typical: "I aint hungry. Keep your muck" [p. 30]) and refuses to pass judgment on him when he is told that

Brown and Christmas are bootleggers. He holds himself responsible for having listened to the gossip: "And so I reckon I aint no better than nobody else" (p. 47). He thinks of Miss Burden and her reputation and the negative judgment the town makes of her; he makes no such judgment. He is a friend of the ruined outcast minister Hightower, not simply "befriending" him, refusing to share the town's harsh judgment, but recognizing in him a kindred spirit, seeking him out for advice, paying him the compliment of putting burdens upon him that he would ask no one else to bear. He pities and tries to help not only Lena and Hightower but Christmas's grandparents, bringing them to Hightower for advice. He extends his compassion to Christmas himself and might have been effective in his intended aid if Hightower had not refused until too late to accept the responsibility Byron tried to get him to see was his.

Byron Bunch has learned to bear the burden of being human. Generally inarticulate, he yet manages several times to define that burden for Hightower: "I mind how I said to you once that there is a price for being good the same as for being bad; a cost to pay. And it's the good men that cant deny the bill when it comes around" (p. 341). What Byron knows, he has had to learn in painful experience. We see him repeatedly tempted to deny the bill. No man, he often feels, should have to bear what he has to bear. But in the end he discovers that he can bear even the thought that all his efforts have succeeded only in getting Lena married to Burch. "It seems like a man can just about bear anything. He can even bear what he never done" (p. 401). His burden, finally, is total recognition of the impurity, the injustice, the unresolvable irony of life itself. When he has learned this, he knows not to ask for justice but for mercy and the strength to persevere. Like Lena, Byron is travelling the road recommended by the saints.

And Hightower. Here the picture is more complicated, so complicated that many readers have had difficulty putting the pieces together. Fundamentally, Hightower is a romantic idealist who, confronted with a reality less pure and heroic than his dreams, has retreated to a spot where he hopes life cannot reach him to hurt him again. His master symbol is the galloping horsemen; he cannot steadily face the fact that the horsemen were engaged in raiding a chicken house. When he sits at his window at sunset waiting for the dusk and the image of the galloping horsemen, a part of him knows that he is really waiting only for death,

> waiting for that instant when all light has failed out of the sky and it would be night save for that faint light which daygranaried leaf and grass blade reluctant suspire, making still a little light on earth though night itself has come. (pp. 51–52)

"Daygranaried": the natural light imagery here cannot be freed of its religious associations. The light of his religious faith has gone from Hightower and he has nothing to wait for now but the little light reflected, stored up perhaps from the source, but now coming, or seeming to come, from the earth itself, before the final coming of night. When he is about to die he thinks he should try to pray, but he does not try.

> "With all air, all heaven, filled with the lost and unheeded crying of all the living who ever lived, wailing still like lost children among the cold and terrible stars." (p. 431)

Yet he finally atones for whatever sin has been his by trying to protect Christmas from his pursuers, at a terrible cost to any pride he has left. Like Joe Christmas, Hightower thinks on one occasion that all he has ever really desired was peace; thinking too that it should rightly be his now, that he has earned it through suffering endured. It is Byron Bunch who teaches him that peace is not to be had by retreat, by taking no chances, that the purity achieved by denying the bill, refusing the risks of his humanity, is more like death than like life. As Hightower explicitly recognizes when he thinks Byron has left town without saying goodbye, Byron has restored him to life, or life to him. And so at the end he acts for once not like the romantic idealist and absolutist he has always been, but like Byron, the practicing Christian, the doer of the word who can submit to unreason and persevere in good works. Telling the pursuing men that Christmas was with him on the night of the murder, Hightower takes on himself the opprobrium of the town's worst surmise.

Before his death Hightower has learned that he is not simply a victim, that in some degree at least he has brought his martyrdom on himself. He sees that he has been "wild too in the pulpit, using religion as though it were a dream" (p. 53), getting religion and his romantic idolization of the past all mixed up together, using perhaps, he suspects, even his wife as a means to the end of his self-inflicted martyrdom. If he could pray at the end of his life he would pray not simply for peace but for mercy, as a sinner. He learns late what Byron Bunch has known all along. Before this when he and Byron sit together he looks "like an awkward beast tricked and befooled of the need for flight. . . . Byron alone seems to possess life" (p. 338). Yet at the end, if he has neither faith nor hope, he has shown himself capable in the supreme test of acting in terms of love, "the greatest of these." Hightower too is finally a redeemed and potentially redemptive character.

Joanna Burden is more complex than Byron Bunch and perhaps more perfectly realized than Hightower. Faulkner's critics have generally passed her over in silence, leaving her unrelated to the central themes of the book. But I think that if we consider the clue offered by her name, we shall find a key to at least the most significant aspect of her symbolic role. To do so seems not to be capricious in considering a book filled with suggestive names: Hightower, who spends most of his life *above* the battle and only at the end of his life comes down into the common life of man; Bunch, whose name suggests something common and solid and unromantic; Grimm; Christmas. Miss Burden, then, may be seen in a preliminary way as one who has taken the opposite road from the one followed by Hightower during his years of isolation. She accepts the burden of working for human betterment and the other, often painful, burdens it entails. Her isolation in a hostile community has been the price *she* has had to pay, in Byron's terms, for working for the cause of Negroes. For her, the white man's burden is her own burden.

But her conscience is not just sensitive, it is sensitive in a special way, the way of her grandfather the abolitionist. Though she has responded to life by commitment instead of flight, she is fundamentally as "idealistic" and "absolutist" in her reactions as Hightower. She accepts Joe Christmas, paradoxically, because he is, or she thinks he is, a Negro, not because he is a human being. The crisis in their relationship comes when she tells him her plan to send him to a Negro college. Her very idealism forces her to *place* him, in black or white. Thus she ends by reinforcing for him the terrible need that has driven him all his life, the need to know what he is. He has become her world, and she cannot accept a mixed, impure, ambiguous world, any more than Joe himself can, or Hightower before Byron teaches him. Like Melville's Pierre, she finds "the ambiguities" intolerable, just because she is so much an idealist. Her cause is finally more important to her even than Joe, and in her inflexible conscientiousness she drives him to murder her.

She is not, of course, an obvious sinner like Doc Hines and the other "righteous" characters in the story. There is real nobility in her that sets her quite apart from all the "idealists" but Hightower. She pays the price of goodness unflinchingly. But she can function only in a world of black and white; gray leaves her baffled, helpless. There is one burden, then, she cannot bear: precisely Byron Bunch's burden, the perception of essential irony. She is murdered by a man neither white nor black, but in a deeper sense she is destroyed by her abolitionist grandfather, for whom moral issues were perfectly clear and unambiguous.

In these people and their relationships the theme of the novel finds whatever expression it gets. There are no author's intrusions, no pointing fingers to tell us what it means. The meditations of Hightower come closer than anything else in the book to the voice of Faulkner the moralist but Hightower is portrayed as so clearly the victim of his own delusions that we are left to make our own decision as to which of his ideas are sound and which mere symptoms of his spiritual sickness. Byron Bunch is nearly as inarticulate as Lena, and we are given every opportunity to dismiss them both as essentially creatures of tender comedy in a pastoral idyl. The only characters of whom we may say that a definite and single judgment is required are McEachern, Hines, and Grimm; these are the only important characters approached wholly from outside, without any sympathetic identification with them on Faulkner's part.

Yet the novel "says" some things clearly enough. To the region in which it is laid it says that its racial injustice is a sin of the most terrible proportions and consequences (not merely a mistake or an accident—there is no moral relativism here or anywhere else in Faulkner) but also an opportunity for moral action. It says that suffering is the universal lot of mankind: in every man's death, even in that of a Joe Christmas, there is a kind of crucifixion. It says that the test of character is the individual's response to suffering: the hatred of Joe Christmas, the

flight from responsibility of Hightower, the humble engagement
of Lena and Byron.

The fact that these two open and close the novel seems to me
crucial and not to have been given sufficient weight in most
interpretations. It is not enough to say that the beginning and
end are comic relief from the pure tragedy of the major part
of the work. Lena and Byron *are* comic, of course, and the ending is an anticlimax, but it is also an affirmation of the possibilities of life. The voice of the traveling man from Memphis
is the voice of sanity which makes no excessive demands on life,
the voice of "realism," if you will, but a realism capable of
seeing two people of precisely Byron's and Lena's qualities as
those who offer hope. That only Byron and Lena, in the end,
are capable of carrying on is to be expected. We have been
prepared for this kind of affirmation by Dilsey and Cash. Certainly one meaning of the ending is that though knowledge of
absolutes is not granted to man, yet what he is given to know
is enough, if he has the moral and religious qualities of Byron
and Lena. If this is the central meaning of the ending, the final
implication of the book is a kind of Christian existentialism
which could be explicated in terms of the theology of a Tillich
or a Bultmann. Byron and Lena have the courage and the faith
to *be* in a world where man does not see God face to face and
any localizing of the absolute is a mark of pride.

This much is tolerably clear, but there is a good deal that is
not, and even this is likely to seem most plausible if we keep
our attention centered on the contrast between Byron and
Lena, on the one hand, and Hightower, Christmas, and Joanna
Burden, on the other—as of course the structure of the book in
the largest sense suggests that we should. There is a theological
ambiguity and a moral one, each of which tends in some degree
to run counter to what I have described as the implication of
the ending. The theological seems not crucial in the context
which the story itself has created. Whether ultimate meaning
here should be thought of in a humanist or in a Christian sense,
in Hightower's way or in Byron's way, it is perfectly clear that
the humble commitment of Byron and Lena is presented as the
only alternative to suicide or destruction. If God exists, and
cares, he demands this of us; if he does not, we must live, if we
are to live at all, by the old virtues anyway. Humanists may be
living only by "daygranaried" light, light stored up from a
higher source that now only *seems* to seep up from below; or

the light may really come from below, from the earth. In either case, the "old truths of the heart" are valid. The theological ambiguity is not crucial to an interpretation of the main thrust of the novel.

But the moral ambiguity is not so easily disposed of. It concerns, as so often in Faulkner, the problem of freedom and responsibility. We have seen Hightower as one who has demanded purity and, not finding it, has tried to isolate himself from an impure world; in this sense he is a victim of his own delusion and so in another sense not a victim at all but a man who has been mistaken. But most of the time during his years of seclusion he sees himself, and Faulkner seems to see him, as an innocent victim of other people or of life. His parishioners, the townspeople, the church, his wife, God, all seem to him to have failed him; and since we see them from his point of view, it is not entirely clear that he is wrong. Or at least it is not until toward the end. Then he thinks, "After all, there must be some things for which God cannot be accused by man and held responsible. There must be" (p. 427). Presumably there must, but it is not entirely clear to Hightower or to the reader what they are. It is significant, I think, that after Hightower achieves this insight and the reader comes to see him in terms of what it implies, the man himself becomes clear and believable to us at last. His dying meditation is one of the most powerful passages in all of Faulkner.

The same ambiguity is more troublesome in the portrait of Christmas. We see him chiefly as a "bad" man who cannot help being what he is. Living and dead he is a condemnation of an unjust society and a perverted religious conscience. But it is difficult if not impossible for us to picture a man as *simply* a victim. We may withhold judgment, refusing to try to decide what he can be held responsible for in the last, and true, judgment, but we must assume that he has some degree of moral responsibility if we are to see him as fully human. Apparently Faulkner must, too. Though the chapters on Christmas's childhood and boyhood, constituting a kind of case history of the growth of a sadomasochist, seems to remove from him all responsibility for what he later becomes, there are passages in which choice is imputed to Christmas. There are others in which, choice being denied but felt by the reader, the effect is sentimental. A couple of examples will serve to illustrate the point sufficiently.

When, after striking McEachern in the dance hall, Christmas runs away, there is a definite imputation of choice:

> The youth . . . rode lightly . . . exulting perhaps at that moment as Faustus had, of having put behind now at once and for all the Shalt Not, of being free at last of honor and law. (p. 180)

But the point of the Faustus myth is that Faustus, with full knowledge and acceptance of responsibility, made a choice. Most of the portrait of Christmas has the effect of suggesting that he was simply a victim, made no choices.

Again, and in contrast to the Faustus passage, the treatment of Christmas's experience with Bobbie Allen culminates in an apparent acceptance by Faulkner of Christmas's own view of the experience, a view which makes this the final betrayal, the last bitter blow of fate. "Why, I committed murder for her. I even stole for her" (p. 189), Christmas thinks. But that is not quite the way it was. As for the stealing, he had been stealing for some time before, and this particular "theft"—he took Mrs. McEachern's money in her presence, knowing well that she would have given it to him gladly—was not so much a theft as a final premeditated blow to the woman who had tried to help him. As for the "murder," whether or not McEachern died from the blow we are not told, but we do know that the boy had been waiting for the opportunity to deliver it for a long time and "exulted" when the opportunity came to "get even." It was not then in any real sense a murder committed "for her." Yet there is no indication in the writing at this point that these rationalizations of the boy's are not to be accepted at face value. The effect of the passage is sentimental.

A final example. As a part of the summary of Christmas's years between the time when he ran away from the McEacherns and the time when he came to Jefferson, we are told of the effect on him of his first experience of sexual relations with a white woman. "He was sick after that. He did not know until then that there were white women who would take a man with a black skin. He stayed sick for two years" (p. 196). I am afraid I shall have to say that this seems to me just plain nonsense. The implication that he was sick for two years not simply "after that" but because of "that" is wrong from several points of view. Would this amazing discovery make a well man sick, and for two years? Anyway, he does not have a "black skin." It is already perfectly clear, and even explicit, that he was very sick indeed psychologically long before this discovery, and is sick long after the two years are up. The passage is melodramatic in its imputation of too great an effect to too little a cause, and it is sentimental in its implication, once again, of innocence betrayed. It tells us more about Faulkner's own mixed racial feelings than it does about Joe Christmas.

No doubt this was how Christmas remembered the incident, but the passage could be effective only if there were some indication that Faulkner himself did not accept Christmas's sick notion of cause and effect. Faulkner's submergence of himself in his characters, which accounts for some of his greatest triumphs, also sometimes accounts for his failures. Here he has become Joe Christmas, sickness and all, as he thinks "back down the street, past all the imperceptible corners of bitter defeats and more bitter victories" (p. 201).

It seems to me, finally, that all the street and corridor imagery, applied chiefly to Christmas but also, less conspicuously, to several of the others, comes to less than it should. Perhaps its chief effect is to imply that for a person with (possibly) mixed blood life is a one-way street with no exit, no escape, leading inevitably to defeat and death. This at least is the effect of the passage in which Christmas finds that the street has turned into a circle, that he is inside it, and that there is still no escape. But this idea is both banal and untrue, or true only in a sense that needs just the kind of qualification a novel could give it. Only one aspect of this too prominent image pattern seems to me interesting, and that one only partially justifies the elaborate and repeated treatment of the pattern. There is some indication that Lena is in a street or a corridor too, as in the passage which begins "Behind her the four weeks, the evocation of *far*, is a peaceful corridor paved with unflagging and tranquil faith and peopled with kind and nameless faces and voices . . ." (p. 6), or in the description of Armstid's wagon as "a shabby bead upon the mild red string of the road" (p. 7). It depends, apparently, how we *take* our corridor, whether it is "peaceful" or bitter, a string of beads, each bead intrinsically valuable, or an avenue of flight. Percy Grimm too has his corridor and to him it means an escape from the necessity of choice: "his life opening before him, uncomplex and inescapable as a barren corridor" (p. 395). With her face lighted by the "unreason" of her faith, Lena finds friendly and helpful people everywhere, while Christmas finds only hatred and frustration.

These technical failings have the cumulative effect of creating an undeniable element of obscurity in a work nevertheless distinguished by its passion and immediacy and the seriousness of its imaginative grasp of reality. The obscurity here is quite different from the intentional ambiguity of *The Sound and the Fury* or *As I Lay Dying,* and different from the ultimately functional obscurity of *Absalom, Absalom!* This obscurity must be seen as an aesthetic weakness. But perhaps we should say only that *Light in August* attempts more than Faulkner could perfectly accomplish.

Light in August offers hope, but only by shifting levels, changing perspectives. The central story of Joe Christmas is unrelieved tragedy; the story of Lena and Byron is tender comedy. The hope is real, but inevitably qualified by our feeling that we must smile at Lena and Byron even as we admire them: *we* are more like Hightower or Miss Burden, or even Joe Christmas. I have argued that we must not undervalue Lena and Byron, that certainly we must not dismiss them as bumpkins before we see their moral and religious implications; but I should certainly not want to imply that we can take them in the same way that we take Hightower or Christmas.

Hope may be found in *Light in August* only by giving up the intellectual and emotional struggle for ultimate certainty embodied in Hightower and Christmas and turning to the humble and unself-conscious engagement of Lena and Byron. Because this means, in effect, turning to what is likely to strike us as a lower level of apprehension, the novel is perhaps in its final effect more unrelievedly tragic than *The Sound and the Fury*. If we agree that Dilsey has truly heroic qualities we may say that redemptive hope in *The Sound and the Fury* lies within the tragedy itself. Because we feel Dilsey's nobility, we feel that we move upward to identify with her and to achieve her view of life. But because we smile at Lena and Byron, though by an act of judgment appreciating their virtues, we must in a sense move down to a vision less serious than the tragic to reach the hope which they alone offer in *Light in August*. As we sit with Hightower in the twilight, we are likely to feel that the darkness is more powerful than the light.

Commentary

Waggoner does, it seems to me, what few have done before with *Light in August*. He finds not merely an attack on the perverted Christianity of McEachern and Hines, on the agonized and uncertain Christianity of Hightower and Joanna Burden, and on the victimization of Joe Christmas by ostensible Christians, but he finds in the story of Lena and Byron a true religious center around which these abuses of Christianity are grouped and in the light of whose standard they are judged. This much seems clear and unassailable.

There is another aspect of *Light in August*, however, which Waggoner touches upon but does not develop at length. It is the deliberate parallel between Joe Christmas and Jesus Christ. We are asked, Waggoner says, "to consider this man's death as parallel to the crucifixion of Christ." There have been attempts to spell out this parallel more in detail, notably by C. Hugh Holman in a provocative essay on "The Unity of Faulkner's *Light in August*" (*PMLA* 73 [1958], 155–166). Holman argues cogently that the Christ imagery of *Light in August* is not only not introduced "casually or irresponsibly," as some have suggested, but is in fact the novel's principle of unity. He finds not only the Joe Christmas story but also the stories of Gail Hightower and of Lena and Byron to be patterned on the life of Christ. "None of these characters," Holman asserts,

> are in themselves alone adequate representations of the Christ story or of those elements in it which have special meaning for Faulkner; but each of them is a representation of certain limited aspects of Christ, so that we may look upon them all and the complex pattern of actions through which they move and see, as it were, the dim but discernible outline of Christ as the organizing principle behind them.

From this he concludes to a "nontheological" interpretation of the book in which Christ is "the suffering servant of *Isaiah*, the archetype of man struggling against the order and condition of himself and his world" (p. 166).

One may no doubt cavil at this interpretation of the Hightower story and the Lena-Byron story, but its application in some form to Joe Christmas seems called for. Faulkner has set up too many resonances of the life of Christ for them to be ignored. And yet

Waggoner, who clearly follows this kind of interpretation, is perhaps wiser merely to point to the parallels, suggest their relevance, and leave the rest to the reader. We are meant, Waggoner seems to imply, simply to be aware of the analogy without analyzing it too closely. We are meant merely to be aware from time to time that this figure, so unlike Christ, "epitomizes the human situation"—as Christ does.

Is this necessarily a "nontheological" interpretation, as it is in Holman's view? Clearly Waggoner does not think so. And if we recall that the religion of Faulkner's novels is, as we have suggested before, primarily a religion of practice, it will not seem strange that he is interested in the Christian way of life (exemplified positively by Lena and Byron, negatively by McEachern, Christmas, Joanna Burden, Hightower, and others) rather than in its dogmatic and metaphysical foundations. This way of life is not theology, to be sure, but it contains profound theological implications.

It might merely be added that the role of Joe Christmas as victim, so cogently discussed by Waggoner, is underscored by a kind of "ritual" quality, a sense of ceremonial, about much of the novel. This is strikingly illustrated in the parallelism set up between the birth of Joe Christmas and the birth of Lena's child, which are recounted only twenty pages apart (pp. 332 and 353). Immediately after birth each child is lifted up, in a kind of ritual gesture of offering. Joe is held aloft by the mad Eupheus Hines, unrelenting in his condemnation of his daughter, Joe's mother; Lena's baby by Mrs. Hines, in conscious repudiation of her husband's hatred. Joe is dedicated to hatred; Lena's child to love.

Later, in discussing Faulkner's allegorical *A Fable*, we shall speak of the nature of allegory and myth in Faulkner, but it might be suggested here that *Light in August*—while no doubt not an "allegory"—does share to some extent in the nature of allegory and myth, bringing the emotional and imaginative resonances of the passion of Christ to bear (by what Waggoner calls "frequent symbolic pointers") on the anguished life and death of Joe Christmas.

9 ▬▬▬

The reader may wish at this point to refer back to Chapter 5, in which John W. Hunt established the premises of his argument for the "theological complexity" of Faulkner's fiction. Taking as his touchstone of the nature of religious meaning the approach to the problem of evil—its origin and nature —Hunt argued there that Faulkner's "religious center" is a tension between the Stoic and the Christian views of man's situation with respect to this problem. The central tension between the two views is focused in the question, "whether man's basic problem is finitude or sin," and in the related soteriological question, "how, *qua* human and only finite or *qua* human and guilty before his creator, the resources for overcoming evil or sin are made available." In the following essay, Hunt studies *Absalom, Absalom!* in terms of these premises.

This essay first appeared as a chapter of Hunt's study, *William Faulkner: Art in Theological Tension* (Syracuse: Syracuse University Press, 1965), pp. 101–136. It is here used with permission.

John W. Hunt

THE THEOLOGICAL CENTER OF
ABSALOM, ABSALOM!

"SOMEWHERE IN THE HEART OF EXPERIENCE," SAYS DARLEY,
Lawrence Durrell's narrator in *Justine,* "there is an order and
a coherence which we might surprise if we were attentive
enough, loving enough, or patient enough."[1] *Absalom, Absalom!* is Faulkner's attentive, loving, and patient exploration
into the heart of experience, past and present, to trap its meaning in an aesthetic mold. Here again he is on theological
center, probing reality imaginatively through multiple percep-
tions to lay bare its order and character and to render the
meaning carried in the face of it by the facts of experience.

The initial task, and the final one also, in an analysis of
Absalom, Absalom! is to determine accurately the controlling
function of its narrative method. This is not to say that the
novel marks a radical departure in method. Reality is rendered
symbolically and mimetically; events and meanings, actions
and symbols are fused through character. Some of the narrative
devices are, however, in many ways singular. The final vision
of reality is not Quentin's. It is a larger reality in the context
of which the one created by Quentin's imagination is made
credible. Sutpen's history is only what Quentin is able, with
the help of others, to make of it, and what he can make of it
is conditioned by the limitations of that sensibility already presented in *The Sound and the Fury.* Quentin reconstructs the
history in such a way that it posits a reality infected with a
meaning peculiar to him. The imaginative act by which he
creates the story is of the same order as the imaginative act of
the author who shows Quentin unable to understand the meaning of his own creation. With Quentin as with the author, the
imaginative process begins with the creation of the facts them-

141

selves; even the final explanation of the central mystery in Sutpen's story (why Sutpen's design failed) is really only an intuitive judgment on Quentin's part of what "must have been" and has no foundation in an "objective" fact provided by the author.

Special attention must be paid to point of view, focus of character, and focus of interest, because in their complex relationship lies the key both to the nature of the final reality posited and to the kind of meaning implied by experience of that reality. Attention is initially forced upon point of view, since the question of reliability arises almost immediately for the reader when with Quentin he is in the presence of Rosa's nearly disembodied voice as she conjures with the obvious distortion of intense frustration and hatred a demonic image of Sutpen from "old ghost-times."[2] After some relief from ambiguity at the beginning of Chapter II, Mr. Compson's memory narrative begins to dominate. Its initial tone of authority quickly vanishes; his tired skepticism embellished with a seedy sophistication evidences the character of his own distortions.

When Quentin and Shreve take up the narrative, again private interests determine both subject matter and interpretation. Their guesses about what must have been are based upon facts which Mr. Compson (in much of his narration) and Rosa (although she alone of the narrators knew Sutpen well during his lifetime) did not have before them, but the reader's discovery of this fact only undermines the reliability of Mr. Compson and Rosa as narrators without giving him confidence in Quentin and Shreve. Shreve and Quentin's relationship as northerner and southerner, novice and expert, their "youthful shame of being moved" (p. 280) in each other's presence, and their great sense of personal identification with Bon and Henry charge the latter half of the novel with an emotional intensity which does little to enhance the reader's comfort about the reliability of their dual narrative.

Nor is there significant relief from ambiguity of fact and meaning in the implied author's contribution. At few points can the reader assume with certainty that he is getting the facts of Sutpen's life, and at fewer points can he rely upon the author for direct interpretation of either Sutpen's or Quentin's story. The author is usually less than omniscient and more than an observer; he describes outward, physical setting, gesture, and speech but intrudes usually with more than surmise and less than omniscience into the thoughts, motives, and states of feeling of the other narrators and the characters. With Quentin, Shreve, Mr. Compson, and Rosa he indulges in guesswork, using words such as "maybe," "probably," and "perhaps" to weaken further the insecurity of the reader's knowledge.

Into this narrative maze the reader is drawn and compelled to participate in the unraveling of the story. Until the end of the novel he shares Bon's feeling that *"you cannot know yet whether what you see is what you are looking at or what you are believing"* (p. 314). But he does have one advantage. His distance—moral, intellectual, and emotional—from Sutpen's story diminishes less rapidly than that of any of the narrators because he sees them correcting one another to such an extent that final judgment can be withheld until the end of the novel. Only when all of the various sensibilities have presented their "facts," have assigned causes appropriate to the facts, and have shown their reactions to them does the reader feel obliged to make the crucial choices regarding the meanings carried by those facts. During the experience of reading, the reader has before him only the process of the creation of the story through recollection, interpretation, and imagination. When the story is over, the fluid images of the tale solidify, enabling the reader to form his judgments on the basis of the norms rendered by the novel as a whole.

Attention to the problem of point of view forces a formal distinction between the tale told and the telling of it, since, like *The Sound and the Fury,* the novel presents two main actions. The present-tense action is Quentin's telling, or being told and remembering. Backstage is the history of Sutpen, never clear, always fluid, known only as it filters through several sensibilities into the tale being told. This means that the novel's focus of character is divided between Quentin and Sutpen. The image of Sutpen, the central figure of the tale told, emerges as Mr. Compson's image, or Rosa's, or Shreve's, but finally Quentin's.

So it is that investigation of point of view leads to the problem of focus of character. That Sutpen's real story is never known is the clue here: there is no single true story apart from its interpretation. The events of his life take on meaning as causes are assigned to them according to the penchant, the personal history, and the intellectual bias of the several narrators. The novel is not history, not even in form, but art; that is, it records the events of Sutpen's life not in the order in which they took place but in the order in which they become significant in the recollection of the characters telling the story, and especially in Quentin's experience of recreation.[3] Had Faulkner wanted simply to give the story of Thomas Sutpen, the character-narrators would be superfluous. What he has given indicates that his purpose is more comprehensive than a history of Sutpen or even a history of the Deep South. The way in which he has given Sutpen's story indicates that the greatest tool for his purpose is the character of Quentin Compson— Quentin, because it is with him that the book opens, in his presence that the narrative proceeds, and with him and his reaction to the total impact of the imaginatively constructed history that the book closes. What the backstage action both is and means is how it occurs to Quentin; its meaning as well as its character lies in the context and manner of its emergence— the intellectual, moral, and emotional present in which it comes to life—and this context is finally Quentin himself.

This is Quentin's story as much as, and in a different way from, Sutpen's. The present-tense action gives us Quentin's reaction to the Sutpen saga. In the dramatic detail of Quentin's confronting the past, it provides a long footnote on the character and content of that Southern past in the face of which he forged his final truant strategy. The reader is forced to focus upon whatever it is in Sutpen's story *qua* Quentin's creation that holds such fascination for Quentin and, indeed, binds the two actions—the tale told and the telling of it—to render one effect. That is, the reader's focus of interest is upon the novel's theme, its import, its meaning, not simply for Quentin but for himself, although he arrives at its theme through the way the novel as a whole evaluates the evidence presented by Quentin's creation.

It is significant that when Quentin's eye turns to the past it rests upon one who is not an exemplar of the aristocratic tradition with which *The Sound and the Fury* supposedly showed him to be the most concerned. Malcolm Cowley once pointed out that Sutpen was not an aristocrat of the Compson-Sartoris-McCaslin order, but one of the "new men," the huge plantation owners who, with the aristocrats, "were determined to establish a lasting social order on the land they had seized from the Indians (that is, to leave sons behind them)."[4] Just how valid Cowley's distinction is and just what its implications are need to be made clear, since it is crucial in two ways for an understanding of the novel. It is crucial first of all for Quentin, and, in the second place, for Faulkner.

When Quentin is asked by his Harvard contemporaries to tell about the South, he responds with the story of Sutpen. In some way, Sutpen's story holds for him the key to the whole Southern experience. If he could explain Sutpen, if he could account for the fact that a Sutpen could exist and that he could not but fail of his "design," he could also explain the South. As the story develops, it becomes apparent that he cannot simply contrast traditional and untraditional men. Though wanting desperately to believe that the distinction to which Cowley points is valid, he senses that Sutpens are possible because of something in the traditional society itself. In order to explain the one he must illuminate the other. Quentin never becomes clear about either; he grasps intellectually the difference between the tradition's ideal claim and Sutpen's untraditional actions, but reacts only with violent emotion (even with a physical spasm) to his vague sense that in Sutpen's story the actual tradition is dramatized, stripped of its ideal vision. Rather than explaining either Sutpen or the aristocrat, he judges both and in such a way that neither offers any hope for meaning in his own experience. At the end of his story he admits failure. The question is posed again: "it's something my people haven't got," Shreve says, "What is it? something you live and breathe in like air?" "You cant understand it. You would have to be born there," Quentin replies—this after three hundred and fifty pages of trying to understand it himself. "Do you understand it?" Shreve asks again, and Quentin says, " 'I don't know. . . . Yes, of course I understand it.' . . . [And] after a moment Quentin said: 'I dont know' " (pp. 361–62).

The novel does not leave us, however, only with Quentin's despair. It is legitimate to look upon the novel, taken in its total performance, as a witness to Faulkner's own judgment of the Southern past. Here—and Quentin should not be confused with Faulkner—both the tradition and the modern world are tested in an aesthetic mold for their truth, the insight they yield into the value and meaning of any man's experience. It is wrong to assume that because Faulkner allows his investigation to proceed under Quentin's limited sensibility the book's illumination of the past is only as clear as Quentin's understanding of it. Quentin himself is under investigation in the novel. Faulkner's total fictional strategy is, in a limited sense,

the same as Quentin's. He too uses the story of one of the new
men to illuminate the inadequacy of both traditional and modern assessments of reality. But Faulkner becomes clear about
the implications of the evidence Quentin presents, while Quentin remains confused. Faulkner's look at the past is aesthetically
controlled to allow a deliberate judgment from a point of view
wider than Quentin's. When we understand the character of
the aesthetic judgment, we understand the character of Faulkner's theological center in this novel. We will look first at
Quentin's attempt to deal with the Sutpen story.

The distinction between traditional and untraditional societies Quentin wants to bring to Sutpen's story is explained, in
another context, by Allen Tate, who contrasts the relationship
within each of them between the economic and moral orders.
Using the word "morality" to mean "responsibility to a given
set of conditions," he finds the traditional society to be one
which hands on "a moral conception of man in relation to the
material of life," and the untraditional society, of which our
modern society is a prime example, to be "hostile to the per-
petuation of a moral code" because the "economic system can
be operated efficiently regardless of the moral stature of the
men who operate it." Traditional men "are making their living
all the time, and affirming their humanity all the time,"[5] while
modern men "are no longer capable of defining a human objective" and "capitulate from their human role to a series of
pragmatic conquests."[6]

The Unvanquished provides a short account of Sutpen from
one of his contemporaries who stood in the aristocratic tradition. Bayard Sartoris, in unequivocal terms, says of Sutpen:

> He was underbred, a cold ruthless man who had come into
> the country about thirty years before the War, nobody
> knew from where except Father said you could look at him
> and know he would not dare to tell. He had got some land
> and nobody knew how he did that either, and he got money
> from somewhere . . . and built a big house and married
> and set up as a gentleman. Then he lost everything in the
> War like everybody else, all hope of descendants too (his
> son killed his daughter's fiancé on the eve of the wedding

and vanished) yet he came back home and set out single-
handed to rebuild his plantation. He had no friends to
borrow from and he had nobody to leave it to and he was
past sixty years old, yet he set out to rebuild his place like
it used to be; they told how he was too busy to bother with
politics or anything; how when Father and the other men
organised the night riders to keep the carpet baggers from
organising the Negroes into an insurrection, he refused to
have anything to do with it. Father stopped hating him
long enough to ride out to see Sutpen himself and he (Sutpen) came to the door with a lamp and did not even invite
them to come in and discuss it; Father said, "Are you with
us or against us?" and he said, "I'm for my land. If every
man of you would rehabilitate his own land, the country
will take care of itself" and Father challenged him to bring
the lamp out and set it on a stump where they could both
see to shoot and Sutpen would not. (pp. 255–56)

Bayard here emphasizes those aspects of Sutpen's career and
character which set him apart from the aristocratic ideal: lack
of breeding, ruthlessness, suspicious origin, and unwillingness
to participate in accepted forms of social behavior except when
there is personal advantage. Quentin's grandfather, who also
knew him, is quick to point out that Sutpen, lacking a received
tradition, confused shrewdness with unscrupulousness, "or
maybe," General Compson says, "that was what he meant by
courage" (*Absalom, Absalom!*, p. 250). Mr. Compson believed
that Wash Jones, admittedly of the landless white class, shared
with Sutpen a morality "that told him he was right in the face
of all fact and usage and everything else" (p. 287). Rosa, more
ignorant than any of the narrators of the facts of Sutpen's life,
yet more directly a part of it, calls him a man "with valor and
strength but without pity or honor" (p. 20). By his own confession, the sum of Sutpen's learning from the incident of the
"monkey-dressed" Negro at the Virginia plantation door was
that "to combat them you have got to have what they have that
made them do what the man did. You got to have land and
niggers and a fine house to combat them with" (p. 238).

Sutpen and his biographers thus testify that he is set apart from the aristocrats by a lack of humanity in Tate's sense of the word. Prior to his experience at the plantation door,

> he no more envied the man than he would have envied a mountain man who happened to own a fine rifle. He would have coveted the rifle, but he would himself have supported and confirmed the owner's pride and pleasure in its owner-ship because he could not have conceived of the owner taking such crass advantage of the luck which gave the rifle to him rather than to another as to say to other men: *Because I own this rifle, my arms and legs and blood and bones are superior to yours.* (pp. 228–29)

The incident itself came as such a shock that he figuratively crawled back into the womb (literally, a cave) to be reborn to another world of experience, because his life had contained no experience "to compare and gauge it by" (p. 234). He was reborn to a vision of his own "innocence," for "it was like that," Sutpen said, "like an explosion—a bright glare that vanished and left nothing, no ashes nor refuse; just a limitless flat plain with the severe shape of his intact innocence rising from it like a monument" (p. 238). He emerged from his shock with a rec-ognition of what he took to be his destiny and his fate: he was sent to the door *so that* the Negro could affront him, *so that* he could learn what it took to combat them. In Greek fashion, his fate became an extension of his will; in vindication "of that little boy who approached that door fifty years ago and was turned away," Sutpen told Quentin's grandfather, General Compson, "the whole plan was conceived and carried forward" (p. 274).

But the human—or inhuman—content of the Negro agent's action suffers in time from abstraction. Fifty years later "that little boy" was merely a "boy-symbol at the door," "just the figment of the amazed and desperate child" (p. 261). Conse-quently, when in the figure of Bon "the forlorn nameless and homeless lost child" (p. 267) comes fifty years later to knock at his own door, Sutpen turns him away. Because he was his son, Bon's human claim upon Sutpen was greater than Sutpen's upon the plantation owner. Quentin and Shreve believe that Bon "wanted so little" (p. 321), just the human recognition, "just the saying of it—the physical touch even though in secret, hidden—the living touch of that flesh" (p. 319), a touch which Rosa believes precipitates *"the fall of all the eggshell shibboleth of caste and color too"* (p. 139). The humanity—so little—he wanted from his father, Bon in his turn denied his own son, Velery, so that the Justice of the Peace was vexed to the symbolic question, *"What are you? Who and where did you come from?"* (p. 203). The incident of the octoroon's photograph in Bon's wallet, however, is interpreted by Quentin to mean that he did not fail completely of humanity in his most trying moment.

Because he had all along failed to comprehend what was actually involved in his initial experience and therefore to incorporate into his design the moral integrity (expressing itself in "humanity") which supposedly gave the tradition its "unity between [man's] . . . moral nature and his livelihood,"[7] Sutpen could assign the cause of the design's collapse only to "an old mistake in fact which a man of courage and shrewdness . . . could still combat if he could only find out what the mistake had been" (*Absalom, Absalom!,* pp. 267–68).

There are also other ways by which Sutpen is set apart from the aristocrats. Lacking the humanity they espoused and therefore unable to affirm the integrity of their total way of life, Sutpen emphasized the material side. He assumed that possession of house, land, and slaves was the entire content of the aristocrat's distinction. And one must be careful to note that he was led to this conclusion by an incident in which the tradition had not functioned according to its ideal spirit. His conclusion was correct on the basis of his evidence: "to combat them you have got to have what they have *that made them do what the man did*" (italics mine). What the man did was to act untraditionally (without the humanity), and his action was licensed by sheer economic power.

It is Drusilla of *The Unvanquished* who points up Sutpen's moral isolation from the community. When Bayard, after summarizing Sutpen's career, says, "Nobody could have more of a dream than that," Drusilla replies, "Yes. But his dream is just Sutpen. John's [John Sartoris'] is not. He is thinking of this whole country . . ." (p. 256). The aristocrat takes responsibility for the entire way of life of the community, not out of love for his fellow man, but out of a dispassionate sense of duty. Received and handed on in the traditional society are the automatically operative values of the entire community (whether they are worth preserving is, at this point, not at issue) which express themselves in the culture's unwritten mores.

Sutpen had no feeling, no automatic receptivity, for these values. He simply recognized them where recognition of them was pragmatic, followed social usage as long as it was advantageous and abandoned it when it was not, maintaining always an "alertness for measuring and weighing event against eventuality, circumstance against human nature, his own fallible judgment and mortal clay against not only human but natural forces, choosing and discarding, compromising with his dream and his ambition" (*Absalom, Absalom!*, p. 53). For example, he "marked down Miss Coldfield's father with the same cold and ruthless deliberation with which he had probably marked down the French architect," came to Jefferson "to find a wife exactly as he would have gone to the Memphis market to buy livestock or slaves" (p. 42), and wanted a big wedding with "the full church and all the ritual" (p. 49) because he calculated that the success of his design required "not the anonymous wife and the anonymous children, but the two names, the stainless wife and the unimpeachable father-in-law, on the license, the patent" (p. 51).

His attitude toward his first wife and toward Bon also involved no personal feeling about Negro blood; they were simply not "adjunctive to the forwarding of the design" (p. 262). And his attitude toward women was alien to those who stand within the received tradition. Quentin's grandfather finds it incredible that Sutpen could presume to buy immunity from his first wife "for no other coin but justice": "didn't the dread and fear of females which you must have drawn in with the primary mammalian milk teach you better?" (p. 265). General Compson's incredulity is significant because the tradition's attitude toward women was fundamental to its whole spirit. As seen in *The Sound and the Fury*, the central position of women in the matriarchal society was associated with their natural function of fertility, and involved, ultimately, the tradition's vision of evil. Shreve, speaking also for Quentin, shows understanding of this when he says of Henry and Bon that "they both knew that women will show pride and honor about almost anything except love" (p. 341). The tradition held women to be amoral, not evil but also not not evil; women were simply natural, beyond good and evil.

The features setting Sutpen apart from the tradition's ideal

—his lack of humanity, his moral variance and isolation from the community, his impersonal pragmatism, his acquisitive drive, his sense of personal destiny and fate—are a large part of what Quentin senses when he says that "Sutpen's trouble was innocence" (p. 220). To the implication of this statement we must give some attention.

In many outward respects, Sutpen would seem to exemplify rather than to contradict the tradition's Stoic rationalization. But this is true only if one takes the word "innocent" to mean something neither Quentin nor Faulkner means by it. The word cannot mean, in this context, "not guilty," for sin and guilt are not at issue; rather, it refers to Sutpen's ignorance or lack of awareness or insensitivity or, finally, lack of knowledge of the nature of things. Cleanth Brooks says that for Faulkner Sutpen's innocence is "about the nature of reality" itself.[8] The nature of things of which he is ignorant is first of all that nature of things envisioned by the tradition's theological realism which was largely Stoic. In this sense, Sutpen is innocent of both nature and human nature. This much Quentin seems to understand, but he is only vaguely aware that Sutpen is ignorant in the second place of the reality envisioned by Christian religiousness.

In a mood of "sober and quiet bemusement" (p. 273), indicating "that he had long since given up any hope of ever understanding it" (p. 263), Sutpen recapitulates his story for General Compson, trying to "discover that mistake which he [still] believed was the sole cause of his problem" (p. 271). He is "fog-bound by his own private embattlement of personal morality," by a "picayune splitting of abstract hairs" (p. 271), and will not act again until he has found out what the mistake was. In his "innocence," Quentin says, he "believed that the ingredients of morality were like the ingredients of pie or cake and once you had measured them and balanced them and mixed them and put them into the oven it was all finished and nothing but pie or cake could come out" (p. 263). Since his morality does not root in a realistic assessment of the nature of things, he meets his defeat at the hand of forces he never realizes to be operative. The *"old impotent logic and morality which had betrayed him before," "had never yet failed to fail him"* (p. 279–80), could only lead him to the conclusion *"that he had been right, just as he knew he had been, and therefore what had happened was just a delusion and did not actually exist"* (p. 280) because it did not take account of the fortuitous evil with which the tradition's Stoic morality, made realistic by the cumulative concrete experience of the historical community, was geared to deal.

The tradition's morality because it was not innocent attained wisdom. By balancing the ideology of the ruling class against its experience, it attempted to allow man to live meaningfully without presuming any ultimate order of things which would guarantee the success of the enterprise. Fate was never to be coerced, and though the source and ultimate nature of retribution remained mysterious, its inevitable manifestation at points of outrage was a social and political fact. Sutpen's morality, because it was unrealistic, abstract, and merely logical, obscured the concrete evil from constant view. When its manifestations burst upon him, his impotent logic could only produce results which to him were "absolutely and forever incredible" (p. 263).

So far, we have measured Sutpen's innocence against the tradition's more sophisticated view of life which required that man forego his state of innocence and take on the risk of the human situation—at the price of possible tragic defeat, perhaps, but even then with the possibility of gaining a whole realm of meaningful human experience. We must now ask how much of this Quentin sees. Certainly we can understand how the Quentin of *The Sound and the Fury* could interpret Sutpen from the standpoint of a Puritan moralist. Because he shows ability to appropriate at least the rationalization of the tradition, he can pass judgment from a Puritan rather than a Stoic point of view that Sutpen was unable to comprehend the collapse of his design as "moral retribution," not the "sins of the father come home to roost . . . but just a mistake" (p. 267). But can Quentin also understand the vital spirit of the tradition, that vision of reality and especially that feeling for the evil, or at least the amorality, behind the face of reality which generated the rationalization? Evidence from *The Sound and the Fury* would indicate that he could not. Yet one does not have to refer to that novel for a definition of Quentin's sensibility. Within the first few pages of *Absalom, Absalom!* and with as omniscient a voice as he ever attains, the author provides the clue:

> Quentin has grown up with that [talk about Sutpen]; the mere names were interchangeable and almost myriad. His

childhood was full of them; his very body was an empty hall echoing with sonorous defeated names; he was not a being, an entity, he was a commonwealth. He was a barracks filled with stubborn back-looking ghosts still recovering, even forty-three years afterward, from the fever which had cured the disease, waking from the fever without even knowing that it had been the fever itself which they had fought against and not the sickness, looking with stubborn recalcitrance backward beyond the fever and into the disease with actual regret, weak from the fever yet free of the disease and not even aware that the freedom was that of impotence. (p. 12)

Faulkner gives us, in short, the double fact of Quentin's southernness and his impotence as the initial condition, the *donnée* of his character. The fullest definition of his sensibility, however, is dramatic rather than descriptive. Just how deeply he is able to penetrate the tradition is measurable by the character of his solution to the problem of why Sutpen's design failed. Quentin begins his review of the story in boredom, shut up with Rosa in the "dim hot airless room" (p. 7), asking himself if he must go through it all again. He ends obsessed, lying on his bed in the Harvard dormitory unable to sleep, jerking violently in a physical spasm, and at last lying quietly, "breathing hard but slow, his eyes wide open upon the window, thinking 'Nevermore of peace. Nevermore of peace. Nevermore Nevermore Nevermore'" (p. 373). Between the boredom and the despair, two crucial events occur. He visits Sutpen's mansion with Rosa and he reviews Sutpen's history with Shreve.

Just what happened that September night at Sutpen's mansion is unclear except as it can be reconstructed from the evidence of its interpretation. Shreve and Quentin do not begin to glare and stare at one another and to think as one person until they come to the story of Henry and Bon (Chapter VIII). One can easily see that the incest theme would interest Quentin and this must account for part of his obsession. As they merge identities with Henry and Bon—"four of them and then just two—Charles-Shreve and Quentin-Henry" (p. 334)—Quentin's identification with Henry becomes so complete that he easily assigns to Henry his own inverted Puritan evaluation of incest as a strategy for attaining being by affirming the possibility of sin:

> *and Henry said 'Thank God. Thank God,'* [when Bon decided to marry Judith] *not for the incest of course but because . . . at last he could* be [emphasis mine] *something even though that something was the irrevocable repudiation of the old heredity and training and the acceptance of eternal damnation* [a shift here, as in *The Sound and the Fury*, from the Stoic orientation to an attenuated Christian one]. . . . *he could say now, 'It isn't yours nor his nor the Pope's hell that we are all going to: it's my mother's and her mother's and father's and their mother's and father's hell.'* (p. 347)

And there are other reasons for special interest in Henry and Bon. Bon and Henry meet each other at college, one is to the other something of a foreigner, and, of course, in a simple way one might view Quentin and Shreve as two boys in a college dormitory talking about love, "creating between them, out of the rag-tag and bob-ends of old tales and talking, people who perhaps had never existed at all anywhere" (p. 303).

But the focus of Quentin's interest is upon the reason why Henry killed Bon. Just before the setting of the novel's present-tense action shifts to the room at Harvard where Shreve and Quentin take up the narration, we are told that Quentin stops listening to Rosa's long, self-justifying monologue:

> But Quentin was not listening, because there was also something which he too could not pass—that door, the running feet on the stairs beyond it almost a continuation of the faint shot, the two women, the negress and the white girl in her underthings . . . pausing, looking at the door, . . . as the door crashed in and the brother stood there, hatless, with his shaggy bayonet-trimmed hair, his gaunt worn unshaven face, his patched and faded gray tunic, the pistol still hanging against his flank: the two of them, brother and sister, . . . speaking to one another in short brief staccato sentences like slaps, as if they stood breast

to breast striking one another in turn neither making any
attempt to guard against the blows.

Now you cant marry him.
Why cant I marry him?
Because he's dead.
Dead?
Yes. I killed him.

He (Quentin) couldn't pass that. (p. 172)

Until he can "pass that door," that is, establish the motive for
Henry's murder of Bon, Quentin cannot answer the more basic
question of why Sutpen's design failed. In the last four chapters, Quentin and Shreve piece "the rag-tag and bob-ends of old
tales and talking" together with Quentin's personal experience.

Quentin's final solution to the mystery comes by an intuitive
inference of what "must have been." Rosa and Shreve prepare
us for his dependence upon such an inference. Rosa speaks of
"a might-have-been which is more true than truth" (p. 143),
"that might-have-been which is the single rock we cling to
above the maelstrom of unbearable reality" (pp. 149–50).
Shreve, in a characteristic variation of Rosa's words, changes
the "might-have-been" to "just have to be": "there are some
things that just have to be whether they are or not, have to be
a damn sight more than some other things that maybe are and
it dont matter a damn whether they are or not" (p. 322). Rosa
and Shreve state what in effect is the burden of the uncertain
private reality Quentin creates with his solution to the mystery
of why Henry murdered Bon and why Bon forced him to do it,
for the solution embodies not only his judgment upon Sutpen
and the tradition but also implicitly a more fundamental judgment about the nature of human experience in reality.

Prior to Quentin's solution, the explanation of the mystery
passes through two stages, each explanation assuming a vague
incestuous love in Henry for his sister. At first, Mr. Compson
assigns the source of the trouble to Bon's legal (though not
binding) marriage ceremony with his octoroon mistress. He
accounts for the ceremony's importance by an emotionally credible hypothesis about Henry's provincial Puritanism and by pro-
jecting onto Bon's character his own sybaritic tastes and indifferent fatalism. He admits, however, that his solution is "just
incredible. It just does not explain" (p. 100). Miss Rosa never

learns the second explanation, namely that Sutpen told Henry that Bon is his half brother.

The final solution, Quentin's own, is prepared for but not unambiguously revealed at the time of his September evening journey with Rosa. Neither his grandfather nor his father had known what Sutpen meant by that "factor" which caused him to put his first wife aside. "And when your old man told it to you, you wouldn't have known what anybody was talking about if you hadn't been out there and seen Clytie. Is that right?" (p. 274) asks Shreve. Quentin confirms his statement. Later, Shreve continues to talk about what Quentin learned from seeing Clytie:

> And she [Clytie] didn't tell you in so many words because she was still keeping that secret . . . she didn't tell you, it just came out of the terror and the fear . . . and she looked at you and you saw it was not rage but terror, and not nigger terror because it was not about herself but was about whatever it was that was upstairs, that she had kept hidden up there for almost four years; and she didn't tell you in the actual words because even in the terror she kept the secret; nevertheless she told you, or at least all of a sudden you knew— (pp. 350–51)

The question becomes, then, what did Quentin learn "all of a sudden" from the terror in Clytie's face? The passage indicates that he learned "about whatever it was that was upstairs." However, following this passage comes an account of what Quentin and Shreve imagine to be a scene, set in Carolina in 1865, in which Sutpen reveals to Henry at last that Bon has Negro blood. This is the first time that the fact is plainly given anywhere in the book. One would think that something in his encounter with Henry led Quentin to this conclusion; yet when the scene in which Quentin discovers Henry in the upstairs room is presented (following the imagining of the Carolina scene), there is no hint that Quentin finds out anything other than that it is Henry, that he has been in Sutpen's decayed mansion for four years, and that he has come home to die.

Now, perhaps by the ranging of these scenes in the above order Faulkner expects the reader to surmise that something in Clytie's terror or in Henry's face informs Quentin that Henry shot Bon because of the threat of miscegenation. If this is the case, Faulkner is requiring that the reader make the same incredible effort of imagination that Quentin would have to make, and then he undercuts both Quentin and the reader by giving the interpretation no foundation in objective fact. Or perhaps Faulkner simply withholds the full scene from the reader. If this is the case, one can charge Faulkner with bad writing, with pointless mystification; this means, in effect, that he has accidentally or deliberately scuttled the whole novel. But we need make such a charge only if in a total reading of the novel we fail to find another and more functional reason.

One credible explanation is that Quentin's solution to the central mystery is in the present tense, that the imagining of the scene in Carolina in 1865 occurs for the first time in the present-tense scene with Shreve, just as the imagining of the rest of the story about Henry and Bon in Chapters VIII and IX occurs at Harvard with Shreve. Some features of the scene could have been imagined at no other time than the present tense. For example, Sutpen remarks to Henry that he had heard of his being wounded at the battle of Shiloh (p. 353). That it was Henry who was wounded rather than Bon is a "fact" created for the first time by Shreve only a few pages earlier (p. 344).

A correlate of this conclusion is that in the September, 1909, scene we are given the entire dramatic exchange between Quentin and Henry, and the scene functions chiefly as a way of removing the whole Sutpen saga from the realm of an old ghost tale. "This meeting," as Hyatt Waggoner says, "was a confrontation with a flesh-and-blood ghost. Here is proof that the past is 'real.' "[9] Quentin finally "passes that door": Henry is real to Quentin for the first time; the past is now a twentieth-century, contemporary, present-tense reality. This must be what Harvey Breit means in his introduction to the Modern Library edition of *Absalom, Absalom!* when he writes that Quentin "is made by Faulkner to be an embodiment of the presentness of the past" (p. vii). Faulkner makes him thus by letting him encounter Henry in the flesh. In a sense, two revelations of the fact of Bon's Negro blood occur, the first in the story told, the second in the telling of it. But only when the second revelation occurs does the imagining of the first take place; thus, in another sense there is only one revelation, and when it occurs, the whole story falls into place for Quentin and for the reader both in "fact" and in meaning.

There is some evidence, however, that Quentin has already discovered the solution—from his grandfather or when he saw Henry—by the time he talks with Shreve. He tells Shreve that his grandfather did not know "what second choice he [Sutpen] was faced with until the very last word he spoke before he got up" (p. 272). Further, Shreve refers to what Quentin learned from Clytie as giving Quentin understanding of what both Mr. Compson and General Compson were talking about (p. 274). Finally, the movement of the story Shreve is building up around Henry and Bon requires that it reach a climax in the revelation of Bon's Negro blood. In whatever way one interprets the evidence, the reality of the past becomes present reality to Quentin when he meets Henry. The Carolina scene, if it is not imagined for the first time in Harvard, is imagined there with such force (partly because of its placement in the novel) that Quentin does not doubt that it is true "a damn sight more than some other things that maybe are and it dont matter a damn whether they are or not."

By an act of the imagination, Quentin thus solves the mystery of why Sutpen's design fails. The character of his solution is important because it embodies a view of the past which leaves him in despair over the possibility of meaning in the present. His sensibility in this novel has the same limitations it had in *The Sound and the Fury*. Neither Sutpen (modern man) nor the tradition (Stoic man) did in fact envision a world which is meaningful in the only way he is capable of admitting it can be meaningful. This judgment remains implied rather than explicit, however, because although he can isolate intellectually the formal element which led to the destruction of both Sutpen and the tradition, his assessment of it is only emotional.

Quentin sees that Sutpen's story and the tradition judge each other. Each fails in the same respect although not for the same reason. The tradition, finding Sutpen lacking in "humanity," can explain his failure in the general terms of retributive justice. Sutpen's innocence precludes his success because it means that he is ignorant of the nature of things and especially of the fact of evil. But the tradition also fails of the same humanity. Quentin shows how Sutpen's design was born at the moment when, in the person of the Tidewater plantation owner's Negro agent, the tradition showed an image of itself divested of its humanity, an image of naked economic power. Sutpen tells

General Compson that at the moment of his shock before the plantation's "white door" (p. 232) he suddenly recognized things he had forgotten he had even remembered. A part of him seemed to "turn and rush back through the two years they had lived there . . . seeing a dozen things that had happened and he hadn't even seen them before" (pp. 229–30).

What he saw was images of himself, his sisters, and his father in attitudes of outrageous frustration, victims and agents in a dehumanizing situation they could not even describe or understand. He remembered the "flat level silent way his older sisters . . . had of looking at niggers, not with fear or dread but with a kind of speculative antagonism not because of any known fact or reason but inherited, by both white and black" (p. 230). He thought of evening scenes at the fireside, the women's voices "calm, yet filled with a quality dark and sullen" and one of the men breaking "out into harsh recapitulation of his own worth," both men and women "talking about the same thing though it had never once been mentioned by name, as when people talk about . . . sickness without ever naming the epidemic" (pp. 230–31). He recalled throwing clods of dirt after a retreating carriage which forced him off the road, the Negro coachman shouting to his sister, who had refused to budge from the road, "the two faces beneath the parasols glaring down at his sister," and he knew "it had not been the nigger coachman that he threw at at all" (p. 231). And finally:

> He thought of one night late when his father came home, blundered into the cabin; he could smell the whiskey even while still dulled with broken sleep, hearing that same fierce exultation, vindication, in his father's voice: 'We whupped one of Pettibone's niggers tonight' and he roused at that, waked at that, asking which one of Pettibone's niggers and his father said he did not know, had never seen the nigger before: and he asked what the nigger had done and his father said, 'Hell fire, that goddam son of a bitch Pettibone's nigger.' He must have meant the question the same way his father meant the answer. (p. 231)

These are images of the ultimate degradation of the human spirit, where Negro and white are set against each other by a system each fears and is corrupted to support. Sutpen knows in each case that "they (the niggers) were not it, not what you wanted to hit" (p. 230). Nor would killing the plantation owner restore his shattered spirit. *"But I can shoot him,"* he argues to himself, "Not the monkey nigger. It was not the nigger anymore than it had been the nigger that his father had helped to whip that night" (p. 234). The monkey-dressed Negro at the door, Quentin conjectures, was a city-born, house-bred servant, and as such was the hothouse fruit of the aristo-crat's withdrawal from the land to the ballroom. The plantation owner did not plant or harvest, but "spent most of the after-noon . . . in a barrel stave hammock between two trees, with his shoes off" (pp. 227–28) and with "a special nigger to hand him his liquor and pull off his shoes that he didn't even need to wear" (p. 229). Nor did the white superintendents work the soil, but watched the Negroes plant and harvest.

Sutpen's own career shows something of the plantation society's devolution from the source of its vitality. At the period of his life when he is most vital, he is stripped to the waist, laboring with his twenty wild West Indies Negroes to raise his mansion from the primordial mud. He catches them at the right moment by gesture or example to gain their maximum effort. When he attains his immediate ends—land, a big house, slaves, an upright wife, a son—his life reaches a plateau where he acts out a role of arrogant leisure and ostentation but with-out grace or heart. Of course, all along his vision and ambition is to achieve the status which represents a corruption of the traditional ideal. His most serious "mistakes" arise from the abstract character of his conception of what his design should involve. For example, his conviction that his daughter's mar-riage must be one free of Negro blood shows that his under-standing of the tradition is purely rationalistic, since the traditional mores demanded only that the male line remain "untainted." But for all his outward similarity to the corrupt aristocrat, he remains essentially different because of his inno-cence. His is the innocence of any materialist from Quentin's brother Jason to Flem Snopes who tries to solve or bypass the problem of evil with will and reason devoid of love. Sutpen's failure is crucial to Quentin partly because it is the character-istic failure of modern man.

Where the tradition actually exhibited the humanity for which it stood, its Stoic strategy for investing experience with meaning was successful. But it did not sustain its own moral vision because it could not; it became, in effect though not in essence, what Sutpen never ceased to be. The tradition lost its wisdom, whereas Sutpen simply kept his innocence. Looked at in one way, the tradition's failure was the more serious, for the tradition could not plead ignorance. It failed on its own moral terms. The question posed by Quentin's reconstructed history is why Sutpen and the tradition fail in the humanity they need. Quentin despairs of an answer, despairs of man, despairs of himself. This question is answered by a sensibility that is not Quentin's, by a vision which sees what he sees but in the context of a reality allowing one to see more than he sees, by an aesthetic organization that is Faulkner's and of which the despairing Quentin is only an element.

Although he works under the limitations of Quentin's sensibility, in contrast to his strategy in *The Sound and the Fury,* Faulkner does not leave his own position ambiguous. He does not speak in his own voice, but, like Quentin's, his position is implied by the way the tale is told. Specifically, he presents Quentin despairing over the implications of Sutpen's and the tradition's failures but allows, in the process, an alternative to Quentin's despair to emerge from Quentin's telling of the tale, an alternative of which Quentin, because of his limitations, is not aware. Through the entire performance of the novel, Faulkner implicitly judges from what must be called a Christian humanist point of view that both Sutpen and the tradition fail because they wrongly assess the nature of reality and especially the nature of man.

In a word, they fail to recognize the "strange work" of love, as Luther called it. Paul Tillich's clarification of this notion can help us to understand the thrust of the novel's judgment:

> The tension between love and justice refers basically to salvation. . . . Love destroys, as its strange work, what is against love. . . . Love, at the same time, as its own work, saves through forgiveness that which is against love. . . . How can these two works of love be one? They are one because love does not enforce salvation. . . . Love must destroy what is against love, but not him who is the bearer of that which is against love. For as a creature, he remains a power of being or a creation of love. But the unity of

his will is destroyed, he is thrown into a conflict with himself, the name of which is despair, mythologically speaking,
hell. Dante was right when he called even Hell a creation
of the divine love. The hell of despair is the strange work
that love does within us in order to open us up for its own
work, justification of him who is unjust.[10]

Quentin is too limited and too close to the process Tillich
describes to understand it. He shows awareness that the tradition and Sutpen fail because of something neither of them can
explain, and in his dramatic reconstruction of Sutpen's story
he provides evidence for what it is: the strange work of love.
It is not too much to claim, I think, that this is a novel about
love, just as *The Sound and the Fury* is about love. Even Quentin and Shreve sense that all of their talking and thinking previous to the Henry-Bon-Judith affair was "just so much that
had to be overpassed . . . in order to overpass to love, where
there might be paradox and inconsistency but nothing fault
nor false" (p. 316). The novel is about love in a sense wider
than theirs and close to Tillich's, who states in theological
terms what Faulkner achieves in aesthetic mode.

The Christian humanist point of view from which Faulkner
judges owes a great deal to the South's Stoic vision. The tradition is no straw man for Faulkner: it represents a signal
achievement. Images of rational man willing his destiny, of
finite man affirming himself in the face of fate and death, are
both attractive and powerful. Words such as honor and pride
and courage are not hollow and "obscene" as they were for the
young Hemingway of *A Farewell to Arms;* they refer to human
virtues worth achieving. But Faulkner also shows the tradition's limitations. Though it was concerned with justice and
its attendant virtues, it does not appear in Faulkner's picture
to have concerned itself with the virtues of love. It could not
have done so without abandoning its own vision, for then it
would have admitted that tension to which Tillich refers as
leading to the Christian notion of salvation. In other words, the
tradition was Stoic rather than Christian. Salvation (and, consequently, love) is the answer to the problem of sin rather than
of ignorance. The notion of sin implies that man is estranged,
because of his own guilt, from his essential (rational) nature,
that his reason and will cannot rescue him because they *are* his

problem. The traditional and Stoic doctrine of man calls for knowledge rather than love. If there is any salvation needed, it is not rescue from sin by the justification brought by love, but resolution of ignorance by the knowledge brought by the exercise of will and reason. Man's problem is finitude, not guilt, and when things go wrong the responsibility is fate's and not man's. The notion of love completely undercuts Stoic tranquility because love cannot be rationally calculated, measured, and controlled.

The tradition fails because its moral vision substituted duty for love, or, put another way, its humanity was only rational and therefore incomplete rather than fully human and therefore rational and complete. One must be careful not to make a simple pietistic judgment here. The tradition aimed high, but it was doomed in Faulkner's sense of the word: its inner nature generated an outward manifestation which in turn destroyed it; sooner or later it had to reap the consequence of the deficiency of its moral vision.

When Quentin shows Henry killing Bon because of miscegenation, he gives dramatic embodiment to the tradition's moral deficiency. The deficiency was not slavery but, negatively, lack of love, or, positively, spiritual pride; slavery was merely the accidental, historical form in which the deficiency expressed itself. There were other forms of its expression: for example, the social order which made the landless whites into objects—things—not free, responsible, deciding persons, but

> cattle, creatures heavy and without grace, brutely evacuated into a world without hope or purpose for them, who would in turn spawn with brutish and vicious prolixity, populate, double treble and compound, fill space and earth with a race whose future would be a succession of cut-down and patched and made-over garments bought on exorbitant credit because they were white people, from stores where niggers were given the garments free. (p. 235)

Quentin reports this as his grandfather's surmise of Sutpen's discovery as he tried to think through what to do about the affront at the plantation door. The deficiency also expressed itself in the military organization:

> battles lost not alone because of superior numbers and

failing ammunition and stores, but because of generals
who should not have been generals, who were generals not
through training in contemporary methods or aptitude for
learning them, but by the divine right to say 'Go there'
conferred upon them by an absolute caste system; or
because the generals of it . . . on one night and wit! a
handful of men would gallantly set fire to and destroy a
million dollar garrison of enemy supplies and on the next
night be discovered by a neighbor in bed with his wife and
be shot to death. (pp. 345–46)

Wash Jones's story is another case in point. Jones placed
ultimate confidence in Sutpen's moral character: "Because you
are brave," he says to Sutpen. "And I know that whatever your
hands tech, whether hit's a regiment of men or a ignorant gal
or just a hound dog, that you will make hit right" (p. 284).
Sutpen's inhuman pragmatism at last becomes clear to him
when he hears Sutpen dealing with his granddaughter as if she
were less a person even than his animal: "Well, Milly; too bad
you're not a mare too. Then I could give you a decent stall in
the stable" (p. 286). At that moment, Wash too finds reality
incredible and like Ellen succumbs to the shock of reality entering his life. *"I kaint have heard what I know I heard. I just
know I kaint"* (p. 288). And later: *"Better if his kind and mine
too had never drawn the breath of life on this earth. Better that
all who remain of us be blasted from the face of it than that
another Wash Jones should see his whole life shredded from
him and shrivel away like a dried shuck thrown onto the fire"*
(pp. 290–91). Wash feels "no earth, no stability" (p. 288) in
a land where such men "set the order and the rule of living . . .
[and] for the first time in his life he began to comprehend
how it had been possible for Yankees or any other army to have
whipped them" (p. 290).

Such a society is doomed from within. In Rosa's sense, the
South was "a land primed for fatality and already cursed with
it" (p. 21) not only because in the nature of things there is that
principle by which love must destroy what is against it, but also
because of the fate within evil itself. That the evil results from
a deficiency rather than from sin is a Stoic and not a Christian
judgment. "Deficiency" for the Christian is too weak a word. It
is not a defect or a lack that is responsible for evil, not a weak-

ness of man's nature, but man himself, all of himself. Quentin is correct in seeing that Sutpen and the tradition judge each other. But Faulkner sees that the tradition failed itself, its own aims and virtues, because it wrongly assessed the nature of man, seeing only defect where there was actually sin. From within the Stoic tradition, it is correct to say that the curse of slavery destroys the society. (To the true Stoic, of course, slavery was always somewhat embarrassing, for it contradicts the Stoic doctrine of the divine spark.) From without the Stoic tradition, however—that is, from the Christian point of view— the judgment that slavery destroys the society is superficial. Man destroys the society because of his sin. Specifically, the sin emerges historically and concretely as slavery.

Absalom, Absalom! shows that Allen Tate is both wrong and right when he says that "it was not that slavery was corrupt 'morally.' Societies can bear an amazing amount of corruption and still produce high cultures. Black slavery could not nurture the white man in his own image."[11] Tate points, in this fashion, to the historical and social means by which the society's destruction was accomplished. In another place, he makes it more explicit: "the Negro slave was a barrier between the ruling class and the soil" (p. 272). Faulkner goes beyond Tate to show an intimate connection between the moral corruption and the alienation of the ruling class from the source of its values. In Reinhold Niebuhr's terms, a deep irony arising from a Christian realism is involved, a strength becoming weakness because of vanity prompted by the strength, virtue becoming vice "through some hidden defect in the virtue," catastrophe arising from "an unconscious weakness rather than . . . a conscious resolution."[12] Quentin's account, taken from his grandfather, provides ample evidence of how the white man is cut off from the source of his values.

When we turn to the way in which love accomplishes the destruction of what is against it in Sutpen's history, as compared with the tradition's, we find the same forces at work but against a lack of humanity in a distinctly modern sense. The tradition's human failure is, in a way, more easily dealt with in Christian terms because the Stoic society at least recognized that life is not unambiguously good, while Sutpen is "innocent" of the distinction between good and evil.

In the persons of Judith, Henry, and Bon, love works in a positive way to destroy Sutpen's design. Their love for each other only partially yields to his attempt to calculate, measure, and manipulate it because each of them finally forgives. A good case for calling Judith's action a renunciation and an expiation of her father's design is made by Cleanth Brooks, who sees the crucial difference between Judith and her father to lie in the fact that Judith is a woman who has a capacity to love. No wonder, then, that Mr. Compson can explain her only by reference to a "true pride which can say to itself without abasement *I love, I will accept no substitute; something has happened between him and my father; if my father was right, I will never see him again, if wrong he will come or send for me; if happy I can be I will, if suffer I must I can*" (*Absalom, Absalom!*, p. 121). Brooks goes on to point out that after Bon's death, and Sutpen's, it is Judith who makes "the acknowledgment of blood kinship" with Bon and his descendants. Thereby "Sutpen's 'design' is repudiated; the boy, even though he has the 'taint' of Negro blood, is not turned away from the door."[13]

Mr. Compson observes that Henry's love for Judith when compounded with his traditional upbringing puts him in a situation where he must make a tragic choice between sister and brother. "He felt, and acted immediately. He knew loyalty and acted it, he knew pride and jealousy; he loved grieved and killed, still grieving and, I believe, still loving Bon" (*Absalom, Absalom!*, pp. 96–97). Of course, Mr. Compson says this in ignorance of Henry's real motive, but his words remain true to the spirit of Quentin's recreation of Henry's tragedy. Sutpen had correctly calculated Henry's traditional response, but even he knew that the playing of his "last trump card" (p. 274) would destroy his design and mean that he would have to begin a third time. Henry's choice was tragic, I should add, only within the situation as he perceived it. Henry did not rise above the tradition as did Judith, but Clytie claims forty-five years later that "whatever he done, me and Judith and him have paid it out" (p. 370).

Quentin and Shreve see Bon as sharing something of his father's calculating, positivist spirit, for Bon manipulates Henry and Judith to force Sutpen's recognition. His need in this instance is essentially the one Sutpen experienced as a child—to be treated as a person and not a thing—and he tries, like his father, to fulfill it by treating others as he has been treated. Yet Quentin and Shreve also make a clear case for Bon's capacity to love. They "correct" Mr. Compson's version of the withdrawal to Pittsburgh Landing at the battle of Shiloh. It is Bon who rescues the wounded Henry. And when Henry comes to Bon after his interview with Sutpen, in Carolina in 1865, Bon's first act, a fully compassionate one, is to put his cloak about Henry's shoulders. But the greatest act of love is in the matter of the octoroon's photograph found by Judith on Bon's body:

> And your old man wouldn't know about that too: why the black son of a bitch should have taken her picture out and put the octoroon's picture in, so he invented a reason for it. But I know. And you know too. Dont you? Dont you, huh? . . . It was because he said to himself, 'If Henry dont mean what he said, it will be all right; I can take it out and destroy it. But if he does mean what he said, it will be the only way I will have to say to her, *I was no good; do not grieve for me.*' Aint that right? Aint it? By God, aint it? (pp. 358-59)

In a negative way, love also works to destroy Sutpen's design. Because he lacks the full humanity with which love could endow him, his own calculating efforts are in vain. Quentin and Shreve believe that one simple act of recognition from Sutpen toward Bon would have saved his whole design:

> —*And he sent me no word? He did not ask you to send me to him? No word to me, no word at all? That was all he had to do, now, today; four years ago or at any time during the four years. That was all. He would not have needed to ask it, require it, of me. I would have offered it. I would have said, I will never see her again before he could have asked it of me. He did not have to do this, Henry. He didn't need to tell you I am a nigger to stop me. He could have stopped me without that, Henry.* (p. 356)

And Sutpen himself is finally cut down when Jones attempts to teach him what he was incapable of learning even from time itself. Quentin thinks at first that the *"clock and calendar"* (p. 181) must have taught him at last, but then visualizes eternity with Sutpen asking Jones, *"What was it, Wash? Something happened. What was it?"* (p. 186). Love cannot force salvation.

When Quentin settles upon the blood conflict between races as the key to Sutpen's failure, he also isolates the historical and formal element in the tradition which leads to its destruction. The novel gives us no reason to think that he has seen clearly into the heart of the tradition's vision of reality, the vision which generated its formal embodiments in social behavior and organization, or even that he understands fully the implications of Sutpen's innocence. But it does show his violent response to the failures of both traditional and modern men. One can compare his reaction with a reader's response to a poetic image. The power of the image does not depend upon the reader's cognitive understanding of the idea the image enacts. Nor does the creator of a powerful image need intellectual control of the idea. At the beginning of Chapter VI, we learn that all of *Absalom, Absalom!* is Quentin's answer to the demand that he *"tell about the South. What's it like there. What do they do there. Why do they live there. Why do they live at all"* (p. 174). Quentin answers with the image of Sutpen and becomes caught up in his own image-making. In other words, Quentin evaluates the failures of traditional and modern men emotionally rather than intellectually. "Nevermore of peace" is the despairing summary of his search.

In the meantime, however, he has provided evidence both in the tale he tells and in the telling of it which is evaluated by Faulkner's aesthetic organization. It has been my thesis that the final view of reality emerging from the novel is not simply Quentin's or Sutpen's or the tradition's, but that it is the larger reality in the context of which the other realities emerge as dramatically credible. The context of the backstage action, I have said, is Quentin. But the final reality is the Christian one posited by a reading of the novel as a whole work of art, and it can be taken to be, if not Faulkner's own, at least the one to which he has in this novel given the broadest aesthetic embodiment and in terms of which he has made his most general judgment.

Absalom, Absalom! marks a shift in Faulkner's theological and fictive strategies. In *The Sound and the Fury* the Christian vision is juxtaposed with a modern one. Dilsey and Benjy stand over against Jason and Quentin. The tradition is treated only indirectly—as it emerges, that is, in Quentin's effete intellect—and the Christian vision is given embodiment in a fully developed character. Faulkner does not choose between his two main themes. In *Absalom, Absalom!* Faulkner goes behind Quentin, by going through him, to the tradition itself and also to the springs of the modern sensibility. He evaluates both not by embodying their Christian alternative in a main character but by setting them against each other in a Christian context which is wider than either.

In this novel, Faulkner is at once clearer about the content of the tradition, harder upon it, and less willing to sell it short by letting it be presented only in its decadent phase. He brings the Christian and Stoic alternatives together, tips the theological balance in favor of the Christian, but does not break their essential tension. The novel represents a movement but not a basic change within his theological center. The movement is subtle, though not as cautious as in "The Bear." The novel ends with an image of the despairing Quentin, still a "commonwealth" racked with disease and lying impotent in the grip of an inherited evil which overwhelms him. But Faulkner's Christian critique of the modern and traditional visions owes much to the Stoic. The tradition is judged but not rejected; its human virtues are still virtues but are to be attained in love rather than in spiritual pride. An essentially different spirit than the Stoic one is necessary even to attain the Stoic virtues. The novel shows Faulkner still engaged in the theological enterprise of defining the nature of reality by an aesthetic testing of the facts of experience.

Commentary ▬▬

Even to the veteran reader of Faulkner it may come as something of a shock to hear it claimed that what Faulkner is really getting at—in the midst of predestination, corruption, greed, and lust—is love. And yet it seems true enough that one must distinguish in Faulkner between what he says the situation *is* and what he says it *ought* to be. Faulkner is often, at least implicitly, considering an ideal of love. Occasionally this ideal is "incarnated" in a specific character, like Dilsey or Lena Grove. More often, as in *Absalom, Absalom!*, it is not clearly typified in a single character but is implicit in the judgments Faulkner makes about those who fail to achieve it. In *Absalom, Absalom!*, as Hunt argues very tellingly, this ideal of love is implicit in the judgment of the two failures which are delineated, that of the traditional man whom Sutpen vainly tries to emulate and that of the modern man whom he truly represents. Love is presented positively and "head-on" in *Absalom, Absalom!* not in a fully developed character but in those who are (though essential to the action) somewhat on the fringes of the story—Judith, Henry, and Charles—and there only in hints and fragmentary glimpses.

It may be that Faulkner is in this matter typical, rather than otherwise, of much of modern literature. In an age when conflict and war and alienation have come so much to the fore, perhaps an ideal of love can be forcefully portrayed only by indirection: in its failures, and in momentary and passing glimpses. One thinks, for example, of T. S. Eliot—not only the Eliot of *The Waste Land* but also the Eliot of the *Four Quartets*—or of D. H. Lawrence or Graham Greene. And yet it remains no less an ideal.

We have referred already (in Chapter 5) to Lennart Björk's essay on the "moral framework" of *Absalom, Absalom!*, and it may be helpful to recall it in the context of the present chapter. His high-lighting of the attitudes of the Old Testament and of Greek tragedy in the novel ought perhaps to be added to the complexity of the "theological tension" enunciated in the preceding essay. In view of the fact that Faulkner deliberately uses as rough paradigms of Sutpen's tragedy the tragedy of Agamemnon and the story of David's sons Absalom and Amnon, it seems legitimate to suggest that at least some of the "Stoic" elements—courage, endurance, uncoercible fate—have their roots equally deep in the ground of Aeschylus and of the Old Testament.

This is not to say that Faulkner uses every element of each of these stories. Obviously he does not. They are in fact far apart in certain of their attitudes: the curse on David's house is as little to be equated with the sense of doom in Aeschylus' play as is Yahweh of the Old Testament to be equated with the impersonal Fate judging and condemning Agamemnon. What Faulkner has done is not to create identical situations, but to use these different traditions to create a broader context for moral judgment. By writing not only within a Christian tradition but within the Hebrew and Greek traditions as well, he has gained, as Lennart Björk suggests in the essay we have cited, "a widely embracing referendum for moral behavior" (p. 202). By bringing into his tragic vision, Björk continues, "the different values, old and modern, of Western civilization, Faulkner enables the readers to estimate the hero from different points of view." Men like Sutpen are condemned in terms of any moral code: "David was punished within the Hebrew culture; Agamemnon within the Greek. The Christian culture, in many ways an assimilation of the two preceding ones, effected the punishment of Sutpen" (p. 203).

With this last sentence we are brought sharply back to one of the central implications of Hunt's essay: Sutpen, as an "innocent"— amoral, ignorant of the real "nature of things"—cannot be punished. One can judge his vision of things to be deficient, but since he is amoral, one cannot pass a moral judgment on his actions. He is beyond good and evil.

But perhaps the two views are not, in the last analysis, incompatible. There is moral judgment implicit in the novel, but it is a judgment of the attitudes—that of the tradition and that of modern man—not of the individuals. Sutpen cannot be condemned, because he "knew not what he did," because he had no moral vision. The Southern "tradition," however, and the moral failure of modern man *can* be judged; and those who embrace them knowingly— knowing good from evil—must be condemned.

10 ≣≣≣

The essentially simple story line and the evident and explicit elements of Christian allegory in "The Bear" are often a trap for the unwary. The story may not be quite as straightforward as it seems and the allegory may turn out to be symbol or myth. The following essay by Herbert A. Perluck contends that its often-ignored irony of tone and attitude militate against the more common "romantic" reading of the story. He explains what he means by this "romantic" reading, and how it differs from his own.

Perluck's essay first appeared in *Accent*, XX (1960), pp. 23–46, and is here used with permission.

Herbert A. Perluck

"THE BEAR": AN UNROMANTIC READING

THE USUAL READING OF "THE BEAR" MAKES OF ISAAC Mc-
Caslin a kind of saint who, by repudiating his inheritance—the
desecrated land upon which a whole people has been violated—
performs an act of expiation and atonement which is a model
for those acts that must follow before the curse upon the land
is lifted. Ike's repudiation of the land, at twenty-one, with
which the tortuous inner section of "The Bear" opens, and over
which he and his cousin, McCaslin Edmonds, debate in the
commissary, is seen in terms of what the reader understands
Ike to have learned and attained under the influence of Sam
Fathers in the untainted Wilderness: the "freedom and humility and pride." The story is of one man's repudiation of the
forces of greed and materialism that have all but extinguished
God's hope for man of freedom and generosity.

The whole sequence of the commissary, the Beauchamp
legacy, and the later life of Isaac McCaslin, is thus ordinarily
taken as a sort of complementary sequel to what may be called
the hunt-narrative; Part IV in the total structure and intention
of the work is a filling-out, past and future, of the "story
proper," as it is sometimes regarded: the hunt-narrative and
especially the episode of the fyce, in which the later renunciation, at twenty-one, is prefigured.

There is much, however, in this difficult portion of the work
that suggests a contrary view. Instead of a romantic Christian
pastoral of redemption, in which the repudiation of the land
and earlier the apparently selfless rescue of the fyce from under
the erect bear are seen as almost sanctifying gestures of renunciation, a searing tragedy of human desire and human limita-
tion evolves, chiefly through ironic means. From McCaslin's

173

scornful skepticism as he listens to Ike's account of God's cir-
cuitous providence, and the "lip-lift"[1] of contempt when he
realizes that even Ike does not wholly believe in his "freedom,"
to the almost hysterical laughter with which Part IV concludes,
the principal effects are ironic.

The central thematic irony, however, upon which these
effects are grounded, is slowly constructed of larger elements.
The repudiation in the commissary *is* prefigured in the hunt-
narrative; something of a parallel does develop between the
selfless non-possession of Ike's gesture at twenty-one and the
repudiation of passion earlier—that effort to preserve the idyll
of the Big Woods, in the reluctance of both Ike and Sam
Fathers to slay Old Ben. But the point of the parallel is not
merely to provide background and extension to the "story-
proper"; it is drawn and pressed home by McCaslin Edmonds
on Ike because in both gestures there is weakness and something even sinister which cannot become clear to McCaslin,
or to the reader, until the dense and complex drama of the
debate in the commissary is enacted.

The terrible irony of Part IV develops in the growing awareness in the reader, as well as in the characters, of the discrepancy between what we and Ike supposed him to have achieved,
to have attained to, and what in fact his repudiations actually
represent. The whole inner section of "The Bear" reflects back
on the hunt-narrative and forward into the last sequence: Ike's
return at eighteen to the woods, which are being destroyed by
the lumber company; his vague, troubled guilt at the sight of the
nearly demented, grieving Boon. Coming where it does in
the story structure, Part IV has the effect of making the reader,
as it makes Ike and McCaslin, remember and painfully reinter-
pret the earlier events as of some dream-idyll of human perfection, of perhaps a kind of angelic pre-existence, now dissipated
in the wakeful glare of the human reality. Slowly and relentlessly, Faulkner's intention takes hold in Part IV, in the tragic
incompleteness of man, as the gulf is drawn between action, life
as lived, and the memory of action and events, in which our
dreams of life, our poems, are created.

"The Bear" is no Saint's Life; on the contrary, what it
expresses ultimately is that there is no "freedom" in renunciation, no sanctity through repudiation—that actually there is no
such thing as human sainthood as we have conceived it. If
Isaac McCaslin is a saint at all, it is not in the traditional

ascetic sense of a successful renunciation of the world and the flesh in atonement and expiation; it is rather a "sainthood" of *un*success, an unwitting, unwilled elevation produced in the tragic *defeat* of spirit and soul in the "uncontrollable mystery" of the world which men and "saints" must live in perforce. In much the same way that Kafka's Bucketrider is unaccountably (to him) "upraised" into the "regions of the icy mountains and [is] lost forever," Isaac McCaslin ascends without comprehending wherein that only "sainthood" man is allowed resides: in the anguished, complex heart. "The Bear" is a story of a renunciation that fails, as they all must. It is also the story of man's ineluctable fate of being only man. And on another level, it is a parable of man's pride, in his trying to be more than man, and of the evil this pride accomplishes in its condescending ascription of all that man does not want to see in himself to a certain few untouchables, the Boons of the world.

Let us begin with the passage in Part IV, which may be called the Ode sequence, where Ike and his cousin McCaslin are suddenly brought back to an incident that had taken place seven years before this moment in the commissary, because it is the interpretative heart of the story. In the debate, or dialogue, between Ike and McCaslin, the former has been trying all along to explain God's ways of instrumenting his hope, which he knows is doomed to unfulfillment, that man will learn humility, will be redeemed, through suffering. To McCaslin's amazed and sardonic incredulity ("Turned back to us? His face to us?" [p. 285]), Ike has argued that God used the war as an instrument for bringing about the redemption of the South ("So he turned once more to this land which he still intended to save because he had done so much for it. . . ." [p. 285]). McCaslin remembers the bad luck of the South in the war, the mere chance, frequently, by which that gallant manhood was defeated by a really unimpassioned, materialistic, and somewhat effete North. "How else have made them fight? Who else but Jacksons and Stuarts and Ashbys and Morgans and Forrests?" Ike asks (p. 287). "Well, maybe that's what he wanted," McCaslin grudgingly admits. "At least that's what he got" (p. 289). And there is a pause as they consider silently the aftermath of the war, "that dark corrupt and bloody time" of Reconstruction (p. 289). And then McCaslin merely lifts his arm toward the desk in the commissary where the current ledger sits, "that dark chronicle which was a whole land in miniature, which multiplied and compounded was the entire South, twenty-three years after surrender and twenty-four from emancipation . . ." (p. 293). His gesture signifies, without words, his ironic commentary on the fruition of God's devious providence, as if he had said, Well, what good has it done, the war and the aftermath? They are still slaves!

Ike understands the gesture: "Yes. Binding them for a while yet, a little while yet." "But not always," he continues, "because they will endure. They will outlast us because they are . . . better than we are. Stronger than we are" (p. 294), he at last forces himself to admit, but only after momentarily hesitating to say that much, to admit what was heresy even to him in this very time and act of his repudiation, of his atonement. He recognizes in his faltering hesitancy that there is more in him of Grandfather, whom Ike is in a sense repudiating by giving up his inheritance—more in him of the general evil that his grandfather represents than he has wanted to acknowledge. He proceeds, shaken with this insight, not lost on McCaslin, to that provocative admission, around which the whole of Part IV, and the rest of the story, is constructed, that the Negro will endure and outlast the white man, because, inheriting freedom from the "old free fathers," he has been "a longer time free than us because"—and they stop at this, looking at each other, knowing that at last the important thing is about to be uttered— "we have never been free" (p. 295).

The convulsion of the spoken and the unspoken admissions leads directly, in the drama of the debate, to the Ode sequence. The dramatic explanation of how these are related—*why* they stop at this particular point in their discourse—concerns us now, and interpretation here illuminates much of the rest. Why should they halt, as if struck—especially McCaslin—and remember events and talk that had taken place so long before?

This time, instead of looking toward the shelf of ledgers, they look at each other, remembering the time seven years before, when Ike and Sam Fathers and a little nameless fyce ambushed Old Ben and could have killed him, but neither one did. There had been time to shoot before the heedless and blindly courageous dog went in at Old Ben; they were only twenty yards away, and couldn't have missed; but instead Ike dashed in under the bear to save the dog—or so at least he (and later, when Sam Fathers told him about it, his cousin McCaslin too) had understood it. "And you didn't shoot," McCaslin had said later when they discussed it together. "How close were you?"

> "I don't know," he said. "There was a big wood tick just
> inside his off hind leg. I saw that. But I didn't have the
> gun then."
> "But you didn't shoot when you had the gun," McCaslin
> said. "Why?" (p. 296)

His cousin had got up suddenly at this point, and crossing the
room, brought back a book, from which he read Ike the "Ode
on a Grecian Urn."

> "She cannot fade, though thou hast not thy bliss,"
> McCaslin said: "Forever wilt thou love, and she be fair."
> "He's talking about a girl," he said.
> "He had to talk about something," McCaslin said. Then
> he [McCaslin] said, "He was talking about truth. Truth is
> one. It doesn't change. It covers all things which touch
> the heart—honor and pride and pity and justice and cour-
> age and love. Do you see now?" (p. 297)

All this, and more, that they had then spoken and thought
passes through their minds, as they merely look at each other.
In this moment, the memory, never really far submerged, comes
flooding back: that time seven years before when McCaslin
tried to explain to Ike, by quoting the "Ode," why Ike saved
the fyce instead of killing Old Ben, or at least what McCaslin
had thought then—that the humility and pride Ike had wanted
to learn in order to become worthy of the Wilderness and of a
manhood in which the Bear was hunted by men like Sam
Fathers, Major de Spain, Walter Ewell, and McCaslin, that
these he had just learned, had come to possess, through forbearance and selfless courage, through, in short, a kind of renunciation, *non*possession. McCaslin's purpose in quoting Keats had
been to show Ike how we may pursue bravely and fiercely and
yet not kill, out of pity and love; how we may love by not loving; how we may be proud and humble, fierce and gentle, at
the same time; how by not possessing in the heart we may
possess all. The heart, which contains these beautiful para-
doxes, "knows" truth, the only truth worth knowing, the only
truth one needs to know. "Courage and honor and pride,"

McCaslin had repeated at the very end of the discussion, "and pity and love of justice and of liberty. They all touch the heart, and what the heart holds to becomes truth, as far as we know truth. Do you see now?" he had asked once more (p. 297).—But he didn't tell him, and probably didn't know it himself until much later, in the commissary with Ike, forced by his cousin's argument and repudiation of the land to defend his own entire existence, that this is only the heart's "truth," and is not all we need to know, that there is difference between knowing in the heart or in a poem and the imperfect knowing of life, between *any* sort of knowing and living.

"Because we have never been free," Ike has just hesitantly admitted, and they pause, looking at each other, both remembering, McCaslin, however, with something of bitterness and irony, with a "faint lip-lift which would have had to be called smiling" (p. 297). He "smiles" now because he understands that this present repudiation of the land is a repetition of the gesture made first seven years before, and that Ike himself, in despair, as the words he has such difficulty uttering fall between them in the commissary, knows it. He understands, as he hadn't before, that Ike's failure to kill Old Ben was a way out, an escape from himself; that Keats had only helped him to repudiate, and so think he had *freed* himself from, what being human and alive in time imposes on a man. McCaslin hadn't told him that what we may know in the heart is not what we are allowed to live. The non-possession, the renunciations, and thus the "freedom" which may be realized in the heart—this Ike has tried to *live*. "Sam Fathers set me free," he protests to McCaslin (p. 300). But the freedom he had indeed obtained was only the "freedom of the heart," which Sam Fathers showed him how to achieve by virtue of giving himself up to the Wilderness, as he does when he "relinquishes" his gun and compass and goes alone to see and be seen by Old Ben—much as Henry Fleming, in that other story of a boy's initiation into manhood, comes to touch the great god Death and discovers it is only death after all. He momentarily reliquishes self and pride, in effect—the way they are relinquished provisionally in a poem— the better to confront that naked red heart of the world, the Wilderness of the human heart, which is "free" only when it is so confronted and acknowledged. This "freedom" is from the blind, uncomprehending *fear* of the "Wilderness" and its creatures, but is not, as Ike would desire it—a confusion that leads

to his agony in the commissary—a freedom from the necessary
human commitment in acts and time. The moral freedom to
choose *not* to act does not exist, except in the heart, where it is
not a moral but a spiritual or aesthetic freedom. Sam Fathers
set Ike free only in the sense of his enabling him to look at *all*
that a man can feel and do, *all* that the "Wilderness" contains;
he could not free him from himself. So it was not the fyce that
had kept him from shooting—out of love and forbearance; he
had, in fact, blanched from that full sight of himself as a man,
who at the same time he was humble and loved the thing he
pursued, was a slayer and ravener.

The "poem," as it were, that Ike has tried to live is one
in which his hunting of Old Ben but his not having to kill
him is the chief symbol—as it is even now in the commissary.
And it *was* very much like the girl and the youth on the Urn,
although Ike had not quite been able to see the analogy. He
has wished, Hamlet-like, to kill and yet not kill, to realize fully
a state of "being" out of time, which is realized only in a play,
in art, and in the complex heart. But the Prince must slay, the
hunter must slay; they cannot, if they would be princes and
hunters, preserve that moment of excruciated sensibility in the
timeless drama of the heart. The "Old Free Fathers" were
aware of this painful human paradox of action, in which man
commits himself in the irrevocable, and they celebrated it in
the sacramental gesture of grief and responsibility (but there
was also pride) for the life they spilled: a consecrating gesture—
the smearing the warm blood of a youth's first kill on his forehead—which absolved a man from *regret* but not from *grief*.[2]

Ike would be absolved from both. He remembers having
thought, when his cousin read him the "Ode," that his not
killing Old Ben had been

> ... simpler than somebody talking in a book about a young
> man and a girl *he would never need to grieve over* because
> he could never approach any nearer and would never have
> to get any further away. He had heard about an old bear
> and finally got big enough to hunt it and he hunted it four
> years and at last met it with a gun in his hands and he
> didn't shoot. Because a little dog—But he could have shot
> long before the fyce covered the twenty yards to where the
> bear waited, and Sam Fathers could have shot at any time

during the interminable minute while Old Ben stood on his hind legs over them. . . . (p. 297; my italics.)

But it had been the same thing. Saving the fyce had meant a repudiation, like the present one in the commissary, of a necessary suffering, an escape, a *freedom* from grieving.

He was "repudiating immolation," as he tells McCaslin earlier, before the full implications become clear to them both through the memory of the fyce and Ike's tortured "admission," because "fatherless"—and he might have added son-less—he was "therefore safe declining the altar" which an already outraged God was preparing. He could repudiate, or forestall, his own self-sacrifice, because in anticipating God by "accepting," he could avoid grieving, and because in surrendering all, in relinquishing the human desires which made God see his whole race as "all Grandfather all of them," there would be nothing for him, no son to sacrifice, nothing to be taken away. Fatherless and solitary, Ike has felt that he was excepted, exempted, from a father's guilty wish and hope of sacrificing his dearest possession to the demanding, wrathful God in atonement and expiation. The sins of the South were his *fathers'* sins, not his, and so he can repudiate immolation, his fathers' sacrifice, being fatherless, by repudiating his fathers' accursed possessions—his inheritance and heritage. He may "decline the altar" because, guiltless (*he* will not have enslaved the Negro, *he* will not have killed Old Ben, *he* will have no possessions), he would be purposelessly taken, instead of the kid this time, by a finally hopeless and impatient God. In his own eyes—or so he wants to understand it—Ike is "escaping," as he admits to McCaslin, to be able to cut off, at least as far as his family is concerned, the line of blood guilt and injustice to the Negro and the land ("The Bear," p. 283). Now, McCaslin "smiling" (p. 297), each knowing that the other is remembering the same events, McCaslin recognizes the repudiation of the land for what it is —an escape from an immolation required of all men, from an immolation that defines man.

But Ike has been approaching this recognition on his own. Even at the time of the fyce incident he had been uneasy ("Because a little dog—But he could have shot. . ." [p. 297]); even then there had been in the back of his mind considerable doubt as to why he had not shot. Now, in the debate with his cousin, brought to the difficult admission that "we have never been free," McCaslin "smiling" as he sees the truth being pressed home on Ike, he still resists it, still struggles to push aside the real knowledge. Indeed, we may say that the power, the dramatic tension which underlies this entire section is generated here, in exactly this half-knowledge of the rationalization he has constructed for himself. What follows in the remainder of the commissary sequence is strongly informed by this tension.

So the interpretation of the Ode sequence—its function in Part IV, and indeed of the whole section and its relation to the rest of the story—must be made on the play between what the incident of the fyce meant to the characters when it took place, seven years before Part IV opens, and what it means now as it is remembered in the commissary and as it is being reinterpreted. We must read the meaning of the Ode sequence dramatically, so to speak, before the larger meanings begin to unfold.

Returning to the debate where we left it—the Ode sequence, the "pause" concluding—we may now read those final remarks between the two men in a dramatic setting which alters their meaning considerably from what they may seem to be "saying." The tension just mentioned can be read most clearly here. *How* they are said, especially Ike's words, is the important thing.

McCaslin sneers, at least "smiles," as we have seen, and Ike senses the ground of his rationalization crumbling before McCaslin's cold irony. McCaslin breaks the silence, the "pause": "*Habet* then.—so this land is, indubitably, of and by itself cursed." He has seen in Ike's admissions and in the fact of his being taken immediately back by them to the fyce episode that Ike knows too that they and the land are cursed. And Ike echoes, "Cursed," nevertheless still excepting himself from it, still persisting in his belief he can remove himself from its burden (p. 298). Relentless, McCaslin urges again upon Ike the difficult truth, so much more pointed now, which he has been trying all along to make him take up:

> "And since I know too what you know I will say now, once more let me say it: And one other, and in the third generation too, and the male, the eldest, the direct and sole and white and still McCaslin even, from father to son to son—" (p. 299)

But Ike interrupts here: "I am free," he protests, not really believing, himself, that he can be free. McCaslin merely looks at him, perhaps with the same ironic "lip-lift," a look which implies

> . . . the frail and iron thread strong as truth and impervious as evil and longer than life itself and reaching beyond record and patrimony both to join him with the lusts and passions, the hopes and dreams and griefs, of bones whose names while still fleshed and capable even old Carothers' grandfather had never heard. . . . (p. 299)

And Ike, still protesting, although with an anguished defiance, weak in conviction: "And [free] of that too" (p. 299)—the human inheritance of lust and passion, which he would repudiate along with the land. But even this, as we see in the paroxysm of the conclusion to Part IV, he must come to realize is impossible for him.

The dialogue proper of Part IV—McCaslin still ironic and somewhat contemptuous—ends with McCaslin's defense of his own existence as a Southerner and a McCaslin, and with Ike still protesting:

> "Chosen, I suppose (I will concede it) out of all your time by Him, as you say Buck and Buddy were from theirs. And it took Him a bear and an old man and four years just for you. And it took you fourteen years to reach that point and about that many, maybe more, for Old Ben, and more than seventy for Sam Fathers. And you are just one. How long then? How long?" and he
>
> "It will be long. I have never said otherwise. But it will be all right because they will endure—" and McCaslin
>
> "And anyway, you will be free.—No, not now nor ever, we from them nor they from us. So I repudiate too. I would deny even if I knew it were true. I would have to. Even you can see that I could do no else. I am what I am; I will be always what I was born and have always been. And more than me. More than me, just as there were more than Buck and Buddy in what you called His first plan which failed": and he
>
> "And more than me": and McCaslin

"No. Not even you. Because mark. You said how on that
instant when Ikkemotubbe realized that he could sell the
land to Grandfather, it ceased forever to have been his.
All right; go on: Then it belonged to Sam Fathers, old
Ikkemotubbe's son. And who inherited from Sam Fathers,
if not you? co-heir perhaps with Boon, if not of his life
maybe, at least of his quitting it?" and he
"Yes. Sam Fathers set me free." (pp. 299–300)

This last Ike repeats preoccupied, hearing but not hearing
McCaslin, who is speaking a truth Ike does not want to hear
because he knows it only too well; it is said loudly, almost
hysterically, terrifiedly.

And the rest slopes off in intensity as the dialogue ends and
we proceed to the Beauchamp legacy, that empty coffee-pot
grail, and finally to the moving sequence that describes Ike's
later submission to what he secretly knew without McCaslin's
telling him: that "no man is ever free" (p. 281), that "they
were all Grandfather all of them" (p. 283). The section ends
with ironic laughter, corresponding in a way to McCaslin's
"lip-lift." Ike's wife, in her naked sexuality, forces upon him
a submission to life as it must be lived—as Addie Bundren had
to live it—in action and commitment of the blood, not in words
or poems or even in the heart. " 'And that's all,' " Ike's wife
tells him. " 'That's all from me. If this dont get you that son
you talk about, it wont be mine': lying on her side, her back
to the empty rented room, laughing and laughing" (p. 315).
So he too, even Ike who had renounced all, had wanted a son;
but he had not wanted, at the same time, the commitment to
life and passion, to possession, and the desire to pass things
possessed down to sons—even if it is just an *idea*—which such
commitment necessarily involves.

When we look back at the rest of the tale, it takes on a
different and more profound aspect. We cannot stop, as virtually all commentaries on "The Bear" do, with a reading which
interprets Boon's slaying of Old Ben as the triumph of the
"new order" (Boon is not "pure"—a hard-eyed, moronic half-
breed) over the Old Dispensation and the pure in heart. Altogether too much has been made of the socio-historical theme in
"The Bear," a version of the oversimplifying Snopes-Sartoris

polarity of Faulkner criticism. Unquestionably this note is
struck in "The Bear": a certain sentimental and romantic tex-
tural layer; but it is really a dramatic element, one aspect of the
dramatic indirection of the work. The romantic "meaning" is
Ike's "meaning"—the way he would prefer to view the events
in which he has participated and his own motives—but it is
not ultimately Faulkner's.

The romantic note, to hypothesize a possible "genesis" of
the work, enters by way of the earlier versions of the tale, and
since whole passages from particularly the short stories "The
Bear" and "Lion" are moved verbatim into the longer final
story, we might expect something of the old flavor and meaning
to become imbedded in the new, misleading readers who fail
to push on through the informing renitencies of Part IV. (It
would be a mistake, however, not to consider the romantic
"meaning" as part of the full-length story *by design,* as well.)
The earlier versions of the story *are* romantic and nostalgic, but
the present work is not a mere fleshing-out of the same story;
the earlier works are different, substantially as well as in tone
and ultimate intention.

A comparison of the several versions suggests that the longer
Faulkner thought about his originals the more the meaning
shifted, the more he himself saw in the symbolic structure he
had created in the hunt-narrative. And the more he reflected
on the subtle meanings the symbol is capable of giving up, the
less satisfied he became with the romantic, sentimental theme
of the defeat of the "old order" by the materialistic New World
—the less truth he found in it. In the final version of "The
Bear," we must attribute it not to Faulkner himself, who is
using it dramatically and in so doing transmuting it into a
much harder truth, but to Isaac McCaslin.

To take this "genesis" of the work a step further, the deliberate and strategic removal of the Ode sequence from the conclusion of the short story "The Bear" to the central position it has
in Part IV, together with certain changes in its tone and language, reflects this altered view of the narrative-symbol that
Faulkner finally took. His attitude towards Ike's rescue of the
fyce, for one thing, which is the whole matter of the short story,
deepens—the way McCaslin's attitude does. Ike's concluding
lines in the short story, which are spoken in answer to his
father's (his cousin's in the present work) question, "Do you
see now?" are changed from: "Sam, and Old Ben, and Nip [the

fyce], he thought. And himself too. He had been all right too. His father had said so. 'Yes, sir,' he said."—this reply to the question, and his thought at the time, are changed to: "He didn't know. Somehow it had seemed simpler than that. . ." (p. 297). The analogy, in the short story, the father wished to make by quoting the Ode is comparatively simple and straight-forwardly romantic, and the general tone of the story bespeaks merely a certain sentimental nostalgia for the Old Times, and a boy's growing up. So he must have dwelt on the conclusion to the short story until it gave up an even more profound para-dox than it did originally. And this is what drew him to ponder further the hunt symbolism itself, a composite mainly of the pursuit of Old Ben in the short story "The Bear" and the slay-ing of Old Ben in "Lion." ("The Old People," written as I suppose after the revised central story—although it precedes it in *Go Down, Moses*—and "Delta Autumn," which follows "The Bear," also show the same deepened theme. "The Old People," however, because it stands somewhat transitionally in theme and tone between the early and later stories of the Isaac McCaslin tale, could possibly have been written before the revi-sion of "The Bear" but after the whole conception of the hunt and of Isaac McCaslin had begun already to be transformed in Faulkner's imagination. "Delta Autumn," the romantic theme now completely absent, or rather exorcised, clearly follows the full, harrowing, shuddering discoveries of "The Bear." It could not have been written without first undertaking that journey through the underworld and can only support the reading of "The Bear" itself that is being advanced here.)

Thus the structure of the revised work corresponds to Faulk-ner's own process of discovery, and, more important, to Ike's: the final meanings are discovered in the *memory* of action, of life, in poetry and in the heart, meanings which convulse the heart in its arriving at them, but meanings which nevertheless, even when they are found, cannot be lived in time and space. Life proceeds in action; there are no meanings until we reflect on acts, in a "poem," in words, either in the effort to compre-hend what has been lived, or in the "poems" we conceive and propose for our futures. And so life for Faulkner and for his characters is hard to live, as poor bedevilled Addie Bundren knows (the only "reason for living was to get ready to stay dead a long time," her father had told her), because the "poems" we invent to explain life and to make it bearable never correspond to the actual living. We romanticize the irredeemable past the way Ike remembers his dream-frieze of hunter and hunted, always pursuing and so never needing to grieve, and we dramatize, in ideal day-dreams of achievement and virtue, the appalling open-ended prospect of the future.

Ike's "poem" was, in fact, a renunciation of life, as all our "poems" tend to be—the "poems" we try to live, at any rate. And Ike is made to confront this in Part IV. The turgid rhetoric of the section, enforced by McCaslin's scorn, reflects the struggle Ike is undergoing. The lucid grace, on the other hand, of the narrative portions is Ike's remembered "poem"—and it is remembered in pain. Our "poems" are all the more lucid and graceful the more the chasm gapes for us between life as lived (as Ike, in this case, must begin to live) and what we would want life to be, what it can be only in art, and in the anguished heart. Our "poems" are more painful the more lucid and graceful they are. This is the hurt of art—why beauty is painful, seems to fall heavily across the heart: it recovers, or reclaims, partially and tentatively, a timeless state of Being, in which an original angelic integrity is re-constituted. Beauty is a form, rather a *type,* in the seventeenth-century sense, of the remembered Eden of the race, which we know only in the rare moments our dissociated faculties achieve a reintegration in art.[3] Faulkner's peculiar nostalgia, that constant suffusing tone of sometimes anguished memory in much that he has written, is a response to this condition of man's existence.

There is, indeed, a sort of lucid, dream-like, "remembered" quality, or tone, about the narrative portions of "The Bear," as we are reading it, but especially *as we remember it* in Part IV, where the lucidity of narrative is replaced by the tortured rhetoric of reason and reality, reason being in a way more like life—probationary, tentatively incomplete, not abstract; groping, fragmentary, imperceptive, not logical—than art is. The tone—most clearly felt when the war is considered, but really ubiquitous in his work—reflects, as perhaps R. P. Warren might put it, Faulkner's "pure" poetic in conflict with intransigent experience, with the irremediable past of our acts, either idealizing it in lucid narrative or, as it is more common in Faulkner and in modern writing in general, aggravating its refractory obtuseness in tangled rhetoric and atomized forms, both being art's chief strategies (if we may imply anything at all of the deliberate in it), both deriving in the racking antinomy of art and life. The juxtaposition of *both* strategies in "The Bear" is primarily what gives the work its peculiar tragic form, made palpable largely by a kind of statuary imagery[4] which fixes—or better suspends—in the mythic dimension the contradiction of art and life, being and becoming, stasis and movement. (What remains in the imagination long after one has puzzled through the difficult *argument* of "The Bear" is the fixed, frieze-like image of the hunt, in which the ennobling pursuit *and* the slaying, the "poem" *and* life, are inextricably suspended. Ike himself sees it in these terms: the great bear "ran in his knowledge before he ever saw it. It loomed and towered in his dreams before he even saw the unaxed woods where it left its crooked print. . ." [p. 193]). The thwarted, wounded sense in Faulkner of the flow and passage of acts in time is thus manifested usually by images which are the opposite of movement but which convey in tragic tension the completeness of being, of art, and the incompleteness of becoming, of life. The one really makes the other possible in the virtually magical and fortuitous engendering of images. (But "engendering" says perhaps more than it was meant to say. "Materialization" would do the same thing, however: the one gives life, the other substance to the aesthetic phenomenon, which is neither, and at the same time both more and less, better and inferior, to life and substance.) Possibly all art achieves its effects through this opposition, in one form or another, between art and life. The whole painting, poem, novel, etc., is a "statuary image" in which being and becoming, the "poem" of life and life itself, merge. Faulkner, in any event, accentuates, exaggerates this aesthetic principle. His work, like a good deal of modern art, self-consciously exploits the principle of art; it is, in a sense, art about art.

This phenomenon, however, is not strictly a modern one, *Hamlet,* for example, showing the same concerns, although not with the same self-consciousness. Let us stay clear of invidious, treacherous comparisons and suggest merely an analogy: Faulkner has that certain Shakespearian melon-sense of the round ripe world, the world which, try as one may, like Hamlet, to embrace it all at once, to comprehend it, and so "be," defeats the human reason and finally even art. "The Bear," it may be ventured, is Faulkner's *Hamlet.* As in Shakespeare's play, its rich and subtle interweaving teases us out of thought, confounds us too, and for the same perhaps self-defeating reasons: what is being "said" in and by art is that art and beauty—not to mention reason—are *not* truth, life's truth; that art, the "play," "being" are not life. Both *Hamlet* and "The Bear," in their ultimate intentions, are not wholly successful attempts to express what "life" is like, in works of art which enforce, I think deliberately, the sense of the difference between art and life, the sense of art's inadequacy before life, its failure to express, or "know" it. But how can one transcend the platform from which one sees or knows *anything* so as to be able to see and know that platform itself? If art is in part a form of cognition functioning by an imitation of life, and if art, the moment it "fixes" life, becomes, or creates, something other than life (and it is perhaps exactly that flux, that *un*-fixedness, that we wish to "know" in art), then it must inevitably fail, in its cognitive function at least, and express whatever it can, whatever it is *possible* for it to express about life itself, being, only in an attitude of the artist's that we find reflected by the work as a secondary effect or function, by *tone,* as Eliot has said of *Hamlet.* This is the Shakespearian "melon-sense" of the world: that anguished, thwarting feel of the really inexpressible and inimitable.

Certainly no romantic conception of art and life comes out of all this, as has been inferred, but rather a harsh *naturalism* of the relation of the two which seems truer although more difficult—and in this Faulkner's great value consists. For Keats, for example ("Do I wake or sleep?"), reality and truth are in the dream, in the poem, and this is the only truth we need to know, the only reality. (Although in Brooks's and Tate's readings of Keats, the underlying tension in "Ode to a Nightingale" and "Ode on a Grecian Urn" is created by Keats's tacit apprehension that the immortal nature of the bird and the dynamic "life" of art are, after all, human death.) Faulkner, on the other hand, forces us not only to acknowledge the great discrepancy between life and art, but insists on the validity of the former as our "reality." Beauty isn't truth; it is rather a valuable sort of *un*-truth which helps make the truth of life bearable, as Nietzsche has said, even though it does so through pain. And we value beauty most, and correctly, when we are most aware of the truth we live. The heart may contain antinomies, as the Ode and the Urn do, but there is a fearful abyss between what the heart and poem hold, or "know," and what we may know in life, in time. Faulkner's rhetoric evolves from his awareness of the irremediableness and irredeemableness of time and action; his art reflects his strained effort to hold or fix *all* that man is and feels, what cannot be held or fixed in life. And this he is able to express only with that weak instrument of the reason, language, which is *bound* by time and logic (the "platform"). So even the men who tried to express God's truth were "liars," in a sense:

> "Yes. Because they were human men. They were trying to write down the heart's truth out of the heart's driving complexity, for all the complex and troubled hearts which would beat after them. What they were trying to tell, what He wanted said, was too simple. Those for whom they transcribed His words could not have believed them. It had to be expounded in the everyday terms which they were familiar with and could comprehend, not only those who listened but those who told it too, because if they who were that near to Him as to have been elected from among all who breathed and spoke language to transcribe and relay His words, could comprehend truth only through the complexity of passion and lust and hate and fear which drives the heart, what distance back to truth must they traverse whom truth could only reach by word-of-mouth?" (pp. 260–261)

To come back, reflection on the events of the Ode sequence, as it may have been the focal point of Faulkner's growth of insight, becomes for Ike, in the terms of the story, the fulcrum of his spiritual moving. And for the reader, the process of discovery is the same. Part IV, in a rhetoric that is more "statement," in its wrestled argumentativeness, than the preceding narrative, brings into an *abstract* tragic clarity the antinomies of life, which the narrative, while it is proceeding, when it is most like life—but only in the sense of its movement and commitment in action—cannot "state" or express clearly at all. The narrative-symbol becomes symbol only after it is concluded and we look back on it in its totality, in its self-containing integrity, which life as it is being lived cannot have. This is what Part IV brings us to perform, and why the organization of the work is such a consummate form: it compels us, as the debate in the commissary compels Ike, to remember, to try to "fix." The reader is thus brought to feel, so much more intimately than he could otherwise, that same poignant sense of time-remembered that Ike feels and with which the entire story is suffused. We remember, with the same sense of the irremediable past, already committed in time, the narrative action which is now transformed into symbolic meaning—those same events and thoughts which Ike remembers and finds tragic meaning in, in the "heart's driving complexity." It could be shown that much of Faulkner's most effective work is similarly formed: a time remembered, a piecing together of the past, in which the reader himself becomes engaged.

We had been saying that the main action—the years of pursuit and the final slaying of Old Ben—must be reinterpreted in the light of a close reading of Part IV, and that, specifically, the romantic theme of the conquest of the "old order" by materialism is inadequate. The fyce episode has already been considered in its doubleness, but what are we to make of the more important aspect of the plot, Boon's slaying of Old Ben? How must we read this, and the final scene of the story where Boon hammers at his gun under the squirrel-filled tree, if the other elements are seen to contain ironies?

"So he should have hated and feared Lion," Part II begins (p. 209). The words recur in this section which relates how the fierce, indomitable hound is at last found who will enable them to kill Old Ben, and they appear again at the very end of the section when the reluctant knowledge has grown into the certainty of the end of something they all have cherished. In the romantic reading of the work, these words mean only that the ferocious hound, whose eyes reflected "nothing of petty malevolence in them, but a cold and almost impersonal malignance like some natural force" (p. 218), and who represented the un-pitying not-man, or un-human, aspect of the world, had arrived to despoil the idyllic relationship of man and beast and Wilderness. This is the romantic and sentimental nature-vs.-materialism theme, which appears to be enforced by the association, in the story, of Lion and Boon, who lovingly and with great respect, or awe, cares for the fierce hound in his life and in his death. But unless this theme is understood dramatically, not as the total theme but as the meaning of events only as seen through Ike's eyes, we fail to see the further meaning in the recurrent words. If we assume Ike's point of view as our own, then Ike "should have hated and feared Lion" because he meant

merely the end of something noble and worth preserving—
"*should* have" because unexpectedly, for some reason, he *didn't*.

> It seemed to him that there was a fatality in it. It seemed
> to him that something, he didn't know what, was begin-
> ning; had already begun. It was like the last act on a set
> stage. It was the beginning of the end of something, he
> didn't know what except that he would not grieve. He
> would be humble and proud that he had been found
> worthy to be a part of it too or even just to see it too.
> (p. 226)

His not hating and fearing Lion is thus accepted, as through
Ike's eyes, as some wondrous act of generosity and humility.
But Boon, in a sense, although for different reasons, hasn't
hated and feared Lion either; the differences are important.
Ike has accepted the inevitability of the end. He would not
grieve, didn't *have* to grieve, because removing himself from
life's commitment, he could view the approaching event in his
play-acting Hamlet-like aesthetic perspective, as the "last act
on a set stage," and thus obviate the necessity to *live* the shattering event. Moreover, it would be Lion, that impersonal "natural force," that would do the slaying; it wouldn't be his fault,
or even man's fault: unfeeling, implacable nature, the not-man,
would be responsible—the Lions and the degenerate, half-breed
Boons. "Should have" becomes thus, in a larger view, "*ought
to have.*" He ought to have hated and feared Lion because
Lion, who "inferred not only courage and all else that went
to make up the will and desire to endure beyond all imaginable
limits of flesh in order to overtake and slay" (p. 237), is as
much a part of him—which he would repudiate—as pity, love,
courage, and humility are. His not hating and fearing Lion
was, after all, for the wrong reasons, unlike Boon's. He could
not look at what he sensed was there in the Wilderness, at
what the hunt and the Bear had really taught him—at what
Kurtz and Marlow look at in the "Heart of Darkness"—and so
he rationalized it out of consciousness by his "saintly" repudiation of the Lion in us, and by his acceptance of inevitability.
So actually he *did* secretly and unwittingly hate and fear Lion!
Boon, however, because he wasn't as smart as the others,
couldn't hate and fear Lion, which requires a certain spiritual

sophistication; he was, rather, powerfully drawn to him, and stood in awe of what his shocking power represented, because in his own inarticulate way he understood the "Wilderness" better than Isaac McCaslin did. For Faulkner, perhaps it is only the spiritually unsophisticated who have the capacity for "sainthood."

It is significant that Faulkner made a considerable change in the conclusion of "Lion"—where Boon sits under the tree hammering at his gun—before he used it to conclude the present story. This is how it reads in the former (it is important too that we recognize the boy as the narrator in this early version):

> Then I saw what Boon was hammering at. It was a section of his gun; drawing nearer, I saw the rest of it scattered in a dozen pieces about him on the ground where he sat, hunched over, hammering furiously at the part on his lap, his walnut face wild and urgent and streaming with sweat. He was living, as always, in the moment; nothing on earth —not Lion, not anything in the past—mattered to him except his helpless fury with his broken gun. He didn't stop; he didn't even look up to see who I was; he just shouted at me in a hoarse desperate voice.
>
> "Get out of here!" he said. "Don't touch them! They're mine!"

Here it is obvious he is trying to put his gun *together*—this uncomprehending, insensitive brute who had slain Old Ben in a fierce animal protectiveness or vengefulness, and had so hastened the end of something, a way of life, he could not understand. He represents, in this earlier romantic view of Faulkner's, the brute destructive force of an encroaching materialism. He is described, in the boy's words just quoted, as having no sense of the historic past, no traditions in the South, and as being unloving, without sentiment. The implications are pretty clear about the intention of the story. But it is not so clear in the present work, largely because so much of the first stories is brought forward intact into this one, but also because of the far more profound theme of the final working. To return, it seems much more likely, in the revised version, that Boon is attempting, in his childlike, hysterical way, to *destroy* the gun, which he had never felt quite at home with and couldn't use proficiently like the others, and which for him is identified with the passing of the wilderness he loved in his own way, and perhaps also with the deaths of Sam and Lion, over whom he grieves more than the others.[5] Whereas Ike "accepts" these, relinquishing passion, renouncing *life*, in effect, Boon must go on living in furious protest against the terrible unjustness of the "inevitabilities," must live in the "wild blood boiling along the earth," as Addie did, because "doing goes along the earth," not in words and "poems." Boon, in the conclusion of the revised story, is protecting the squirrels:

> Then he saw Boon, sitting, his back against the trunk, his head bent, hammering furiously at something on his lap. What he hammered with was the barrel of his dismembered gun, what he hammered at was the breech of it. The rest of the gun lay scattered about him in a half-dozen pieces while he bent over the piece on his lap his scarlet and streaming walnut face, hammering the disjointed barrel against the gun-breech with the frantic abandon of a madman. He didn't even look up to see who it was. Still hammering, he merely shouted back at the boy in a hoarse strangled voice:
>
> "Get out of here! Don't touch them! Don't touch a one of them! They're mine!" (p. 331)

Unlike Ike, Boon, the half-witted and half-bred, grieves. God, in "The Bear," grieves too, in his commitment, and perhaps in this, Faulkner would say, is God's love.

Faulkner's meaning in "The Bear" is that if man would live, he must be prepared for the dying too; if he would love, he must also grieve for the spilled life that loving and living require. Simply to repudiate the spilling, to relinquish the grief, by relinquishing the passion, is to remove oneself from life, and from love, which, like the hunt, necessarily involves us in blood. There is no renunciation of life and the world which we can choose to make, and there can be no "acceptance" of the inevitabilities; we may only choose life. What we may renounce is only renunciation itself, and what we may attain to is not a regenerate state, sainthood, being, but our humanity. We gain life by "losing" it only in the sense of having it *taken away*, of trying to live what is in the heart, and failing. Renun-

ciation, "acceptance," is to surrender life to live in the "pretty
rooms" of sonnets ("and Isaac McCaslin, not yet Uncle Ike . . .
living in one small cramped fireless rented room in a Jefferson
boarding-house . . . with his kit of brand-new carpenter's tools
. . . the shotgun McCaslin had given him with his named
engraved in silver . . . and the bright tin coffee-pot" [p. 300]).

We prefer to think the Boons of this world do the slaying,
and our renunciations are our way of *allowing* them to. We
construct our "pretty rooms" right in the Wilderness where we
play at virtue and perform our purification rites, just as Major
de Spain, Walter Ewell, McCaslin Edmonds and the rest did
each year. The Negroes and their white masters, at the camp
site, lived under an entirely different dispensation from the one
which ordinarily prevailed in town, in real life, where they
were virtually slaves. In the Big Woods they could play at
being untainted, guiltless—there one felt free. The pursuit of
Old Ben over the years is unsuccessful, not merely because he
is a wily old beast, almost supernatural, but because they didn't
want to kill him, and not killing him is the ritual of purification; by this, and by the altered relationship of Negro and
white master, they could free themselves, for a while at least.
Sam Fathers had begun, long before, to live at the camp site all
year round, but when they approach him after he has collapsed,
he murmurs, "Let me out, master" (p. 245), knowing that only
death can really free him, that he hasn't been free at all in the
white man's lodge and woods. The Boons, with the hard button
eyes—the insensitive, un-human destroyers and raveners, as we
conceive them—are there at the last, almost by design, to shatter
the pretty glass room of this dream of redemption: we create
them and then sacrifice them in our condescensions and our
renunciations in this last act of the ritual.

But as McCaslin says, we are rather "co-heirs with Boon"
(p. 300) of Grandfather's legacy. So we are indubitably cursed,
as McCaslin has it—cursed not to be able to live "poems," to
dwell in the "pretty rooms" of the imagination, as Ike and the
others attempt to do. Unlike the frieze of lovers on the Urn,
and unlike what the Ode may contain, life in time requires of
us a constant commitment in irremediable acts of living, an
ineluctable involvement in our accursed fallen state.

But if this were all, we could not bear to read Faulkner. The
work itself, moreover, would be, in a sense, self-denying: a work
of art which repudiates art; a poem which denies poetry. The

point, the difference, is that "The Bear" is no well-wrought urn testifying to, and promising, a healing and annealing power of the imagination, allowing us, by its blandishments, to escape, or renounce, the "heart high sorrowful and cloyed," the "burning forehead and a parching tongue," as in Keats, or mortal solitariness, human isolation, as in Donne—it doesn't allow us to renounce these for the timeless room of art. The wounding beauty of Faulkner makes us more *directly* aware of our human imperfection, or rather incompleteness, if the first term carries with it too much theological freight; it produces no mere *nostalgia* for Eden, but an anguish of the complex heart, a fructifying passion. The hurt is no sweet pining, no languishing upon the midnight with no pain, on the one hand; and instead of "pretty rooms," there are only the pounding chambers of the heart. We are not canonized in Faulkner, we are humanized; there is no beautifying, idealizing transfiguration, no "moral regeneration," either in the work or for the reader, but only an ideal of passion. Thus Faulkner does not deny beauty and poetry, although in a sense all tragedy does in part; he denies only the falsification of life which comes of living a poem. But this is not quite right either. There must *be* the "poems" man attempts to live, but there can be no deliberate renunciation and relinquishment of "doing," as Addie Bundren calls it, in order to escape into the "poem." And there can be no deliberate "acceptance" of life, which is also a kind of escape, a not-life, because it sees *too much,* understands too much, in its aesthetic completeness which regrets everything, pardons everything in advance. The true seeing is only from a kind of sublime blindness, much like the blindness of Lear and Oedipus, in which no inevitability is "accepted" and in which the "poem" and life are taken away. Our "poems" give us the tragic *vulnerability,* the capacity for being hurt and defeated—such as Hemingway's characters show behind their bravado and tight-lipped defense against the world—without which there can be no "world," no life, no love, no tragic greatness. Faulkner's "beauty" thus arises in his truer imitation, in which man at his best is seen in passion.

For the most part, the kind of criticism "The Bear," and Faulkner in general, has received is one whose strategy consists primarily in the discovery and elucidation of symbolic and mythic *analogues,* a criticism that is limited as an analytical instrument from the start. It reduces, right at its very inception, the organic, dramatic substance of a work to a mere *illustration* of a meaning which is already, because of our interpretation and reduction of the original symbolism, too logical, too far abstracted into statement. Instead of myth and symbol, we deal this way with parable and allegory of the simplest sort; instead of allowing the work its *own* mythic energies, its myth-creating power, we read it only as a kind of demonstration of what is, relatively speaking, really platitude. This is, in effect, interpretation twice removed from the work of art—actually, interpretation of interpretation—and in the process what we would wish to fasten our attention on really drops out of sight. Language itself is reduced to communicative counters and loses its expressive, meaning-creative function in this interpretation of interpretation, in the strict analogical criticism. Words, rhetorical and dramatic patterns, become mere clues to a puzzle. This is the true symbol-mongering. The important symbolism is the one the work creates by its own images; it is not the one upon which a work *may*, in fact, be modelled, as many indeed are, in which case the two levels of symbolism, the dramatic and the analogical, must be carefully distinguished, the two, of course, interanimating the total meaning of the work.

It is extraordinary that the literary and philosophical movement which seemed at one point to be destructive of all meaning and value should offer us now the subtle, fruitful meanings we need. Naturalism, by its insistence on the experience of the senses and on an existent "reality," by its rejection of a symbolic, idealistic, spiritual "reality," has perhaps served us better than we know—certainly better than *it* knew. In a roundabout, ironic way, naturalism *restores* the symbolic imagination by destroying the analogical reading of experience and the world, just as Faulkner, in "The Bear," restores the possibility of sainthood by first destroying the platitude, the theology, of sainthood.

"The Bear" is an example of naturalism come of age. We distort the character and value of the movement when we limit the use of the term to the early deterministic and, to some, clinically brutalizing denials of traditional values. In this later phase of the movement, made possible only by the philosophical ground-clearing of the early destructive, negative phase, but actually an extension of the same unembarrassed scrutiny of the "natural" organism in its environment, there occurs something like a rediscovery of the psychological, "natural" grounds of myth and symbolism, which enables us to interpret anew the traditional symbols themselves. Naturalism ultimately reformulates in new symbols the same profound human meanings and requirements of the spirit that were embodied in our mythologies; these have, through the years, fossilized, in a manner of speaking, so that we no longer really find them viable. And frequently, through this fossilization, they grow from the descriptive sort of idealizing poetry they are in the beginning into systems, or theologies, which are no longer chiefly valuable for the "mysteries" they may contain, or *describe,* but for the techniques or programmes they *prescribe* for behavior and thought. The terms somehow remain the same in these "fossils" but the meanings they are able to support are altered considerably: they are reduced to platitudes.

The Christian symbolism and other mythic analogues we may discover in a work like "The Bear" thus really occur only as resonators, as it were, of the newly formed, and forming, meanings, and should be valued only dramatically, as making something else, indirectly, meaningful. Actually, in "The Bear," there is a denial of the traditional symbols as we, at least, have known and used them—that is, in their "theological" character. Faulkner's naturalism consists exactly in this. The naturalistic animus—so much easier to see in the earlier writers, where there was only bitterness, only disillusionment, and manifest more frequently than otherwise in the self-wounding mechanical determinisms which we have misread as "scientific detachment" and brutalism—this animus in Faulkner can be read in his rejection of our theology-techniques, in his telling us, in effect, as the other naturalists do, what the world and living really are like. The coffee-pot grail is empty, contains no answers for the questing knight; the Christ-like carpenter's existence is empty too of meaning—false, actually. Indeed, Ike's whole "poem," as I have called it, corresponds, by implication, to man's day-dream of redemption. What Faulkner rejects, then, is the "theological" Christian symbols, the platitudinous symbolism and mythology of technique; and from being mere animus and self-contempt, self-scourging—better, as a *result* of this necessary initial temper—his "naturalism" ultimately recovers in passion perhaps the most fundamental meaning of Christian symbolism. It has been a most difficult recovery, especially for American writers, who have had to struggle with their Puritan inheritance for their artistic freedom and integrity. (In the

Puritan psychology of faith, passion—as well as the Passion—was not recognized as being worth anything in itself. Where "sainthood" was an achievable human state, if the correct tests and techniques were applied, passion could only signify imperfection, failure, sin.) Most of the great American works give the same indications in their rhetoric and matter, one way or another, of having wrestled severely and, in the view of some of the artists, *heretically* for their freedom. ("I have written a wicked book, and feel spotless as the lamb.") Indeed, perhaps with the Reformation itself there began the "wicked books" which have had to recover our mythologies, over and over again, from theological technique.

So we must in no sense regard "The Bear" as an illustration or exemplification of conventional Christian values. Rather it questions these, denies them, but from this denial finally regains the forgotten human matrix out of which the symbols originally arose. It re-embodies them in new symbols, which have little if anything to do with the "moral regeneration" of the old. And these latter have merely a dramatic function in the work as Ike's "meaning," Ike's "poem." They do not constitute the primary substantial symbolism of the work, which has to do, ultimately, with the human passion that exists in the unbridgeable chasm between the "truth" of the heart, of beauty, art, where man may be *all* that he might want to be, and the truth of the life we live in reality, where we are only what we are at any one committed moment of time. And this passion is valuable in itself, not for what we might obtain by it for ourselves, either in terms of enlightenment or actual ennoblement, in terms of a realizable redemption, but for the unselfconscious and unwitting humanity we attain to. "It is in defeat that we become Christian," another "naturalist" has one of his characters remark.

Commentary ══════

With Perluck's reading of "The Bear" the lines are clearly drawn between two quite different interpretations: one which accepts more or less at face value Ike McCaslin's renunciation of his heritage—including his withdrawal, as an ascetic and a kind of saint, from a world no longer worthy of a Christian; the other which reads the story as a tissue of ironies, culminating in Ike's essentially ironic canonization.

This is not meant to imply that the first of these readings is somehow simple-minded or simplistic; it is often rendered with care and sophistication, and many critics find it far more convincing and satisfying than the other perhaps more nuanced interpretation. Complexity is not necessarily a virtue in itself.

The most equitable way to do justice to the "romantic" reading of "The Bear" is to consult one of its best proponents. Irving Howe (*William Faulkner: A Critical Study* [2nd ed.; New York: Vintage Books, 1962], pp. 92–97, 253–259) is surely one of these. It is clear, first of all, that Howe is well aware of the "unromantic" reading of the story, for he concedes that "some of Faulkner's critics have felt that Isaac's withdrawal, for all its saintly humaneness, does not bear sufficiently upon the condition that has caused it: he leaves the world intact, still caught up in its accumulated evil, and if only for this reason—that he fails actively to engage himself—he cannot be considered a heroic figure" (p. 96). Howe admits that he is not unsympathetic to this point of view, but he feels that such an argument misses one decisive point: "At least intermittently Faulkner seems to believe very deeply in the intrinsic value and ultimate efficacy of passive suffering." Although Howe does not refer to it in this context, one might think of Faulkner's admiring comment on the Negro characters of *The Sound and the Fury*: "They endured." Or again, one might cite his Nobel Prize speech, which extols man's capability for "compassion and sacrifice and endurance." Clearly a case can be made for believing in Faulkner's real commitment to these values.

The problem is, Howe feels, that the modern world does not share Faulkner's valuation of the virtue of passive suffering, and has sometimes tried to read "The Bear" in its own terms. For Faulkner "the image of endurance, related for him both to the agony of Christ and the condition of man, evokes his deepest and sometimes

199

uncontainable feelings." The modern reader cannot fully accept
Faulkner's admiration for this image, with the result that Faulkner,
"despite his modernist techniques, is a writer seriously estranged
from his time" (p. 96). Faulkner believes in "the moral rightness,
perhaps the invincibility, of waiting and powerlessness." In Howe's
view this is not because of Christian commitment so much as from
"a sense of the terribleness of history, a sense which leads him to
reach for a patience beyond hope or despair." He concludes that
Faulkner's readers are bound, not to accept Faulkner's valuation of
the necessity and power of passive endurance, but "only to take it
seriously" (p. 97).

It seems to Howe unquestionable, then, that "Isaac McCaslin is
meant and deserves to gain our moral admiration" (p. 96). Within
the context of Perluck's reading, on the other hand, there may well
be sympathy and involvement of the reader with Ike's decision, but
it would have to be, I think, more of the nature of pity than of
admiration. If it is true that Ike is escaping from life, its limitations
and its responsibilities, then he may have earned our compassion,
but he cannot have earned our respect.

One further note should be added. Although Faulkner is not
always his own best commentator, he did have something to say
about the nature of Ike's renunciation which ought to be thrown
into the balance. In the course of a student conference at the University of Virginia in 1958 Faulkner was asked about Ike's renunciation of his inheritance, and his answer puts him on the side of the
unromantic reading of "The Bear." He begins: "Well, there are
some people in any time and age that cannot face and cope with the
problems." He then goes on to distinguish three kinds of men:

> The first says, This is rotten, I'll have no part of it, I will take
> death first. The second says, This is rotten, I don't like it, I
> can't do anything about it, but at least I will not participate
> in it myself, I will go off into a cave or climb a pillar to sit on.
> The third says, This stinks and I'm going to do something
> about it. McCaslin is the second. He says, This is bad, and I
> will withdraw from it. What we need are people who will say,
> This is bad and I'm going to do something about it, I'm going
> to change it. (*Faulkner in the University*, pp. 245–246)

One should not conclude that this is the only possible reading of
"The Bear," or even that it is Faulkner's only understanding of it.
In practice, it is the reader who will have to decide which reading
he finds more valid in terms of the text Faulkner has left us. As to

the matter of ultimate validity, probably the question will never be settled once for all. And possibly this is the way Faulkner intended it, as an implicit assertion of the final mysterious ambiguity of the human spirit in its motivation and dedication.

11 ═══

One of the greatest sources of difficulty for the reader of
A Fable is the fact that it is essentially an interaction of conflicts. A reviewer (*Newsweek*, August 2, 1954) concluded that
it is "an experience of a study in conflicts, of faith fighting its
own cynicism, of hopes never really cut off from corresponding
doubts." The whole vast panorama of World War I as Faulkner presents it is a tension of opposites, and these opposites
are only resolved (if they are even then) with the martyrdom
of the Corporal and his eventual enshrinement in the tomb
of the Unknown Soldier. It is this very tension, unresolved for
the greater part of the story, which is its vital principle and
the source of its dynamism.

The other source of possible misunderstanding is an unwar-
ranted emphasis on the literal interpretation of the symbolism
of the Passion. Faulkner's use of the passion of Christ as the
background for his story is certainly fundamental to the book,
but it is not its most important element. What is most significant is rather the theme—or themes—enunciated through the
medium of these symbols, whether or not they be taken as
literal transcriptions of elements of the Gospel story.

Both these problematic areas are discussed in the following
essay of Roma A. King, Jr., which first appeared in *Modern
Fiction Studies,* © 1956 by Purdue Research Foundation,
Lafayette, Indiana. It is used here with permission.

Roma A. King, Jr.

A FABLE: EVERYMAN'S WARFARE

BEFORE *A FABLE* WAS PUBLISHED RUMORS SPREAD THAT Faulkner was writing a religious novel, and it was widely assumed that in it he would say something personal, perhaps announce his conversion to Christianity. That the book has an explicit "message," variously interpreted, has been accepted by most reviewers.

Superficially, the novel appears to be a naive re-affirmation of the faith Faulkner expressed in his Nobel Prize speech. The book is, also on the surface, ostentatiously Christian. There are crosses on the dust jacket, the cover, the title page, at the beginning of chapters, between chapters; there is the structural pattern based upon the events of Passion week; and there are the almost laborious parallels between Faulkner's story and the Gospel narrative of the life of Christ.

Faulkner has long been attracted by religious allegory, and many of his characters express a somewhat intellectually deficient, emotionally over-wrought religion. In *A Fable,* as in his earlier novels, there is an element of Christian theology. His view of evil and of man's fallen nature is basically Christian (as that of the "naturalist" is not). In the past he has clearly utilized his understanding not as a dogma but as a point of view from which to express his moral revulsion for man's all too often sordid behavior. In this sense his works have been "moral." His treatment, however, has been emotional, not intellectual; his immediate purpose, to create disgust for the ugly, not to reform the sinner. If in *A Fable* he changes his intent and wishes to reform, his old approach is inadequate for his purpose. He will require a more systematic intellectual grounding, and if he is to write a Christian fable, a more comprehensive theology. This he does not have. His view of man remains Christian, but his view of God, if he has one in this novel, is not. Consequently, as his detractors argue, this book as "message" is intellectually flabby. Indeed, as such, it is naive and sentimental.

But I suggest that the book is not a simple "message" about having faith and stopping wars. The novel is, as the title indicates, a fable. It is a modern morality closer in concept to the medieval *Everyman* than to the modern realistic novel. It is a fable that tells the complex, sometimes irreconcilable, stories of a group of men engaged in a war. Both men and war are allegorical. The men compositely represent Everyman, and their conflicts among themselves may well signify the traditional warfare within man between the forces of darkness and light. The difference between Faulkner and the medieval writer is that Faulkner's point of view is radically different. He is unable to make a simple affirmation of faith and to give his novel a single, clear focus. Typically modern, he sceptically passes from one perspective to another, from one set of experiences to another, searching for, but never quite finding among diverse possibilities, one truth upon which to fix dogmatically and permanently. Indeed, the power of this novel derives from the deepening insights which its dialectical, ambivalent exploration of human experience provides.

In *A Fable* Faulkner is unwilling to permit one character to be all or say all. The old general, ambivalent as he is, must be aided by supporting characters if the "truth" is to be told about man and his wars. Each of these represents one possible perspective from which the human drama may be viewed. Their stories parallel, confirm, supplement, contradict each other. We move from one to another, not causally nor logically, but analogically. We accept each character for no more than he is—one voice among many speaking that portion of truth, or untruth, which he has learned from his experience. Our task is to see the whole, and to discover among the temporal, sequential, ideological, and emotional complexities a unifying theme. Concerned initially with a diversity of experiences, we search for their analogical unity and a new understanding of universal human experience.

The characters fall into two important groups and a third of lesser significance. Roughly, there are those who support war and those who oppose it. Then there are those who neither support nor oppose it but are passively caught by its fury or by their own folly. The first six chapters of the book make these divisions clear. Chapter one takes place on Wednesday. The story, beginning at an advanced stage, the entry of the corporal into the city following the mutiny and his arrest, dramatizes this important event as it is seen imperfectly from the outside, primarily by the uninformed people. We then drop back in time to Monday, and, to understand more clearly the scene we have just witnessed, we watch its development from first one point of view and then another. In chapters two and four we learn about it from those characters who favor war; in three and six, from those who promote peace; in five, from the passive civilian countrymen.

Each character within a group supplements and completes every other character in that group, and each group provides a qualifying or contradictory comment upon the others. At the end of chapter six we are brought back to the beginning of the novel, the entry of the corporal, and are ready to watch events move to their climax.

I suggest, then, that in *A Fable* Faulkner continues to work imaginatively and poetically, that in this novel, as in his earlier ones, he takes the ambivalent, ironic view of man's inner struggle. The book is extremely complex, incapable of being reduced to a simple religious, political, or social thesis. Those who look for a "message" must find it either in passages out of context or in their own imaginations.

If *A Fable* fails, and, certainly, to an extent it does, it is because Faulkner sometimes forgets his main purpose and permits his fable to be lost among naturalistic details and irrelevancies. And, because, further, his intellectual imprecision undermines his dialectical scheme, enervating, as I shall show later, one side of the conflict so that the tension which should be there is, if not missing, considerably weaker than it should be.

The allegorical structure provides the most obvious clue to Faulkner's meaning. The basic symbol is the war, signifying in Faulkner's words "man's deathless folly." It is man's sin against primeval order, a symbol of his selfish brutality and his disregard for corporate society. It is, in Christian theology, called original sin. War, in *A Fable,* is an analogue for a metaphysical truth (as Faulkner sees that truth), providing a point of reference, a basis in reality, from which human experience can be examined and understood.

The theme of the novel is man's tragic involvement in evil,

his struggle to extricate himself, and, ultimately, his possible salvation. Because the powers of "deathless folly" are subtle and the human situation complex, Faulkner has adopted a multiple point of view. The old general is his most comprehensive character. The chief spokesman for war, he is coldly calculating, inhumanely objective, frightening. Indeed, Faulkner continually calls him the "old gray" general, words symbolic of death and decay. His best friend, the Quartermaster General who loved him and expected him to save the world, is eventually disillusioned about him. His son repudiates him. The half sister of his illegitimate son excruciatingly condemns him. Yet, his character is more complex than this listing suggests. Who, actually, is he? He is the devil, the Prince of War; he is also the father of the Christ-figure, the Prince of Peace. To his son, he is, in the Gethsemane scene, at once Caesar, the Lord of the World, and God the Father of Heaven, both tempter and sustainer. To his soldiers, he is the old gray man who plots their destruction, and at the same time, the father-figure who calls them all "my child." He is capable of inspiring fanatical hate and love, sometimes both in the same man.

He is a composite character, reminding us that the warfare between light and dark is localized in the individual. From him the other characters emanate and, of necessity, serve more limited purposes. Before noting their function in the novel we must recall that in a morality characters need not appear as fully developed, flesh and blood men and woman. Functioning in relationship to and as a part of the symbolic whole, they need to be "real" in a sense other than that demanded of characters in a naturalistic novel.

Associated with the old general in evil is a group which corresponds most closely to his darker side. There is, first, the General of the Division, Gragnon, whose troops mutiny. To him war is a profession and soldiering a perverse game in which he must defend his perverse honor. For this purpose he gives his life in ironic contrast to the corporal, who offers his rather than betray the confidence of his followers.

There are the young aviator, the German general, the punk from Chicago, and the British jockey. The young aviator has a diseased, romantic love for a monstrosity which he is incapable of understanding, but to which he is, nevertheless, passionately dedicated. The German general regards war as a way of life, a religion. That he is a caricature makes him more adequately the symbol of his own intellectual and moral partiality. Faulkner's description of him recalls in its symbolic techniques those earlier portraits of robots, particularly those in *Sanctuary*. The young punk takes the war as a training ground for gangsterism and the British jockey uses it to exploit his fellow soldiers.

In none of these characters do we have a complete representation of war but in them compositely we get some idea of its horror. In opposition to them, there are those characters associated with the light in the old general. There is, first, the corporal, the Christ-figure, perhaps the most unsatisfactory character in the novel. In almost laborious detail his life parallels that of Christ, and it is all too clear that he is intended as the instrument of man's salvation. Yet, he has neither the personal magnetism nor the spiritual and intellectual force to oppose the powers of darkness, so effectively symbolized in the old general and his military following. Only in the Gethsemane scene does the corporal convincingly come to life. This is not enough. Perhaps it is too much to ask that he measure up to our expectations; perhaps Faulkner should not have attempted what even Milton failed to do. He not only did, however, but he made the Christ-figure pivotal in *A Fable*, so that his inadequacy seriously reduces the effectiveness of the novel.

This is not all. The corporal's most devout convert, the runner, the Saint Paul figure, is equally unsatisfying. His intellectual naivete is astounding. Having never seen the corporal himself, the runner receives the gospel from an ignorant old porter at an ammunition dump. His simple belief that wars will cease when enough little people "cry enough," lay down their arms, and refuse to fight is far removed from the sophisticated teachings of Saint Paul. As the man who attempts a second mutiny in which he, like Saint Paul, is blinded by a light from heaven (explained here as a blast of shot fired by his own countrymen), as the man who later serves as a missionary to a hostile world, the runner is inadequate.

Of course, this may be said in his defense: even though he received, he never lived an easy gospel, and perhaps his endurance in face of fire and persecution is intended to counteract his intellectual deficiency. After all, he is not opposing an intellectual system but something so rationally evasive as human nature itself. Even so, it seems that endurance requires motivation—either a belief in man and his institutions (which the characters of darkness have) or in God and his grace (which neither the corporal nor the runner adequately demonstrates). The strongest "humanistic" argument is given by the tempter; this the corporal rejects, but what he accepts in its place is inadequately defined.

The old Negro preacher who represents a simple, emotional, anti-clerical Protestantism (or Masonry) is even less effective than the corporal and the runner. His final sacrifice appears futile, and his function in the novel as a whole is vague, if not irrelevant.

The most sympathetic character, the Quartermaster General, can be placed among the corporal, the runner, and the Negro preacher only with reservations since he partakes equally of the darkness and the light. Initially in the service of the old general, he comes finally to detest the machinations of the military organization. Yet, he is unable to free himself completely from his friend-enemy, because, to borrow from Fry, who borrowed from someone else, his dark is not light enough. Although disillusioned about the old way, he still sees no better. At the conclusion of the book, however, he seems to have gained some understanding and perception—enough at least to see that man's rejection of the peace message is a tragedy. He is the only character in the novel who undergoes development.

The point is not just that these characters advance a set of superficial ideas, but that in their weakness, singly and compositely, they fail to create their share of the dramatic tension which might have made this novel the significant achievement Faulkner expected it to be. Although as literary critics we cannot censure him for holding a bad theology, we can regret that an incomplete intellectualization of his problem spoiled the artistic effect of the book.

It should be noted, however, that he does avoid the sentimentality inherent in his over-simplified characters by not insisting that they are spokesmen for the whole truth, and by not asking us to accept either their theology or their faith as a satisfactory solution to the problem of man's warfare. In fact, Faulkner himself shows considerable scepticism. On at least one level, he permits each to suffer defeat. Whatever victory emerges from their failure remains at most only a possibility—an ironic, ambivalent possibility.

The ineffectiveness of Faulkner's advocates of peace enervates their struggle against "man's deathless folly," rendering unconvincing their ultimate salvation. Before we accept their damnation as foregone, however, let us look again at what Faulkner is trying to say, particularly in the last third of the novel. The issues between the two forces are most potently argued in the Gethsemane scene, perhaps the most successful episode in the book. The struggle narrows here to one between the general, spokesman for self-preservation, and the corporal, spokesman for self-denial and sacrifice. Who wins? Both—on a different level. The general eliminates the corporal and continues the war. The corporal triumphs morally over himself, and achieves at the conclusion of the scene an ironic "well done" from the old general, his erstwhile tempter now transformed into his father.

Further, the corporal experiences a kind of "resurrection," literal or symbolic. After his grave has been ripped open by gun fire, bits of his coffin but no trace of his body are found. Clearly the implication is that the body has been completely destroyed (if it has not risen). At the end of this Sunday of Passion week there is at least a possibility that the corporal through self-denial and sacrifice has triumphed over his enemy.

If Faulkner had stopped here, the novel would have been much simpler than it is. But he didn't. He added a chapter called "Tomorrow" in which he attempts to review the life of the Christ-figure in retrospect: what are we now to make of this story of a man who was dead, buried, and on the third day may have risen again?

First, our tendency is to disbelieve so strongly that we willingly accept any alternative, logical or illogical. Faulkner provides that alternative. A body, whole, save for natural disintegration, is taken from a spot near where the corporal was buried, but where Faulkner carefully points out other soldiers, any one of whom might have been killed, engaged in battle. This unidentified body is placed in the tomb of the unknown soldier. It is easy to assume, as most critics have, that the body was the corporal's and that Faulkner is cynically negating the Resurrection. But is he? Maybe. Maybe the fable of a risen corporal (or Christ) is only a pious myth. Maybe, on the other hand, it only seems so because in order to explain it away we are willing to accept the preposterous thesis that the body survived intact the terrific blast, and that it lay openly exposed but somehow invisible to the three women and the step-father, to believe that it was, indeed, miraculously preserved to give the lie to the miracle of the resurrection.

At the end, then, Faulkner remains, or for this novel becomes for the first time, the ironic, ambivalent artist. Both father and son are dead and the world seems little changed because of their lives. Yet, there remains the tantalizing, inescapable possibility that the body in the tomb is not the corporal's. And if it is not? To this question Faulkner, the artist, offers no dogmatic answer. The theology here may not satisfy Christians; the possibility of a resurrection may antagonize non-Christians; but for the discerning among both the situation creates a tension that is essentially good drama. If Faulkner had handled all the novel so well, it would have been, indeed, not only his greatest achievement, but the greatest of his generation.

That the forces of darkness and light are still present in the world is obvious in the final pages of the book. The runner, still believing in the corporal's way of self-denial and sacrifice, appears at the old general's funeral to shout a last defiance at him. But in a world of violence and brute force he experiences the outrage all such people may expect—a kick in the teeth and a bed in the gutter. Such, Faulkner seems to say, is the reception awaiting any Prince of Peace. Yet, even here all is not bleak. The runner, laughing, is able to affirm from the gutter "I shall never die," and the old Quartermaster General, sensing the tragedy of man's often futile struggle, sheds an understanding tear.

Commentary

Roma King has discussed very cogently the interaction of characters in *A Fable*, resulting in a tension at the very heart of the novel. In addition, he has shown how the old General is himself a composite character, and therefore contains a similar tension within himself. I would like to push this analysis a bit further, and suggest that these tensions may interact among themselves even more complexly than King has indicated.

First of all, the prototype of the Corporal is clearly Christ. The General has been taken as representative first of all of God the Father, later of Satan. There are also a number of indications, however, that the General, as well as the Corporal, is meant at times to represent Christ himself. The development of the two characters is in fact, for a great part of the book, almost parallel. For example, Faulkner makes much of the fact that the General, at the beginning of his military career, could have chosen an easy and glorious entrance into service but deliberately chose the humblest (*A Fable* [New York: Random House, 1954], pp. 245ff.). Then there is his retirement into solitude and obscurity (pp. 253–258); his Gethsemane (p. 258); his role as savior of the world (p. 264 and p. 271). With this in mind, I suggest that the shifting symbolism of the General includes Christ himself, God the Father, and Satan.

As King has shown—and as we suggested briefly in Chapter 2— the Corporal and the General are but aspects of one and the same personality, and stand for every human being. They are, taken together, representative of the complete man with his essentially dual nature—earthbound, yet seeking the fulfilment of his spiritual aspirations. The General clearly enunciates this duality in the important Temptation scene, in which he tries to dissuade the Corporal, his son, from going to martyrdom for the sake of peace. This passage has already been cited in Chapter 2, but I think it is important enough to be repeated here. The General says (pp. 347–348):

> . . . we are two articulations, self-elected possibly, anyway elected, anyway postulated, not so much to defend as to test two inimical conditions which, through no fault of ours but through the simple paucity and restrictions of the arena

211

where they meet, must contend and—one of them—perish: I
champion of this mundane earth which, whether I like it or
not, is, and to which I did not ask to come, yet since I am here,
not only must stop but intend to stop during my allotted
while; you champion of an esoteric realm of man's baseless
hopes and his infinite capacity—no: passion—for unfact.

Yet even as he derides his son's championing of the esoteric realm
of "unfact," the General is forced to admit that this "infinite capacity" is founded in the nature of man, and that in the proper order
of things the two drives can exist together in harmony. For he
immediately goes on to say: "No, they are not inimical really, there
is no contest actually; they can even exist side by side together in
this one restricted arena, and could and would, had yours not
interfered with mine."

This explains, I think, why the old General, representing the
earthly element in man, can symbolize in turn Christ, God the
Father, and Satan. In the two former symbolizations he represents
man's use of the world in proper subordination to spiritual principles and values. In the third he represents the possibility latent
in man of substituting earth for heaven, frustrating the drive of
his dual nature.

King's essay has spoken of the same tension—both this central
one and the other lesser analogues of it—in the more generic terms
of a tension between "the darkness and the light." I am suggesting
that this tension may be specified further (at least on one level) as
the tension between the love of man for earth and his longing for "a
new heaven and a new earth," turning primarily about the delicate
moral axis of the conflict between the General and the Corporal.

It is possible to agree quite completely, then, with Roma King's
enunciation of the theme of A Fable: "man's tragic involvement, his
struggle to extricate himself, and, ultimately, his possible salvation."
In spite of the hatred and greed of men who have succumbed to the
General's offer to "take the earth," man still has it in his power to
attain peace by suffering—even suffering death—in fulfilment of his
spiritual aspirations. There has certainly been suffering in Faulkner's books before this, but in A Fable man's suffering seems somehow to have been given new meaning. By means of linking (in
Harvey Breit's phrase) "his dark, textured narrative to the beautifully clear narrative of the week of the Passion of Jesus," Faulkner
has transfigured the one without demeaning the other. He has
associated—not "equated" or "superimposed"—this tangled and
ambiguous human story with what much of the Western world conceives to be the supreme human suffering and the supreme act of
charity, and in the process has given it a universal human signifi-

cance. This is ultimately the function of *A Fable*'s master-symbol, the cross of Christ.

A Fable partakes somehow, then, of the nature of religious allegory. Faulkner himself has said as much. As he remarked in an interview (*Paris Review* 4 [1956], 42): "In *A Fable* the Christian allegory was the right allegory to use." And yet it is not the allegory of *Everyman* or Spenser's *Faerie Queene* or Bunyan's *Pilgrim's Progress*. What the poet Babette Deutsch (in her *Poetry Hhandbook* [2nd ed.; New York: Universal Library, 1962]) wrote of modern poets is true of novelists as well: "Contemporary poets reject allegory because of the oversimplification and didacticism it risks" (p. 77). Allegory, in the sense of a clear one-to-one correspondence between the allegorical figure and the truth it represents, is primarily a teacher's tool. This is not to say that it cannot be used with beautiful effect in the hands of a teacher who happens also to be a master artist. Witness the story of Spenser's Red Cross Knight or of Everyman, both of which are artistic allegories of man's spiritual pilgrimage. Generally speaking, allegory teaches—and what it commonly presumes is a certain truth already achieved by the teacher, to be conveyed imaginatively to the listener. With this in mind perhaps it may be clear why contemporary artists are chary of allegory: today the most urgent problems which engage the attention of the artist are involved with the search for truth rather than with the communication of truth already achieved.

And yet King's essay speaks of *A Fable* as allegory, as did the author himself. At the same time, however, King goes on to speak throughout his essay in terms of symbolism: not a set of simple one-to-one correspondences, but a set of images to which cling an undefined and, practically speaking, unlimited number of connotations —as Yeats, for instance, uses the symbol of a tree or a tower. King's discussion does not yield a simply-defined set of correspondences— as if, for example, the old General were simply to be identified with God the Father, the Corporal with Christ, the runner with Saint Paul. He has quite deliberately and very wisely steered us away from precisely this oversimplification. What Faulkner has done is to build up a system of symbols which offer certain connotations or imaginative resonances, some obvious, some oblique, some deliberately and ironically distorted or ambiguous, some barely hinted at. These resonances include, first and most obviously, the Christ story itself; they evoke the horrors of one of the most awful of all wars; they suggest "everyman," the eternal pilgrim who represents all men struggling against the human condition; they reflect the frustration and seeming futility of modern society. All these, and perhaps much more, are somehow evoked within the same overarching story. As King puts it, Faulkner is "unable to make a simple affirmation of faith and to give his novel a single, clear focus. Typically modern, he sceptically passes from one perspective to another . . . searching for, but never quite finding among diverse possibilities, one truth upon which to fix dogmatically and permanently."

Even beyond this, however, what we have in *A Fable* (and elsewhere in Faulkner) is a conscious artistic use of myth. There are two reasons why it is important to insist that Faulkner has gone beyond mere symbol, to the use of myth. In a sense, a myth is a system or pattern of symbols. It is something much more, however. First of all, a myth is a story, and as such involves movement, passage of time. A symbol, of and by itself, is timeless; it does not of itself involve movement. A myth, on the other hand—as a story—allows for the passage of time, and therefore for dramatic movement: action, complication, resolution. Second, because a myth is built of symbols, it encloses connotations, emotions, affective responses. Therefore whatever dramatic resolution is achieved within the myth is a resolution of things not accessible to merely rational knowledge or argument.

Almost every past age seems to have had its myth, that is, an imaginative story or pattern of events which affords a matrix according to which men may be helped to order their lives, achieve some structure of values, articulate and perhaps resolve their fears and their aspirations. The myths of the gods were such for the Greeks, as the legends of the founding of Rome were for the Romans. Modern man often seems to be without such a viable myth. Babette Deutsch has remarked that a great deal of contemporary poetry has dealt with precisely this problem, this "lack of an acceptable or widely accredited myth, that imaginative ordering of experience which helps the group or the person giving it assent to enjoy life and to accept death" (*Poetry Handbook*, p. 93). The problem had begun, in fact, as early as William Blake, who wrote in his poetic prophecy *Jerusalem:*

I must Create a System or be enslav'd by another Man's.
I will not Reason & Compare: my business is to Create.

I think it likely that what Faulkner has done in *A Fable* (as to a lesser extent in *The Sound and the Fury* and *Light in August* and elsewhere) is to use the Christ story mythically. He has found in it, as other modern artists have done, the almost uniquely "acceptable or widely accredited" story which can serve the function formerly served by myth. This is not to say that either he or his readers do not credit the story as history. But whether they credit it in this way or not, they at least know it, they admire at least many of its ideals, and they find it woven deeply into the fabric of their Western culture. With this story as architectonic structure Faulkner can build his whole complex of resonances, touching on the crucial areas of perennial and contemporary human concern. He has used the Christian story, as one of the few viable myths left to modern man, to convey a whole congeries of problems, values, emotional responses, and imaginative insights. It is not, like simple allegory, the tool of a teacher. It is not merely timeless symbol. It is a dramatic tool, open to the movement of time and action, in the hands of a searcher after meaning and resolution.

Before closing this discussion of *A Fable*, there is one demurrer to be made. Much as I have admired Roma King's fine analysis, I must take issue with one of his conclusions. Analyzing the book as a "fable," analogous to a morality play, King finds what he considers an imbalance in the forces which are meant to create the essential dramatic tension of the fable. The figure of the old General is powerfully drawn, he feels, while the opposing figures—the Corporal and his followers—are too weak to make the dramatic tension credible. Although one can agree with the relative weakness of the portrayal of the Corporal—and King admits himself that even Milton could not solve the problem of portraying a Christ figure effectively—I find it difficult to agree that the same weakness exists in the portrayal of his disciples.

First of all, I find the figures of the Runner and the Rev. Sutterfield much more effective than he does, granting—as King does himself—that they are not meant to be realistic characters in a novel but figures in a moral fable. As such, I think they work wonderfully well. But even more important, King misreads the role of the Groom (later the Sentry), whom King refers to as "the British jockey." The Groom is not, as King suggests, on the side of war. With his deep compassion beautifully undercutting his taciturnity and seeming greed, he actually shares with the Runner—albeit reluctantly—the highest place in the hierarchy of the Corporal's movement for peace. And the Groom, linking as he does the main story with the parallel story of the racehorse—both stories asserting the force of individual freedom and responsibility in the face of dehumanizing authority—is crucial to the dramatic movement of the book. He is powerfully portrayed, both in his bizarre adventures with the crippled and courageous horse and in his equally strange adventures as a Sentry in France. The Groom is quite as mysterious—and quite as compelling in his mystery—as the old General. Like the General, he is an ambiguous figure; he wishes to be let alone and yet is moved seemingly against his will by his instinctive compassion for others. Most readers, I think, find it difficult not to be moved by him. Dramatically, he is at least a match for the old General. And with this compelling figure thrown into the balance, I believe Faulkner's dramatic success in the fable as a whole far outweighs whatever weaknesses there may be.

One further note must be added, which might militate against stressing overmuch an ambiguity in the ending of *A Fable*. Are we meant to doubt whether or not the body of the Unknown Soldier is that of the Corporal? Faulkner's comments about the novel take for granted that the body is the Corporal's. As he remarked at the University of Virginia in 1957: "The notion occurred to me one day in 1942 shortly after Pearl Harbor and the beginning of the last great war, Suppose—who might that unknown soldier be? Suppose that had been Christ again, under that fine big cenotaph with the eternal flame burning on it? That he would naturally have got crucified again. . . . That was an idea and a hope, an unexpressed thought that Christ had appeared twice, had been crucified twice, and maybe we'd have only one more chance" (*Faulkner in the University*, p. 27). But did he rise again from the dead this second time? Perhaps that is what Faulkner means to leave in ironic ambiguity.

12

EPILOGUE

IF THERE IS ANY SINGLE IMPRESSION WHICH EMERGES FROM
the preceding essays, I think it must be a sense of the enormous
complexity of Faulkner's religious attitudes. It is all too tempt-
ing to sum up Faulkner simply as Calvinist, or as Stoic, or as
modern religious humanist. The reality is something far more
complicated, and at the same time far more rich.

It is not, I think, simply the essay of John Hunt on Faulkner's "theological complexity" which gives this impression. We
have seen it asserted, with documentation, that Faulkner's religious stance (particularly in his realization of the possibility
of man's redemption) manifests development; we have seen a
convincing argument, on the other hand, that there is an unex-
pected constancy in his religious viewpoint. We have found
that mythic dimensions of the Christian Scriptures are of great
importance; we have also found that the literal values of Scripture are meaningfully present. Women are the wellspring of
life; they are also the root of evil. Man has a limited freedom
of choice, but not always and everywhere. God is the Savior
who washes men in the blood of the Lamb; he is also the Player
who moves the pawns.

This theological complexity, which is a common note of most
of the essays in this volume, is by no means accidental. Faulkner quite deliberately works in ambiguities. Time and time
again we have seen ourselves left in uncertainty about Faulkner's intentions. This has been especially true of his characterization. The multivalent symbolization of the General in *A
Fable* is a case in point, but any number of others have also
been remarked: Joe Christmas, who is both a Christ figure and
a Satanic figure; Addie Bundren, who is at once a sign of weakness and of redemption; Ike McCaslin, who may be a hero or

who may be a refugee from the problems of the modern world. In short, Faulkner's attitudes—including his religious attitudes —reflect the complexity of the real world.

A second common note which stands out clearly from these essays is the problematic nature of man's freedom. It has run like a refrain through our discussion of Faulkner. It is the problem which haunts him perhaps above all others. Man is constantly striving to act as a free man, but can do so only occasionally and in a limited way. And yet on those rare occasions when one of his characters does act as a free human being, the grandeur of it shines like a shaft of light through the dark. Dilsey is free with a glorious freedom.

Another problem which has recurred is linked with that of man's freedom. It is the anguishing modern mystery of alienation from the community. Cleanth Brooks has suggested that the difficulty of the individual's moral choice may be obviated in some degree by a return to the supporting strength of the community's pattern of values. Amos Wilder has discussed this "radical estrangement" in the light of *The Sound and the Fury,* and the subsequent commentary saw the same problem in terms of still other novels. John Hunt's essay on *Absalom, Absalom!* has focused the same mystery as a failure of love.

A fourth theme which has emerged, somewhat less strongly, is Faulkner's use of myth. The mythic dimensions of Christianity especially have entered deeply into the fabric of many of his novels. We have seen this in a pervasive way in *A Fable,* where the novel is structured upon the pattern of the Christian story. It has also been noted in an important way in *Light in August, The Sound and the Fury,* and elsewhere.

One of the most intriguing themes to stand out in the course of this study is the notion of the positive, redemptive value of suffering. It was perhaps most clearly seen in Irving Howe's remarks on "The Bear," referred to in Chapter 10. Howe expresses it as an ideal of "passive endurance." Ike McCaslin is admirable not because he acts but because he suffers. Although one may or may not agree with this reading of Ike, the conception of such an ideal may shed light on earlier comments in this volume on Faulkner's increasing awareness of a possible value in suffering itself. Earlier novels like *The Sound and the Fury* surely held up as an ideal the "endurance" of Dilsey and her peers: "They endured." In later novels, especially in the explicit association of this ideal with the passion of Christ in

A Fable, new dimensions and perhaps a new urgency are added. It does seem, as I suggested in the essay on Faulkner and the Calvinist tradition (Chapter 2), that later novels like *Requiem for a Nun* and *A Fable* manifest a clearer realization of a possible redemption of man through suffering. It is ill defined, to be sure, and—apart from the mythic dimension—offers no objective ground (Christian or otherwise) for this value, but it does seem to be an advance for Faulkner in the direction of one of the great Christian mysteries, the mystery of the cross.

The wide range of themes and problems we have encountered in the course of this volume suggests the question of possible directions to be taken in future studies of religious aspects of Faulkner's fiction. The authorized Faulkner biography, now being written by Joseph Blotner, will no doubt shed some light on his religious themes and attitudes—how much light we can only guess. Meanwhile, much more could be done by way of close study of Faulkner's use of religious myth and symbol. In addition, although much has been written already on freedom in Faulkner, much remains to be done. The varying conclusions of Douglas and Daniel, of Brooks, and of Hunt on this matter make it clear that the case is far from closed. Then, too, the question raised by Douglas and Daniel concerning the nature of tragedy in Faulkner, especially the extent to which the "conditions of tragedy" are a function of his Calvinist Christianity, merits further attention.

Finally, the question we raised in Chapter 2—"is there a God behind it all, and is he a God who saves?"—remains a haunting one. Although the question will perhaps never find a definitive and apodictic answer, I should like to see further discussion of the existence and nature of God in Faulkner's work. In any such discussion, however, there is one further datum not yet mentioned which must be thrown into the balance. It is Faulkner's review of Hemingway's *Old Man and the Sea,* in which Faulkner, in his own voice, comes down clearly on the side of a transcendent God. The review consists of one paragraph:

> His best. Time may show it to be the best single piece of any of us, I mean his and my contemporaries. This time he discovered God, a Creator. Until now, his men and women had made themselves, shaped themselves out of their own clay; their victories and defeats were at the hands

of each other, just to prove to themselves or one another how tough they could be. But this time, he wrote about pity: about something somewhere that made them all: the old man who had to catch the fish and then lose it, the fish that had to be caught and then lost, the sharks which had to rob the old man of his fish; made them all and loved them all and pitied them all. It's all right. Praise God that whatever made and loves and pities Hemingway and me kept him from touching it any further. (William Faulkner, *Essays, Speeches and Public Letters* [New York: Random House, 1965], p. 193)

This is what Faulkner himself has done, and perhaps this is what any literary artist concerned with religious experience must do: reveal God through human experience—not primarily experience of God (unless one happens to be a Saint John of the Cross), but experience of man among men. Man's nature reveals his Creator. Faulkner reveals God as a "presence" in the lives of men. Faulkner portrays man as one needing protection and love, as one not totally fulfilled even by human love, as one dependent on something outside himself; thus God is present implicitly as the one who created, who pities and loves that "poor son of a bitch," man. And it might be asked, is not this kind of revelation of a presence of God—mediated through men—more real than the more explicit theologizing of professedly "religious" novelists?

There is a remarkable passage in *A Fable* in which the old Negro Baptist minister, Reverend Tobe Sutterfield, is questioned about the nature of his vocation:

> "Are you an ordained minister?"
> "I dont know. I bears witness."
> "To what? God?"
> "To man. God dont need me. I bears witness to Him of course, but my main witness is to man." (p. 180)

Perhaps this is what the artist does in his treatment of man's religious experience: witnesses to man, and by this witness gives witness to God. As Christ, who for the Christian is the epitome of humanity and human experience, has said: "He who sees me, sees the Father who sent me."

There is one other question which perhaps ought to be raised again: what is the relationship of Faulkner to his own day? In his comments on "The Bear," Irving Howe suggested that Faulkner is an artist "estranged from his time" because he holds up an ideal of passive endurance which the modern world cannot accept. It may be that this is a difficult ideal for modern man to accept (though the modern acceptance and use of Gandhian "passive resistance" might be cited as a case in contradiction), but one can just as easily recall themes of Faulkner discussed in the preceding chapters which echo faithfully the concerns of modern man and much of modern literature: the problem of the alienation of men from one another and from their community; the mystery of time; the nature and scope of man's freedom; the decline of order and ethical values in modern society; the perennial problem of evil. In addition, it might be pointed out that (as we have noted already) the religion of Faulkner's novels is above all an ethic, a religion of practice. And is not this the thrust of the greater part of religious discussion in our day: the search for meaningful patterns of action?

One must always be wary, I suppose, about separating out any single aspect of a work of art, for the result will be necessarily only a partial view. If this part is mistaken for the whole, the resulting distortion could be disastrous. In singling out various religious aspects of Faulkner's fiction in the preceding essays and commentaries, there has been no pretense that the process is anything more than part of the entire critical discussion of Faulkner's work. The reader's task will be to return to the novels themselves with whatever insight he has gained from these essays, and to see them whole. One takes a fine watch apart only with a view to putting it together again so that it can work its magic.

If the religious aspects of Faulkner's fiction are only a part of his work, they remain nevertheless an essential part. It might be said they are the soul of Faulkner's art, for it is his religious and human vision that gives shape to the material in which he works. Whether it be Dilsey or Sutpen, Temple Drake or Ike McCaslin, whether it be in Yoknapatawpha County or in the trenches of France, it is this broadly religious vision which is bodied forth. Only by coming to terms with this vision can one come to terms with Faulkner's art.

Notes ══════

NOTES TO CHAPTER 1

Religion and Literature: The Critical Context

1. Nathan A. Scott, Jr., *Modern Literature and the Religious Frontier* (New York: Harper, 1958), p. 46.

2. *Ibid.*

3. Amos N. Wilder, *Theology and Modern Literature* (Cambridge: Harvard University Press, 1958), p. 25.

4. A partial list of such books would include the following: Cleanth Brooks, *The Hidden God* (1963); Edmund Fuller, *Man in Modern Fiction* (1958); Harold Gardiner, *Norms for the Novel* (1958); Roy L. Hart, *Unfinished Man and the Imagination* (1969); Stanley Hopper (ed.), *Spiritual Problems in Contemporary Literature* (1952); Martin Jarrett-Kerr, *Studies in Literature and Belief* (1955); R. W. B. Lewis, *The American Adam* (1955); William Lynch, *Christ and Apollo: Dimensions of the Literary Imagination* (1960); Donat O'Donnell, *Maria Cross* (1953); D. S. Savage, *The Withered Branch* (1952); Nathan Scott, *The Tragic Vision and the Christian Faith* (1957), *Modern Literature and the Religious Frontier* (1958), *The New Orpheus: Essays Toward a Christian Poetic* (1964), *The Broken Center: Studies in the Theological Horizon of Modern Literature* (1966); Sallie McFague TeSelle, *Literature and the Christian Life* (1967); Hyatt Waggoner, *The Heel of Elohim* (1950); Amos Wilder, *Modern Poetry and the Christian Tradition* (1952), *Theology and Modern Literature* (1958).

5. *Theology and Modern Literature*, p. 29.

6. William F. Lynch, *The Image Industries* (New York: Sheed and Ward, 1959), p. 44.

7. *Ibid.*, pp. 40 and 43.

8. *Ibid.*, p. 39.

9. *Ibid.*, p. 38.

NOTES TO CHAPTER 2

Faulkner and the Calvinist Tradition

1. William Van O'Connor, *The Tangled Fire of William Faulk-*

ner (Minneapolis: University of Minnesota Press, 1954), pp. 72–87.

2. Vernon Louis Parrington, *Main Currents in American Thought* (New York: Harcourt, Brace, 1927), I, pp. 5–15.

3. Kenneth B. Murdock, "Writers of New England," *Literary History of the United States*, ed. Robert E. Spiller *et al.* (New York: Macmillan, 1960), p. 55.

4. Perry Miller, *Errand into the Wilderness* (Cambridge: Harvard University Press, 1956), p. 60.

5. *Ibid.*, p. 66.

6. *Ibid.*, p. 69.

7. *Ibid.*, p. 71.

8. Parrington, *op. cit.*, II, p. 436.

9. Irving Howe, *William Faulkner: A Critical Study* (New York: Random House, 1952), p. 104.

10. *Soldier's Pay* (New York: Liveright, 1926), p. 244.

11. *Sartoris* (New York: Harcourt, Brace, 1929), p. 23.

12. *The Sound and the Fury* (New York: Modern Library, 1946), p. 176.

13. *Light in August* (New York: Modern Library, 1950), Introd., p. vi.

14. *Absalom, Absalom!* (New York: Modern Library, 1951), pp. 72–73.

15. *The Wild Palms* (New York: Random House, 1939), p. 174. "Old Man" is published as a part of *The Wild Palms*.

16. *Go Down, Moses* (New York: Modern Library, 1955), p. 278.

17. *Pylon* (New York: Harrison Smith and Robert Haas, 1935), p. 48.

18. *Collected Stories* (New York: Random House, 1950), p. 307.

19. Howe, *Faulkner: A Critical Study*, p. 61.

20. Rabi, "Faulkner and the Exiled Generation," in *William Faulkner: Two Decades of Criticism*, ed. Frederick J. Hoffman and Olga W. Vickery (East Lansing: Michigan State College Press, 1954), p. 135. This article originally appeared in *Esprit*, No. 175 (January, 1951), pp. 47–65.

21. *Requiem for a Nun* (New York: Random House, 1951), p. 276.

22. *A Fable* (New York: Random House, 1954), pp. 347–348.

23. For a fuller treatment of this interpretation of *A Fable*, see J. Robert Barth, "A Rereading of Faulkner's *Fable*," *America*, 92 (1954), pp. 44–46.

NOTES TO CHAPTER 3

Faulkner's Southern Puritanism

1. See references to Southern Puritanism in W. J. Cash, *The Mind of the South* (New York, 1941), pp. 130–33 *et passim*.

2. *Southern Renascence,* ed. Louis D. Rubin, Jr., and Robert D. Jacobs (Baltimore, 1953), pp. 153–69; *The Tangled Fire of William Faulkner* (Minneapolis, 1954), pp. 72–87.

3. "Hawthorne and Faulkner: Some Common Ground," *Virginia Quarterly Review,* XXXIII (1957), pp. 105–23.

4. *Southern Renascence,* p. 156; omitted from the revision.

5. *Tangled Fire,* p. 73n.

6. London, 1934, pp. 42–64.

7. "Faulkner—Sorcerer or Slave?", *Saturday Review,* XXXV (July 12, 1952), p. 10.

8. *Ibid.,* p. 39. This paragraph follows directly on a summary of the passage in *The Sound and the Fury* where Quentin decides to tell his father that he and his sister have committed incest, rather than let him know of her loose behavior with other men.

9. The likeness between the treatment of free will in *Light in August* and in *Oedipus the King* is well discussed in John L. Longley's essay "Joe Christmas: the Hero in the Modern World," published since the present article was written: *Virginia Quarterly Review,* XXXIII (1957), pp. 233–49. According to *The New Yorker,* XXXIII (May 11, 1957), p. 37, Miss Hamilton, now in her ninetieth year, is unregenerate.

10. "Hawthorne and Faulkner," *College English,* XVII (1956), pp. 258–62.

11. *As I Lay Dying* (New York: Modern Library, 1946), p. 466.

12. *Maule's Curse* (Norfolk, Conn., 1938), p. 11.

13. *William Faulkner: a Critical Study* (New York, 1952), p. 81. The disparagement was handsomely retracted in *The New York Times Book Review,* April 24, 1954, p. 22.

14. New York: New American Library, 1953, p. xiv.

15. *The Liberal Imagination* (New York, 1950), pp. ix and 301.

NOTES TO CHAPTER 4

Faulkner's Vision of Good and Evil

1. (Baton Rouge, Louisiana: Louisiana State University Press, 1958), pp. 141–142.

2. *Speculations* (New York: Harcourt, Brace, Harvest Books, 1924), pp. 70–71.

3. Faulkner, a few years ago, in defining his notion of Christianity, called it a "code of behavior by means of which (man) makes himself a better human being than his nature wants to be, if he follows his nature only" (*Paris Review*, Spring, 1956), p. 42.

4. *Sanctuary* (New York: Modern Library, 1932,) p. 221.

5. *The Sound and the Fury* (New York: Modern Library, 1946), p. 115.

6. *Absalom, Absalom!* (New York: Modern Library, 1951), p. 263.

7. *The Unvanquished* (New York: Random House, 1938), p. 244.

8. *Light in August* (New York: Modern Library, 1950), p. 326.

9. "The Bear," in *Go Down, Moses* (New York: Modern Library, 1955), p. 297.

NOTES TO CHAPTER 5

The Theological Complexity of Faulkner's Fiction

1. *The Sound and the Fury* (New York: Modern Library, 1946), p. 194.

2. (New Haven: Yale University Press, 1952), p. 9.

3. *Stoics and Sceptics* (New York: Barnes & Noble, Inc., 1959), p. 66.

4. *Ibid.*, p. 70.

5. "A Free Man's Worship," *Mysticism and Logic* (Garden City, New York: Doubleday Anchor Books, 1957), pp. 45–46.

6. *Ibid.*, pp. 48–49.

7. Quotations from Seneca's *On Providence* are from the Loeb Classical Library edition of *Moral Essays*, I, trans. John W. Basore (Cambridge, Mass.: Harvard University Press, 1958). The quotation from Seneca's *Epistles* is taken from the Loeb edition of *Ad Lucilium Epistulae Morales*, II, trans. Richard M. Gummere (Cambridge, Mass.: Harvard University Press, 1953).

8. *The Greek Experience* (Cleveland: The World Publishing Co., 1957), p. 53.

9. *The Courage to Be*, p. 17.

10. Søren Kierkegaard, *Fear and Trembling and Sickness Unto Death,* trans. Walter Lowrie (Garden City, New York: Doubleday Anchor Books, 1954), p. 77.

NOTES TO CHAPTER 6

Vestigial Moralities in The Sound and the Fury

1. One can apply to her what is said of the Negro servant of Temple Drake in *Requiem for a Nun:* "nurse: guide: mentor, catalyst, glue, whatever you want to call it, holding the whole lot of them together . . . in a semblance at least of order and respectability and peace; not ole cradle-rocking mamma at all" (New York: Random House, 1951), p. 157.

2. *The Sound and the Fury* (New York: Modern Library, 1946), p. 277.

3. *Requiem for a Nun,* p. 135.

4. "Moral and Temporal Order in *The Sound and the Fury*," *The Sewanee Review,* LXI (1953), p. 223.

5. *Requiem for a Nun,* p. 92.

6. "Time in Faulkner: *The Sound and the Fury*," in *William Faulkner: Three Decades of Criticism,* ed. by F. J. Hoffman and O. W. Vickery (New York: Harcourt, Brace and World, Harbinger Books, 1963), pp. 225–232.

7. "His Confidence," *The Collected Poems of W. B. Yeats* (New York: Macmillan, 1937), p. 301.

8. "Crazy Jane Talks With the Bishop," *Ibid.,* p. 298.

NOTES TO CHAPTER 7

The Old Testament Vision in As I Lay Dying

1. *Faulkner in the University: Class Conferences at the University of Virginia, 1957–1958,* ed. by Frederick L. Gwynn and Joseph L. Blotner (New York: Vintage Books, 1965), p. 87.

2. Maurice LeBreton, "Le Thème de la Vie et de la Mort dans *As I Lay Dying*," *Revue des Lettres Modernes,* 40–42 (Hiver, 1958–1959), p. 516.

3. "The Bear," in *Go Down, Moses* (New York: Modern Library, 1955), p. 195.

4. *Absalom, Absalom!* (New York: Modern Library, 1951), p. 312.

5. *As I Lay Dying* (New York: Modern Library, 1946), pp. 410–411. This is in the same volume with *The Sound and the Fury.*

6. William Faulkner, *Essays, Speeches and Public Letters,* ed. by James B. Meriwether (New York: Random House, 1965), p. 120.

NOTES TO CHAPTER 8

Light in August: *Outrage and Compassion*

1. *Light in August* (New York: Modern Library, 1950), pp. 321–322.

NOTES TO CHAPTER 9

The Theological Center of Absalom, Absalom!

1. (New York: E. P. Dutton & Co., 1957), p. 221.
2. *Absalom, Absalom!* (New York: Modern Library, 1951), p. 9.
3. This distinction between history and art comes from *Justine*, p. 115: "What I most need to do is to record experiences, not in the order in which they took place—for that is history—but in the order in which they first became significant for me."
4. "Introduction to *The Portable Faulkner*," in *William Faulkner: Three Decades of Criticism*, ed. by Frederick J. Hoffman and Olga W. Vickery (New York: Harcourt, Brace, and World [Harbinger Books], 1963), p. 102.
5. *On the Limits of Poetry: Selected Essays 1928–1948* (New York: The Swallow Press and William Morrow & Co., 1948), p. 303.
6. *Ibid.,* p. 301.
7. *Ibid.,* pp. 302–03.
8. "*Absalom, Absalom:* The Definition of Innocence," *The Sewanee Review,* LIX (1951), p. 545.
9. *William Faulkner: From Jefferson to the World* (Lexington, Kentucky: University of Kentucky Press, 1959), p. 163.
10. *Love, Power, and Justice* (New York: Oxford University Press, 1954), pp. 113–14.
11. *On the Limits of Poetry,* p. 274.
12. *The Irony of American History* (New York: Charles Scribner's Sons, 1952), p. viii.
13. "*Absalom, Absalom:* The Definition of Innocence," p. 552.

NOTES TO CHAPTER 10

"The Bear:" An Unromantic Reading

1. "The Bear," in *Go Down, Moses* (New York: Modern Library, 1955), p. 297.
2. See "The Old People," in *Go Down, Moses* (New York: Modern Library, 1955), pp. 181–182.

3. See John Crowe Ransom, "The Tense of Poetry," in *The World's Body* (New York: Schribner, 1938), pp. 233–260.

4. See Karl E. Zink, "Flux and the Frozen Moment: The Imagery of Stasis in Faulkner's Prose," *PMLA*, LXXI (June, 1956), pp. 285–301.

5. [Editor's note. A remark made by Faulkner at the University of Virginia in 1957 contradicts this suggestion. In answer to a question about "The Bear," Faulkner spoke of Boon "trying to patch up a gun in order to shoot a squirrel." See *Faulkner in the University*, ed. by Frederick L. Gwynn and Joseph L. Blotner (New York: Vintage Books, 1965), p. 60.]

Editions of Faulkner's Works Cited ▬▬▬

[date of first publication is given in brackets]

Soldier's Pay [1926]. New York: Liveright, 1926.

Sartoris [1929]. New York: Harcourt, Brace, 1929.

The Sound and the Fury [1929]. New York: Modern Library, 1946.

As I Lay Dying [1930]. New York: Modern Library, 1946 (in same volume with *The Sound and the Fury*).

Sanctuary [1931]. New York: Modern Library, 1932.

Light in August [1932]. New York: Modern Library, 1950.

Pylon [1935]. New York: Harrison Smith and Robert Haas, 1935 (reproduced photographically by Random House, 1962).

Absalom, Absalom! [1936]. New York: Modern Library, 1951.

The Unvanquished [1938]. New York: Random House, 1938.

The Wild Palms [1939]. New York: Random House, 1939.

"The Bear," in *Go Down, Moses* [1942]. New York: Modern Library, 1955.

Collected Stories of William Faulkner [1950]. New York: Random House, 1950.

Requiem for a Nun [1951]. New York: Random House, 1951.

A Fable [1954]. New York: Random House, 1954.

Faulkner in the University: Class Conferences at the University of Virginia, 1957–1958 [1959], ed. by Frederick L. Gwynn and Joseph L. Blotner [1959]. New York: Vintage Books, 1965.

Essays, Speeches and Public Letters, ed. by James B. Meriwether [1965]. New York: Random House, 1965.

Index

231